3/19/94

THE ROOT OF ALL EVIL

Whether it's insurance money or the money in a bank vault, a pensioner's pitiful nest egg or a businessman's fortune, the insatiable lust for money drives sometimes sane people to brutal acts of murder.

Now from the authentic files of *True Detective,* America's premier true crime magazine, read these chilling true accounts of cold-blooded GREED KILLERS like: Barbara Gueswelle of St. Louis, who had her husband killed for his 14 insurance policies; Arthur and Irene Seale, who kidnapped Exxon executive Sidney Reso, shot him, and left him to die of asphyxiation in a storage locker; and Robert Maury, who killed three women to collect the reward money for helping California police locate their bodies!

GREED KILLERS

**PINNACLE BOOKS AND *TRUE DETECTIVE* MAGAZINE
TEAM UP TO BRING YOU THE
MOST HORRIFIC TRUE CRIME STORIES!**

FROM THE FILES OF <u>TRUE DETECTIVE</u> MAGAZINE

GREED
KILLERS

Edited by
Rose G. Mandelsberg

PINNACLE BOOKS
WINDSOR PUBLISHING CORP.

The editor wishes to express her sincerest thanks and appreciation to Stan Munro whose relentless efforts in research made this book possible.

PINNACLE BOOKS are published by

Windsor Publishing Corp.
475 Park Avenue South
New York, NY 10016

First Printing: March, 1994

Printed in the United States of America

CONTENTS

"THEY BUTCHERED BENJI IN THE BATHTUB!"

by Gary King

It was 8:10 a.m. on Friday, November 28, 1986, when two tree cutters showed up for work at a Christmas tree farm in Molalla, Oregon, a small town just outside Portland in a rural area of Clackamas County. It was a cold, misty morning, typical of north-western Oregon weather at that time of year. An eerie shroud of clouds and fog clung stubbornly to the tops of the larger fir trees that stood sentry-like at the edge of the farm, as if guarding the smaller trees that would ultimately end up in homes from California to Texas during the yuletide season.

When the two tree cutters, Joe Magee and Tom Wilson, arrived at the farm owned by Molalla resident Carter Nelson, they felt as if the place had been deserted. Nelson subcontracted the cutting of his trees to a California business owned by a man named Lenny Miller. Nelson was away, and the cutting operation's foreman, a Mexican national they knew only by the name of Benji, was nowhere to be found. He wasn't in the area of the forest where he would normally be when the men showed up for work, and he wasn't in the equipment shed where they sometimes found him working on tools.

Not finding the tools they wanted in the equipment shed and not wanting to wait around to receive instructions from Benji, Magee and Wilson went to a travel trailer next to the shed to get a couple of the best-working chainsaws that they knew Benji always kept there. Since their boss couldn't be found to issue them a chainsaw, they reasoned they might as well use the best.

The trailer, which belonged to Lenny Miller's company, was used as Benji's residence. Magee found the front sliding door to the trailer wide open. He saw no one inside and figured that Benji must have gone into town for something or was working somewhere on the farm that they hadn't yet checked. Magee went into the living area, which was just beyond the sliding glass door, and brought out the two chainsaws. He gave one to his partner, and they went to work cutting trees not far from Benji's trailer.

At about 9:30 a.m., Magee encountered a problem with one of the chainsaws and returned to Benji's trailer to get some tools to fix it. He first looked for the tools in the living room but, unable to find them there, he walked into the bathroom. That was when, quite by surprise, he discovered Benji's whereabouts.

Magee stared in horror and revulsion at what had become of his friend and foreman. Benji was lying in the bathtub, covered with blood and stab wounds! Momentarily frozen where he stood, Magee eventually began to shake and cried out to his partner outside. When Wilson came in to see what the fuss was all about, he, too, got the shock of his life.

Horror-stricken and sick, Magee and Wilson left

the trailer as quickly as possible. They notified the Clackamas County Sheriff's Office from a telephone at another location at the farm.

A short time later, Sergeant Pat Tuley and Deputy Howard Fox arrived at the tree farm. They were met by Magee and Wilson, who were still visibly shaken over their macabre discovery. The two tree cutters led the lawmen to the small trailer situated at the end of a muddy, unpaved roadway. Tuley and Fox cringed when they saw the victim, identified by Magee only as Benji, lying in a supine position in the small bathtub. After confirming that the victim was dead and beyond help, Tuley and Fox reported back to C-Com, the Clackamas County Communications Center, to advise their superiors of the obvious homicide.

Meanwhile, in another part of the building, veteran homicide sleuth John Turner and his younger partner Mike Machado were busy catching up on a backlog of paperwork. It being the day after Thanksgiving, Turner and Machado had counted on almost everyone else at the department to take advantage of the paid holiday so they could work undisturbed. Or so they had hoped. Just before 10 o'clock, Lieutenant H. Pat Detloff, in charge of detectives at the time, walked in.

"I want you two down in Molalla," said Detloff. "We've got a body inside a trailer."

Detloff gave the two sleuths the address and they promptly left. Taking homicide kits with them on their way out, they instructed the deputy on duty to pass the word about the body to Deputy John Gilliland, the department's criminalist.

When Turner and Machado arrived at Nelson's Tree Farm at 10:20 a.m., Tuley and Fox briefed them on the situation. Before going inside, the two detectives methodically took in all the details outside. The property, they noted, was on the east side of Molalla Avenue and was heavily forested with Christmas trees. Also located on the property was owner Carter Nelson's home and several outbuildings. The travel trailer, a 1983 Timberbrook bearing New Mexico license number RVN7155, was located near the main residence. The trailer, they observed, also bore a 1986 California temporary registration with license number U166945. Papers that Tuley and Fox found indicated that it belonged to Lenny Miller.

They also noted a 1983 Dodge pickup with California license number 2T04618 parked in front of the equipment shed. Registration papers showed that it, too, was registered to Lenny Miller and was used in Miller's California-based company.

The trailer where the body was located was approximately 20 feet east of the storage shed. The detectives observed a tractor and a flatbed trailer, among various other pieces of farm equipment, inside the shed. Turning back to the Timberbrook trailer, Detectives Turner and Machado noted that it had two doors, one a sliding glass door and the other a single door located near the back. The door at the rear of the trailer, they learned, opened into a single bedroom.

The entire property was muddy and wet from recent heavy rain. The driveway was especially muddy, although in some locations someone had laid down gravel to make driving easier.

After Turner and Machado made a cursory examination of the exterior, Sergeant Tuley and Deputy Fox led them inside the trailer and eventually to the blood-covered body. On their way in, the detectives noted what appeared to be blood on the portion of the sliding glass door that fit into the door frame when it was closed. The blood was on both the inside and outside of the door. They deduced that it must have been left by someone who opened the door from the inside on their way out.

The sleuths noted that the living room also opened into the kitchen. They turned left and walked through the kitchen to the middle section of the trailer, where the bathroom was located. The bathroom was not visible from the living room, and the detectives concluded that that was why Joe Magee had not seen the body earlier when he had retrieved the two chainsaws.

Across from the bathroom, Turner and Machado noticed an upright clothes closet bearing two doors. One door handle had been broken, and they could see pry marks on the door frame. The marks were light in color and appeared to have been freshly made. Inside the bathroom, the detectives observed that the victim, a Hispanic man clad only in boxer shorts, was partially covered by a shower curtain and towel, both of which had apparently been torn down along with the curtain rod during a struggle. The victim's head was at the opposite end from the tub's drain, and his knees were bent. The victim was lying in a pool of partially coagulated blood that had seeped from numerous stab and slash wounds clearly visible over much of his body. The detectives noted several stab wounds to the victim's face and chest, but they did not move the body to look for additional wounds pending the arrival of the medical examiner.

Turner and Machado's preliminary examination led them to believe that the victim was in the bathtub at the time of the stabbing. But because there was no water in the tub and because the victim was wearing boxer shorts, it didn't appear that he had been bathing at the time of the attack. It seemed more likely to the detectives that the killer or killers had either pushed, shoved, or carried the victim to that location to carry out the butchery.

Turner and Machado noticed blood spatters and drops all over the bathroom walls, the shower stall, the sink, and the toilet. The toilet-seat cover had been broken off and was lying on the floor next to the toilet, topside down. They could see blood on the exposed underside. It was possible, they speculated, that the victim had been sitting on the toilet at the time the attack began. The toilet was full of tissue paper, on top of which lay a single cigarette butt. There was little or no water inside the toilet bowl. The probers subsequently learned from Magee and Wilson that the victim did not smoke, a fact that gave the cigarette butt an added significance. They also found a wooden-handled kitchen knife in the medicine cabinet above the sink, but they could not immediately determine whether or not it was the murder weapon.

Later, after a deputy medical examiner officially determined that the victim had died from stab wounds and blood loss and formally released the body, the detectives turned the corpse over and observed several more stab wounds on the left arm, on both hands, and on the right shoulder blade. Many of the wounds, they knew, were defensive, made as the victim futilely tried to fend off the savage attack.

Turning their attention to the bedroom, the sleuths observed articles of clothing scattered about the room. The messy pile of blankets on the bed suggested that someone had been sleeping in the bed, possibly even as the attack began. They also noted what they considered to be "blood transfer" on the fitted sheet near the foot of the bed. Did the violence begin in the bedroom? they wondered. Had the victim been asleep when attacked?

The detectives noticed that the door that led from the outside into the trailer's bedroom had fresh marks on it similar to the pry marks they found on the clothes closet. Someone, they believed, had attempted to break into the locked door, bolstering the possibility that the victim had been attacked while asleep. The door itself was buckled outward at the area of the pry marks.

If, as Turner's gut instinct told him, robbery had been the motive, it was peculiar that the killer or killers had gone to the trouble of breaking into the trailer and killing someone only to leave behind several semivaluable items, including a portable television in the living room and a radio-cassette player in the bedroom. Although such items weren't worth much, the detectives knew they could easily be sold for small amounts of quick cash. Might something or someone have frightened the perpetrators away, causing them to leave the items behind? Had they

13

found cash in Benji's possession and felt no need to take anything else? Or had Benji been killed for another, altogether different reason?

During their search of the trailer, Turner and Machado discovered a jacket, identified by witnesses as Benji's, with its pockets turned inside out. Inside one of the pockets was a single dollar bill. The detectives found no other money inside the trailer and no wallet containing money or identification of the victim.

About 10 feet north of the trailer's rear, Turner and Machado came across a brown knit cap and a dark blue sweater lying between a row of Christmas trees. When they picked up the cap, they discovered a partial shoe print in the mud beneath it. The shoe print appeared to be a straight, multi-ridged pattern, with the ridges about seven-sixteenths of an inch apart.

While awaiting additional crime scene personnel, Turner and Machado interviewed Joe Magee and Tom Wilson, the men who had found the body and called the sheriff's department. Magee and Wilson explained that they worked for Lenny Miller's company from California, which Carter Nelson had contracted to cut the trees on his property. They said they knew the foreman only as Benjamin or "Benji" and added that a fourth man, named Jim had recently begun working with them. Neither Magee nor Wilson knew Benji's or Jim's last names. Magee told the detectives that they had all worked together on Wednesday, November 26th, the day before Thanksgiving, until about noon, when Magee and Wilson stopped work to take off the rest of the day and all

14

of the next day. They related how they had arrived at work that morning and eventually found Benji's body.

Magee told the detectives that Lenny Miller and others had worked at the farm cutting trees until Sunday, November 23rd, at which time everyone except Benji, Magee, and Wilson left for California with a semi loaded with trees to sell. Magee said that Jim was not a member of the original crew but had been hired by Miller late Sunday morning to begin work with the remaining crew on Tuesday, November 25th. Before leaving on Sunday, Miller gave Benji $600 in cash to be used for paying the crew that remained behind. Magee said that Miller also cashed Benji's payroll check for $138, leaving Benji with a total of about $738 in cash.

If robbery was, in fact, the motive for Benji's vicious murder, $738 wasn't much money for a person's life, Detective Turner reflected. But then, he had investigated cases where people had been killed for much less.

Jim arrived for work on Tuesday, November 25th, as planned, Magee continued. At the end of the day, in accordance with the usual procedure, Benji paid each worker in cash. Magee said that Jim even helped Benji figure out the wages for that day. When Magee and Wilson left at noon the next day, Jim told Benji that he would work with him on Thanksgiving Day if he wanted him to. But neither Magee nor Wilson knew if Jim actually did work on Thanksgiving.

Both men described Jim as a Caucasian male, about 25 years old, 6 feet tall, and weighing about

160 to 170 pounds. They said he had a mustache and shoulder-length, sandy-blond hair. They also said he wore a black baseball cap that had an emblem of a steel bar and the word "metals" on it. Magee and Wilson told the detectives that Jim lived in the Molalla area and that one of his relatives worked as a cook at a local cafe.

The knit cap and dark blue sweater found behind the trailer, Magee and Wilson said, were Benji's. Turner and Machado subsequently found a black baseball cap inside the Dodge pickup parked in front of the toolshed. Magee identified the cap as belonging to Jim.

As soon as he arrived, Deputy John Gilliland photographed the crime scene extensively. He would also conduct a cyanoacrylate or Super Glue treatment of the entire bathroom, enabling him to lift prints from several locations.

At the conclusion of the crime scene work, the victim's body was zipped up inside a yellow body bag and taken to the state medical examiner's office in Portland.

The next day, November 29th, Turner, Machado, and Gilliland viewed the autopsy performed by Dr. Larry Lewman, state medical examiner. Lewman informed the detectives that the victim had sustained numerous stab wounds, including ones to the top of the head that exposed the skull bone. Lewman said the probable cause of death was a stab wound to the heart. Lewman pointed out the wounds and told the lawmen that the weapon most likely used was a knife. As best as could be determined, the victim had been stabbed 39 times. Several of the defensive wounds, particularly those to the hands, were knife cuts that went all the way to the bone.

Gilliland thoroughly photographed the autopsy, then obtained fingernail scrapings from the victim's hands. He also obtained inked fingerprints and palm prints from the victim, all of which were turned over to Detective Turner.

The fingerprints quickly paid off. Through them, the victim was identified as Benjamin Paris Hernandez, a Mexican national whom the detectives were able to trace to Modesto, California. Hernandez, they learned, had been involved in a drunken driving incident and had lost his driver's license as a result. Otherwise he did not have an extensive record. He nonetheless went by several aliases, including Mendoza Javier Medina, Benjamin Hernandez Paris, Benjamin Parides, Hernandez Javier Nunes, Medina Javier Mendoza, and Fernandez Perez.

On Sunday, November 30th, Detective Machado reached Lenny Miller by telephone. Miller told him that his tree cutting crew had been working at the Nelson tree farm since the first week in November, and that he had hired Benjamin Hernandez as his "straw boss" or foreman.

Miller said that on Sunday morning, November 23rd, he and his crew were having breakfast at a Molalla restaurant when a person named Jim approached him about work. Miller said he hired Jim on the spot. Miller said he had told Benji, Magee, and Wilson to take off Monday, November 24th, and told Jim to report for work on Tuesday. As he was leaving the restaurant, Miller said, he introduced Jim to Benji. But he didn't know Jim's last name. He left

17

that detail to Benji, he said. Miller described Jim as Caucasian, 21 years old, 5 foot, 9 inches tall and weighing about 170 pounds. He said Jim wore his auburn hair about collar-length.

Miller confirmed Magee's statement about having given Benji $600 in cash just before he and the others left for California. He said the cash was in denominations of $100s, $50s, and $20s.

Later that same day, Detectives Turner and Machado went to the Molalla restaurant where Lenny Miller and his crew had eaten breakfast that Monday before Thanksgiving. The sleuths spoke with a waitress who said she was familiar with the crew and remembered seeing a man who fit the description of Jim that Monday talking to Lenny Miller at the front counter. The waitress agreed to help detectives construct a composite of Jim later that day.

The detectives asked another restaurant employee if she knew any cooks in town who had a relative named Jim. She immediately responded that the Jim they were talking about was probably Jim Cudaback, whose relative worked at that very restaurant.

The employee said that Jim had shown up unexpectedly from out of state recently and that his relatives had seemed shocked when they learned he was in town. She didn't know why they had been shocked about his return, unless it was because he had been gone for so long. She said Jim had been staying with his relatives and that he often came to the restaurant to have coffee with a family member.

That same day, Turner and Machado went to the Molalla Police Department and conducted a routine records check on Jim Cudaback. They located an address for his family in the 16400 block of South Union Mills Road, a slightly-wooded rural setting near the town of Mulino. They also rustled up a 1982 Molalla High School Yearbook in which they found a photograph of James Lee Cudaback. It fit the general description they had so far received of the guy named "Jim."

The two detectives decided to return to the tree farm and speak with the owner, Carter Nelson. Nelson remembered seeing Jim for the first time a few days before Benji's death. In fact, he said, he saw Benji and Jim working together on Wednesday, November 26th.

"Benji was still alive at noon on Thursday, November 27th," Nelson said.

Nelson said that at that time, he asked Benji to move his pickup so he could get a tractor out of the equipment shed. Benji moved the vehicle to the spot where it was found on Friday. As far as Nelson knew, the pickup hadn't been moved since. No one was with Benji and no crews were working the farm that Thursday afternoon. As they parted ways after the pickup was moved, Benji told Nelson that he was going to "siesta." Nelson never saw Benji again.

The tree farmer described Jim as a white male in his early to mid 20s, standing 5-foot-8 to 5-foot-9, weighing about 140 to 150 pounds, with auburn hair and a scraggly beard.

After leaving the farm, Turner and Machado were driving north on Molalla Avenue when, only about 500 feet from Nelson's driveway, they noticed an unpaved road that headed eastward, back into the tree farm. They turned onto the road, drove about 20 feet, and stopped when they noticed fresh tire tracks leading up the road to a turnaround near a grassy area just ahead.

When they got out to take a look, they realized that the grassy area led east to Nelson's tree field. As they looked farther, they observed that the tree field extended to an area just behind Benji's trailer. The two sleuths climbed over a wire fence and began walking southward on a grass path that skirted the rows of trees.

It wasn't long before the sleuths located a set of shoe prints in the pathway. The path, between a row of trees, was muddy and wet. The shoe print was immediately recognizable as of the same pattern as the shoe print they found beneath the cap behind Benji's trailer.

Turner and Machado followed the tracks eastward about 200 feet to where they apparently began. At that point the tracks turned south, ending up at the exact location of the first shoe print they found at the crime scene. They noted that the tracks led from the fence to the trailer and back to the fence. But the spacing between the prints that led from the fence to the trailer was less than those that led from the trailer back to the fence. This prompted the detectives to conclude that the person who made the prints *walked* toward the trailer and *ran* away from it.

At Turner and Machado's request, criminalist Gilliland soon arrived and began taking photos of the tire impressions and shoe prints. He also took measurements and made plaster casts.

Still later that same day, Turner and Machado returned to the Molalla Police Department where they met with the waitress who had seen Jim talking with Lenny Miller. With her assistance, they put together a composite of their "person of interest." Then they returned to the Nelson tree farm. When shown the composite, both Joe Magee and Tom Wilson told the detectives that it very closely resembled the man Lenny Miller had hired whom they knew as Jim.

Turner and Machado went to the home where they heard Jim Cudaback was staying. They were told by a relative there that Jim had not been in the area for at least two to three years. The relative did say, however, that Jim had shown up about two and a half weeks earlier, and that he had been staying in a small camping trailer on his family's South Union Mills Road property.

The relative said he was aware that Jim was working on the tree farm in Molalla recently and that he had worked there during Thanksgiving week. The relative confirmed that Jim got the job from a man who had been in the restaurant where another relative worked.

The relative also told the detectives that he had seen Jim driving the Dodge Ram pickup that belonged to "the Spanish guy," whose name he didn't know. He said that the "Spanish guy" sometimes asked Jim to drive him around because he had no license. The relative said that Jim had mentioned that he liked the "Spanish guy" because he always paid Jim at the end of each workday and because he took Jim to breakfast and to lunch.

Jim, however, did not work on Thanksgiving Day,

the relative said. Instead, he spent the day with his relatives at their home, and later spent some time with a person named Robert Dotts, described as a family acquaintance.

Turner and Machado wanted to know what the circumstances were surrounding the time Jim spent with Dotts.

Jim's relative replied that at approximately 7:30 p.m. on Thanksgiving, he asked everyone to leave because he wanted to watch a movie, undisturbed, on television. They left in Dotts' car and Jim never returned that night.

The next day, Cudaback's relative said, he went to Dotts' apartment, a small, one-bedroom unit in a complex in Molalla, but found nobody home. Knowing that Dotts was a flaky sort, the relative said he looked inside the window to see if they had moved out overnight. All of Dotts' belongings, however, were still inside the apartment. When he returned home, the relative said, he looked inside the trailer where Jim had been staying and saw that his things were still there, too.

The relative also showed the detectives a pair of Jim's work boots that he had found in the trailer. Their curiosity piqued, Turner and Machado examined the sole pattern but quickly found that it did not match the tracks they found on the tree farm. When asked if Jim owned any other shoes, the relative said that Jim had recently purchased a pair of gray, felt-type shoes with "bumps on the bottoms."

The relative said he hadn't seen Jim or Dotts since Thanksgiving evening. The detectives also learned that Dotts had a girlfriend named Maggie Sinclair, who lived with Dotts and worked at a restaurant in Molalla.

First, however, Detectives Turner and Machado, although exhausted from such a long day, returned to the Molalla Police Department where they ran a records check on Robert Dotts. They learned that Dotts' full name was Robert Joe Dotts, and that he was born on December 27, 1962. The most recent address listed in the records was an apartment in the 300 block of Heintz Road in Molalla. Dotts, they learned, had been issued a traffic citation on November 16, 1986, in Oregon City while driving a 1973 Chevrolet station wagon bearing Oregon license number FGW-081.

Next the sleuths went to the restaurant where Maggie Sinclair worked, but they were told by the night manager that Maggie hadn't been heard from in several days. Maggie had last worked on Wednesday night, November 26th, and was scheduled to work on Friday night and Saturday, but she had failed to show up for work.

"It was strange that she didn't show up for work," said the manager. "She is normally very dependable and a good employee. Besides, she should have shown up for work because she has some money coming to her." The night manager said nobody had heard from her and no one she had talked to knew where Maggie was.

The next day, Monday, December 1st, Turner and Machado went to the apartment complex on Heintz Road where the manager told them that Dotts and Maggie lived in apartment number 8. The manager told the detectives, however, that they wouldn't find

Dotts and Maggie at the apartment. The couple had moved out, apparently in the middle of the night, and had not told anyone they were moving.

"They even left behind a hundred-dollar cleaning fee that could have been refundable," said the manager. "They didn't even leave a forwarding address."

The manager explained that neighbors found the back sliding glass door to Dotts' apartment open the night before. When the neighbors looked inside, they discovered that everything, including a stereo they had just loaned Dotts, was gone. The manager told the detectives that she didn't know Dotts and Maggie were gone until the neighbors informed her. She also said that, before the neighbors found Dotts' apartment vacant, a tenant had seen someone knocking at the back door to Dotts' apartment.

Could that have been Jim's relative looking for Jim? the detectives wondered.

The neighbors who found Dotts' apartment vacant told the detectives that Dotts and Maggie had been at home on Thanksgiving Day, at least until 4:00 p.m. The neighbors knew the couple was home because the apartment walls are thin and they could hear Dotts and Maggie arguing about something. The neighbors left at 4:00 p.m. to visit some friends, but when they returned at 9:00 p.m., they heard nothing coming from Dotts' apartment. They did, however, remember hearing noises coming from Dotts' apartment on Friday night at about 8:00, but they didn't investigate. They recalled talking with Dotts on Wednesday night, when he came over to borrow the stereo. Asked if they had seen any blood, cuts, or other injuries on Dotts at that time, the neighbors said they hadn't. They added that they hadn't seen Dotts or Maggie since Thanksgiving, and they had no idea why they left in such an extreme hurry.

A short time later, Turner and Machado spoke to another neighbor at the apartment complex, who told them that she heard all kinds of noises coming from Dotts' apartment on Friday night, November 28th, from approximately 10:00 p.m. to 2:00 a.m.

"It sounded like closet doors were banging, as well as the front door," the neighbor said. "They were home on Thanksgiving until the afternoon. There was a lot of noise coming from their apartment, on into the afternoon, and then it was just quiet. We believed the people had left. Then they came home Thursday night. We could hear them through the walls."

The neighbor said that Dotts and Maggie had two small children and drove a brown, older model full-size Chevrolet station wagon. They said they hadn't seen Dotts, Maggie, the children, or the car for a few days.

The detectives later interviewed another of Jim's relatives, the one who worked at a Molalla restaurant. She told the detectives that Jim went by the name Jimmy Lee Cudaback, but he sometimes used the last name of Canaday. Cudaback, they learned, was born on September 10, 1965, making him 21 at the time. The relative confirmed what another relative had already said, that Jim had been gone about three years but had returned to town about a month before, in early October.

The relative also confirmed what the detectives

25

had already learned about Jim's being hired by Lenny Miller.

On Jim's first day at work, the relative continued, another family member drove him to the tree farm. He worked that Tuesday and again on Wednesday. At about noon on Wednesday, Jim and the foreman, "the Mexican guy" showed up at the restaurant looking for another person to help them. It so happened that another of Jim's relatives was at the restaurant, and he was hired, as Jim had been, on the spot. The foreman, Jim, and Jim's relative left promptly. After work that day, Jim and the foreman dropped the relative off at home at about 5:00 p.m., after which Jim and the foreman went out drinking. The foreman dropped Jim off at home at about 7:30 p.m.

The relative confirmed that Jim stayed home on Thanksgiving Day until 7:30 or 8:00 p.m., when he left with Dotts and Maggie in Dotts' station wagon. She said she told Jim as he was leaving not to forget that he had to go to work the next morning. However, when no one in the family had heard from Jim by the next morning, family members went to Dotts' apartment where they presumed Jim had spent the night. Upon their arrival, they noticed that the station wagon was not there, and they got no response when they knocked on the apartment door.

The relative told the detectives that as time went on, she became more concerned. She went to the apartment herself at about 12:45 p.m. on Friday and then again on Saturday at about the same time. On both occasions, she related, the station wagon was not there and no one answered the door. Concerned about the whereabouts of Jim, Maggie, and Robert,

26

the relative said she returned to the apartment again on Sunday only to learn that Maggie and Robert had moved out unexpectedly.

"The fact that Jim, Maggie, and Robert just up and left was strange," she said. "When we got to the apartment, the station wagon was still gone and we found the back sliding door standing open about one inch. We opened the door and found that the apartment was empty, except for a few of the children's toys lying on the floor. It looked like they had left in a hurry."

The relative told Turner and Machado that Jim, Maggie, and Dotts were all cigarette smokers. She also said that Jim wore boots and a pair of suede-like shoes, and that Robert sometimes wore rubber boots but more often wore tennis shoes.

Later that same day, Detective Turner returned to the apartment complex where Dotts and Maggie had lived. He spoke to another neighbor whose living-room window looked down upon the lot where Dotts normally parked his station wagon. The neighbor said she could also see the sliding back door of Dotts' apartment from her unit.

The neighbor told Turner that she wasn't certain, but she thought it was on Friday, November 28th, about 3:30 p.m. when she saw Dotts' station wagon pull into the parking area and Dotts and his girlfriend get out of their car. She observed that Dotts' right hand was bleeding, and she also saw blood on Dotts' arm.

"He had a towel or cloth wrapped around the little finger and ring finger of his right hand," the neighbor recalled. "He wasn't wearing a shirt, and I saw scratches on the left side of his chest." The neighbor said she believed Dotts was wearing jeans and tennis shoes at the time.

The neighbor also told Turner that the light near Dotts' sliding glass door was normally left on all the time, but that it hadn't been on since Thanksgiving. She said that she thought that was unusual.

Had Dotts been cut during the struggle with Benji? Detective Turner wondered. If he had been, then it was very possible that Benji had been killed early on the day his body was discovered.

It was also possible that the neighbor had been mistaken about the day she saw a bleeding Dotts and his girlfriend in the parking lot. She could have seen them on *Thursday* at 3:30 p.m., not Friday. After all, she said she wasn't certain. She only said it was "possibly" on Friday, November 28th.

Turner and Machado knew, of course, that just because Dotts had been seen bleeding, that didn't necessarily mean he was involved in Benji's death. It did make them suspicious, but they knew it was possible Dotts had received the wounds some other way.

Meanwhile, results of tests on the evidence began to come back from the Oregon State Police Crime Detection Laboratory in Portland. The crime lab determined that blood found on the underside of the toilet seat in Benji's trailer was deposited both as directional spatter and as droplets. It was also found to be type A, which was consistent with Benjamin Hernandez's blood type. Blood found near the body was also consistent with Benji's type. The spatter was indicative of violence that would cause the blood to travel away from the victim at high velocity.

28

On Friday, December 5th, at 10:30 a.m., Detective Machado and criminalist Deputy John Gilliland served a search warrant at the apartment that Robert Dotts had hurriedly vacated only days earlier. They lifted several latent fingerprints from various locations to compare with those found inside Benji's trailer. They also collected blood samples from the bathroom, the bedroom, and the kitchen, as well as from wood chips found inside a kitchen drawer.

Afterward, Machado and Gilliland served a search warrant at the trailer on South Union Mills Road where Jim Cudaback was known to have lived. They lifted latent prints from that dwelling, too, as well as a sample of what appeared to be dried blood on the bed.

As one day followed another, Detectives Turner and Machado hoped their efforts would eventually pay off. They had collected a lot of evidence from a number of locations, but without a suspect to compare it to, they had no way to determine its significance, if any, to the crime.

Shortly after they began focusing on Jim Cudaback and Robert Dotts as potential suspects in Benji Hernandez's slaying, the two detectives issued a nationwide APB for the two men, as well as for Dotts' Chevrolet station wagon. Much to their dismay, however, the suspects and the car seemed nowhere to be found.

Then, as luck would have it, on Thursday, December 11th at 2:00 p.m., Dotts and Maggie Sinclair appeared at the Clackamas County Sheriff's Office in Oregon City. They said they had heard from Maggie's relatives that the detectives wanted to talk to them about Benjamin Hernandez's murder.

Detective Machado spoke to Maggie Sinclair first. Maggie related that on November 28th at about 1:00 a.m., Robert Dotts and Jimmy Cudaback went to Hernandez's trailer to get money that Jimmy said Benji owed him. Earlier, Maggie explained, Jimmy had been talking about how they could all move to Texas where Dotts came from and where Dotts and Maggie had been wanting to move to. They could do it that very night, Jimmy said. He had $100 saved up, and with that and what his boss owed him, they'd have enough to get to Texas. Jimmy even said he would pay all their expenses if they wanted to leave with him that night.

Maggie said that Dotts agreed to go with Jimmy to Benji's trailer. When they returned, Dotts told Maggie that Jimmy had "hit the guy," meaning Benji. Dotts told Maggie that he had parked away from Benji's trailer, out of view. A short time later, Jimmy came running up to the station wagon, pushed Dotts, and said, "Let's go." Dotts told Maggie that Jimmy had fought Benji for the money. Benji threw a punch at him, so Jimmy picked up something and hit him with it. Jimmy said that he succeeded in getting the money. A short time later, Maggie said, they loaded up the station wagon and left Oregon. On November 30th, they arrived in Pauls Valley, Oklahoma, where Maggie and Dotts dropped off Jimmy Cudaback.

Maggie said that at no time did she observe any blood on either Dotts or Cudaback and added that neither man had been injured. She said she could not explain the blood found in the apartment that she

30

and Dotts left so suddenly.

Next, Detectives Turner and Machado interviewed Robert Dotts. Dotts' version of events was similar to Maggie Sinclair's but provided considerably more detail.

Dotts told the detectives that he drove Cudaback to an area later identified as the tree farm, where he dropped Cudaback off on the road so Cudaback could talk to a guy who owed him money.

Dotts said that after he let Cudaback out of the car, he drove up the road a short distance, turned around, and returned to the spot where he'd dropped Cudaback off. He said that Cudaback never told him what had gone on in the trailer. Dotts said he never got out of the car, and that Cudaback never forced him to go back to the apartment. Dotts said that he never saw any blood on Cudaback, nor did Cudaback appear to be injured in any manner. They quickly returned to the apartment, packed up their belongings, and left.

They traveled to Pauls Valley, Oklahoma, Dotts said, where Cudaback decided to stay. As Dotts and Maggie prepared to leave for Texas, Cudaback told Dotts that he had stabbed his foreman "thirty-nine times."

"We started fighting and fighting, and I stabbed him and kept stabbing him," Dotts quoted Cudaback as saying. During the entire trip, but particularly prior to making the purported confession, Cudaback kept telling Dotts and Maggie to stick by him.

When the detectives reinterviewed Dotts on tape, Dotts repeated much of what he had said and was consistent about what had happened both before and after the incident at the tree farm. But he altered his account about how Benji was killed. Instead of saying that Jimmy Cudaback had stabbed him to death, he said that Cudaback had beaten the victim with a two-by-four. He said nothing about the stabbing.

"Why are you changing your story now to a beating, instead of a stabbing?" asked one of the detectives.

"I never said anything about anyone being stabbed," replied Dotts. He denied that Cudaback ever told him about the stabbing, and continued to deny that he had ever told the detectives about a stabbing.

When asked about the blood found in the apartment, Dotts explained that it was his own. He said that earlier in the day, he and Maggie had gone to a store in Oregon City to cash in some pop bottles and cans. One of the bottles had broke, Dotts said, and when he reached into the back to get it out, he cut his finger on the glass. Dotts showed the detectives a cut about two inches long, which was healing, on the knuckle of his left index finger. The detectives observed that the cut was a straight-line cut, not a jagged, random cut. Dotts explained that the cut had bled throughout the day, and that he had to continually wrap the finger with tissue paper.

The next day, Dotts requested that Turner and Machado meet with him again, because he now wanted to tell them the truth about the events surrounding Benji's death. The two detectives contacted Dotts in the town of Mulino, near Molalla.

On the morning that the murder occurred, Dotts

told the detectives, he got out of the car and started to walk down the roadway to where Jimmy Cudaback had gone. It was at that time that Cudaback came back and pushed him, telling him that they had to leave. But Cudaback hadn't told Dotts why they needed to get out of there.

On Wednesday, December 17th, Turner and Machado served search warrants on Robert Dotts and Maggie Sinclair to have their blood samples drawn at a local hospital and to obtain finger and palm prints. They also served a warrant to search Dotts' 1973 Chevrolet station wagon. The car was towed to the sheriff's office impound garage.

The car was in a filthy condition, literally filled with junk and garbage, articles of black clothing, a cooler chest, a gasoline can, and several children's toys. The car was carefully photographed, and evidence was collected and properly tagged.

During the course of their continuing investigation, the detectives also seized two identical hunting knives with six-inch blades. A small amount of blood, identified as human, was removed from the hilt of one of the knives. The blood sample was too small for further testing. The other knife, which had no blood on it, had a bent tip. According to the crime lab technicians, the fresh pry marks on the exterior door to Benji Hernandez's trailer corresponded with the dimensions of the knife bearing the bent tip. As for the cigarette butt found inside Benji's toilet, the crime lab's findings were inconclusive.

After contacting authorities in Wagoner County, Oklahoma, to ask for assistance in locating Jimmy Cudaback, Detectives Turner and Machado learned that Cudaback was working in Wagoner, a small town just outside Tulsa. With the assistance of Oklahoma authorities, the detectives traced him to a specific job site, and then they flew to Oklahoma on Friday, December 19th, a week before Christmas.

Accompanied by a number of deputies from the Wagoner County Sheriff's Office, the lawmen surrounded the job site. When everyone was in place, a deputy ordered everybody "down on the ground." Machado, recognizing their suspect, walked up to a man of medium height and build with longish auburn hair.

"Are you Jimmy Cudaback?" asked Machado.

"Yes, I am."

"You're under arrest for murder from the state of Oregon," said Machado.

"I don't know anything about any murder," responded Cudaback.

"Have you ever heard of the name Robert Dotts?" asked Turner as they put handcuffs on Cudaback.

"Those lousy sonsofbitches!" Cudaback blurted out. "I want to tell my story," he added as he reached out to Machado.

"Shut up!" Turner snapped. "We have to give you your rights."

After reading Cudaback his Miranda rights verbatim, the detectives had the suspect sign a standard Miranda card acknowledging that he understood his rights. Afterward, Cudaback anxiously agreed to have his statement tape recorded. For the next two and a half hours, Turner and Machado couldn't shut their suspect up. During the interview, the detectives continuously reminded him of his rights. But Cuda-

34

back continued to talk.

Cudaback recounted how he and Dotts had gone to the tree farm, possibly as late as 1:00 a.m. on the morning of November 28th. They had talked it over previously, and decided to go to the trailer to obtain whatever money Benji had on him. Maggie Sinclair, Cudaback said, was told to start packing as they left.

Cudaback said that he and Dotts changed clothes prior to leaving, dressing entirely in black, silk-like "ninja" costumes. Their entire faces and head, except for eye holes, were covered. They changed into the ninja outfits at the side of the apartment complex so that neighbors wouldn't see them leaving the apartment. Then they had Maggie drive the car to where they were. Leaving Maggie behind to pack, they left for the tree farm. Each carried a knife.

They parked the vehicle, walked up the road north of the farm's driveway, and entered a wooded area. There they crossed a fence — where Turner and Machado would find the footprints — and then approached Benji's trailer from behind.

Cudaback said he tried the trailer's rear door, but it was locked. He then tried the front sliding door and finding it open, he entered. He started for the back of the trailer, but he found that the bedroom door was closed and locked. He then left the trailer and told Dotts what was going on.

Dotts tried the rear door to see for himself that it was locked. Obviously disappointed, he told Cudaback that they needed the money to go to Texas. Cudaback then reentered the trailer and called out for Benji. When he heard Benji moving, he identified himself as Lenny Miller, Benji's boss. When Benji came out and saw that he had been duped, a fight began and Benji was stabbed to death, Cudaback said.

Following the stabbing, Cudaback went into the bedroom and picked up a pair of plaid pants, feeling a wallet in the right rear pocket. He left the trailer with the pants and went back to where Dotts was waiting. Together, the men removed the wallet and found that it contained approximately $300. Then they left the area, using the same route they had taken to get to the trailer.

While Dotts drove, Cudaback went through the wallet and pants pockets. Afterward, Dotts told Cudaback to get rid of the pants. Cudaback then rolled down the window and threw the pants out. They then drove back to the apartment, loaded up the car, and gave Maggie Sinclair the money they had stolen.

They drove to Oklahoma, leaving Oregon through the eastern part of the state via I-84. At a location somewhere between The Dalles and Pendleton, they threw the victim's wallet into a small river. Upon arriving in Pauls Valley, Oklahoma, Dotts and Maggie stranded Cudaback.

In his statement, Jimmy Cudaback insisted that had Dotts not pushed the issue of getting the money to go to Texas, he wouldn't have stabbed Hernandez.

On December 21st, Turner interviewed Robert Dotts again and confronted him with Cudaback's statement. This time Dotts admitted he had gone to the scene with Cudaback dressed in the dark clothing the detectives had seized from Dotts' car. But Dotts maintained that he had remained outside the trailer

36

during the fight between Cudaback and the victim. Dotts admitted to Detective Turner that he had previously lied about certain details of his actions that night. Dotts told Turner essentially everything that Cudaback had stated, but he left out the part about planning the crime. Dotts maintained that he had no involvement in the victim's death, but he agreed that they had obtained approximately $380 from Benji's wallet. Dotts was initially arrested on charges of first-degree robbery and hindering prosecution, and later of manslaughter.

Cudaback waived extradition to Oregon and was lodged in the Clackamas County Jail on accusations of aggravated murder and robbery. While in jail, he contacted Turner and Machado and surprised them again.

"How do I fire my attorney so that I can plead guilty?" he asked.

After working out a plea-bargain arrangement with the district attorney's office, Cudaback admitted to stabbing Benjamin Hernandez, although he didn't know how many times. Rather than go to trial for aggravated murder, in which he could have received the death penalty if convicted, Jimmy Cudaback was allowed to plead guilty to first-degree murder. On May 5, 1987, James Lee Cudaback was sentenced to life in prison. He will be eligible for parole after 10 years.

Similarly, Robert Joe Dotts worked out a plea-bargain arrangement, and on June 11, 1987, he pleaded guilty to manslaughter and first-degree robbery. He was sentenced to prison for nine years on each offense, with credit for time served in the county jail. Actual time served for both inmates will be determined by the state parole board.

Maggie Sinclair was not charged with any crime.

EDITOR'S NOTE:
Joe Magee, Tom Wilson, Lenny Miller, Carter Nelson, and Maggie Sinclair are not the real names of the persons so named in the foregoing story. Fictitious names have been used because there is no reason for public interest in the identities of these persons.

"THE EXXON EXEC'S 5 DAYS OF HELL!"

by Bud Ampolsk

Shortly before 7:30 a.m. on Wednesday, April 29, 1992, 57-year-old Sidney Reso finished breakfast, wished his wife of 37 years a tender goodbye, and slipped out the front door. Impeccably dressed and looking every inch the top executive of one of the world's leading corporations, the bespectacled president of Exxon International slid behind the wheel of his automobile. Today he would not employ the services of a company driver to make the 10-minute junket from his Morris Township home to the company's headquarters in Florham Park, New Jersey. Today, he'd drive himself.

Essentially a simple man who wore his cloak of authority with a refreshing ease, Reso was used to doing for himself. He would tool his automobile the 200 feet to the road, step out to pick up the morning papers, then be on his way.

At 8:00 a.m., a neighbor whose husband also worked for Exxon saw Reso's car still parked in the driveway, the door open and the engine idling. Her suspicions aroused by the strange sight, the woman put a call through to Reso's office only to be told that he had not yet arrived.

Within seconds, an Exxon Executive called the Reso home to investigate the situation. The accuracy of the report of Reso's abandoned car was confirmed by Reso's wife, to whom fell the nerve-jarring task of determining what was going on at the spot where the Reso driveway met the road.

Even a cursory glance showed that something indeed was very much amiss. Not only was the car door slightly ajar, but the key was still in the ignition, the engine was idling, and Reso's briefcase and topcoat were inside. Yet Sidney Reso was nowhere to be seen.

Informed that one of Morris County's most prominent citizens appeared to have vanished into thin air, the county prosecutor's office and township police launched an immediate probe, even though Reso had been missing for only a short time.

Reso's job description alone would have been enough to trigger such action.

During 1991 alone, the last year for which corporate figures were available, foreign ventures managed by Reso had yielded $6.9 billion of the company's $8.4 billion pre-tax earnings. More than $50 billion of Exxon's $87.5 billion net assets were under his control.

Morris County Prosecutor Michael Murphy Jr. quickly went public with the news that Morris Township police were working with New Jersey State Police and FBI agents in search of the missing executive. The search would be conducted in an area of large homes separated by substantial tracts of land where the deer are slightly more numerous than the millionaires.

Morris Township police cruisers blocked the road as officers on horseback were joined on the ground by search dog patrols and overhead by helicopters.

At day's end, according to Prosecutor Murphy, searchers had come up empty-handed. "We simply do not know what happened to Mr. Reso," Murphy said. "We do not know whether it was a voluntary or involuntary disappearance. At this juncture, we have exhausted our leads in the immediate area."

The prosecutor told reporters he had no reason to believe that anything unusual had prompted Reso's disappearance—there had been no personal problems or large debts, for example. Murphy said he had asked the FBI and the state police to join the search "due to the stature of the person involved." He noted that the case was being handled as a "high-intensity missing person's case."

However, Murphy did not rule out the possibility that Reso might have been "the victim of a forced abduction." The county prosecutor added, "We're not eliminating any possibility."

The bits and scraps of information about Sidney Reso's background that began to filter in gave every indication that the missing man was a "straight arrow" with nothing in his personal or corporate life to explain his sudden disappearance.

From the very start, Sidney Reso had embodied the American dream. He had not been born to wealth but received a greater treasure than that—the nurturing love and guidance of a staunchly religious family.

In his high school days in New Orleans, Reso won

41

the respect of his fellow students with his athletic prowess, his intelligence, and his unassuming ways. A star member of his football team, although standing only 5-foot-10 and weighing 180 pounds, the youngster used his brain power to overcome the size advantage of brawnier opponents.

In the late 1950s, Reso was accepted into the engineering program of Louisiana State University (LSU). One professor who remembers Reso well from those days said of him, "He was confident and streetwise. He'd stand people down, put you in your place quickly. He certainly wasn't a wimp. He was a pretty rugged-looking guy. Women would find him attractive, you bet."

But unlike other jocks, Reso was of a serious mind. He courted one girl and married her while still an undergraduate. The couple's first child was born while Reso was in college. In all, they would have five children together, although one would die tragically early.

In straitened financial circumstances, Reso financed his education with scholarships and working at summer jobs.

Having graduated from LSU, Reso was hired by Humble Oil as a junior engineer. His former professors remained very much in tough with the young man who had caught their eye. Said one, "If you want one single thing he did, he was responsible for the development of newly discovered off-shore oil and gas reserves in the Bass Straits in Australia."

When Humble Oil was absorbed by Exxon, Reso became a division manager in 1973. Only one year later he was promoted to manage production operations in Houston.

Reso went through a series of foreign assignments, serving in Australia and England, before returning to Exxon U.S.A. as vice president in charge of production. He was appointed executive vice president in 1985 and transferred to Exxon International in 1986. In 1987, Reso was named president of Exxon International.

Throughout his career, Reso remained a devoted family man, living a quiet life. He was well known at a Morristown restaurant where he and his wife dined as frequently as three times a month. The big attraction for Reso was the piano music of Mozart and Beethoven that was performed live there.

One employee of the cafe commented, "He talked with a great deal of wisdom about what was real in life. I didn't know he was such a big shot."

Added another, "I'm not naive. But you can tell a phony, and if Sid Reso's a phony, it'd blow your mind."

A longterm friend viewed Reso in these terms. "He's not bible-thumping and all of that, but Sid and [Mrs. Reso] are one of those dying breeds, once committed to each other, committed forever.

"With Sid," the distraught friend told a reporter, "you don't think you're in the presence of God. He breathes different air than I do, but hey, it's hard to believe this guy controls the pulse of a multinational company. If [a kidnapper] does have him, my question would be, 'Why him?' "

An Exxon executive who worked alongside the missing corporate president said of Reso, "If you want to talk about a guy who blends in and doesn't stand out, he's certainly one. He's not flamboyant. He blends into the crowd. He's direct, but he's not abrasive, not a desk pounder, or anything like that."

Despite the general opinion that there was nothing devious about Reso that could have led to his vanishing, Lois Ferguson, a spokeswoman for Prosecutor Murphy insisted, "We're not counting out any possibility." She said she knew of no threats or personal business or labor problems that could be behind his disappearance, "but we're still investigating."

Those familiar with international commerce gave little credence to theories that Reso was abducted by foreign terrorists or by radical environmentalists still raging over the oil spill in Valdez, Alaska.

Stated one stock market analyst who follows Exxon, "When you're in a position like his [Reso's] they give you training in how to protect yourself. When you go overseas to these areas, you're pretty much a marked person."

For their part, lawmen were playing down the possibility that the missing corporate head had fallen prey to kidnappers—at least, they refused to go public with speculation along those lines. But out of the public eye, they were moving in that direction. In short order, literally hundreds of FBI agents, backed by state and local police, had converged on Morristown and its environs, attempting to establish contact with parties who might be holding Reso.

What investigators were not talking about was that on Thursday, April 30th, one day after Reso's abandoned Mercedes had been discovered in his driveway, Exxon executives at Florham Park received a call directing them to nearby Livingston Mall, where they discovered a note telling them to await further instructions.

On Friday, May 1st, a second note, this one found in a park in Morristown some five miles from the Reso home, did little, if anything, to clarify Reso's condition or whereabouts. However, the missive was ominously signed "Rainbow Warriors." The signature suggested the involvement of an unknown extremist environmental group. *Rainbow Warrior* was the name of an environmentalist ship that had been bombed by French secret service agents in 1985 in a dispute over nuclear waste dumping in the high seas.

As late as Thursday, May 7th, following a leak to the press concerning the possibility that ransom communications had been started, Prosecutor Murphy refused to confirm such reports.

The Morris County prosecutor said, "Absent current photographs and/or voice recordings, this office cannot reach the conclusion that Mr. Reso is in the custody of any particular group." He released a statement condemning Reso's kidnapping from the environmental group that had sponsored the bombed ship *Rainbow Warrior*.

One reason officials continued to be reluctant to release details about the investigation to the media was that they did not want to give any kidnappers an unfair advantage in intelligence about their moves. One of the instructions the apparent abductors had given police was for a cellular phone system to be set up for communication with officials. Calls received on such instruments can not be traced electronically.

On May 15th, WWOR-TV of Secaucus, New Jersey, at the request of Exxon officials, broadcast a tape by the missing executive's wife.

Mrs. Reso said, "I am making a personal appeal to some people who I want to believe have my husband with them. I know in my heart that he is alive. I pray that he is healthy. I want you to know that I have received your message."

A source close to the situation said that the message had been received during the day and that it included instructions that Reso's wife make such a statement.

Mrs. Reso continued, "It is so important to me and my kids [that] I have assurance that he is safe and unharmed. I am willing to do whatever is necessary to have him reunited with us. And I hope that he will be released very soon.

"I am asking the news media to stop any speculation as to who you may be and what your goals are. I simply want my husband back with his family."

A source at Exxon said Mrs. Reso had received two communications, but this person did not know what the messages had contained.

An Exxon spokesman stated, "Apparently she received a message and her statement is a response to that message."

It was also learned that Exxon had offered a substantial reward for the safe return of its missing executive. No dollar amount was released.

With every passing tick of the clock, the sense of dread grew among lawmen assigned to the baffling case. The passing of time without any positive developments made it ever more apparent that Sidney Reso had not survived his abduction ordeal. Still, the desperate cat-and-mouse game went on.

By May 12th, a ransom note was received at Exxon's corporate headquarters in Irving, Texas. It called for payment of the abductors' demands and was signed, "Members of the conspiracy."

On May 15th, the day Mrs. Reso's statement aired, Jeremiah Doyle, the FBI's second in command in Newark, reiterated the bureau's demand for proof that the kidnappers were holding Reso and that he was alive and well.

On June 1st, "the members of the conspiracy" mailed a letter from Florham Park, New Jersey, to Exxon's international division, calling for payment of the ransom.

A change of venue of sorts took place on June 8th. This occurred when a call was placed from Pooler, Georgia, to a cellular telephone operated by the FBI for the exclusive monitoring of the ransomers' calls. In it, a man's voice asked why there had been no response to a previous message.

By now the investigative team had swelled to more than 300 people, and the search, prompted by the call emanating from Georgia, had gone nationwide.

On June 16th, Mrs. Reso appeared before the media again and made still another poignant plea for her husband's release. She expressed hope that he would be back with his family in time to celebrate Father's Day with them.

"In my heart, I believe Sid is alive. He's very strong and he's got great faith," she said.

On the very day that Mrs. Reso was meeting with members of the press, FBI agents discovered a peculiar note. It was stuffed in a mailbox on Route 24 in Morris Township. The missive instructed Exxon officials to bundle $18.5 million for ransom in packets of $100 bills. The money was to be stuffed inside laundry bags. The authorities had been tipped to the letter's location by a prerecorded message that had been transmitted to the FBI cellular phone.

On Thursday, June 18th, the case was fast reaching its climax. The kidnappers made two final calls to confirm arrangements for the ransom drops. Teams of FBI agents were dispatched throughout Morris County to watch pay phones there. What lawmen knew was that the series of calls that had been placed to them had been made alternately by a man and a woman.

On Thursday, June 18th, at 9:08 p.m., a call from a pay phone at the train station in Gladstone, New Jersey, gave instructions to FBI agents to pick up an envelope in Morristown.

Following the instructions, a drop-off team rushed to the Ralston General Store in Mendham, about five miles away, where they discovered a note saying that another note awaited them in a building on Route 24 near Chester. Three calls were received at approximately the same time from a pay phone at the Somerset Elks Club in Gladstone. The note found near Chester led to a pay phone near the Komline Sanderson Company in Peapack.

At 10:40 p.m., a man called the drop team from a pay phone at the Chester Mall. At the same time, an FBI surveillance team spotted a man with blond hair who was wearing gloves as he approached the mall phone.

After making a call, the man took off the gloves and drove away in a white Oldsmobile. A rapid check of the license plate by members of the trail team revealed that the Olds had been rented from a Warren County car rental company. The female renter had identified herself to the firm's owner as Irene Seale.

At 11:16 p.m., a woman resembling the description by car rental sources of Irene Seale was seen near pay phones in the Somerset Hills Elks Club in Gladstone. As the trail team watched, the woman walked toward a white Mercedes Benz.

At 11:53 p.m, a man was seen getting into the white Oldsmobile at the Far Hills train station. He appeared to the FBI trail team to be driving erratically, as if to avoid surveillance. At one point, the driver apparently became rattled at the sight of a police roadblock that had nothing to do with the kidnapping probe. The man made a quick U-turn and was lost by the trail team.

At 12:50 on Friday morning, the man proceeded to the car rental company parking lot where still another FBI team awaited him. Questioned by agents, the man told them he was waiting for his wife to pick him up.

Soon afterward, the woman answering Irene Seale's description drove into the parking lot at the wheel of the Mercedes.

Immediately taking the pair into custody, the lawmen made a quick inspection of the Mercedes and came up with a number of damning pieces of evidence. Included were four laundry bags similar to those the Reso kidnappers had ordered. There were also clothes, gloves, and a briefcase containing a 1985 directory of the home addresses of Exxon executives in the U.S.

The arrested pair was identified as Arthur D. and Irene J. Seale, both 45, of Changewater in Hunterdon County, New Jersey.

In a bizarre twist, lawmen described Arthur Seale as a former Exxon employee who may have worked in security. However, no other details about his employment were immediately available. An Exxon spokesman refused to comment on Seale's possible association with the energy firm, saying only that Exxon was aware of the arrests and was continuing to cooperate with the authorities.

In a report filed with the complaint against the couple, FBI Agent Richard C. Smith said Exxon had received a ransom demand the day Reso was abducted. The kidnappers had demanded that a cellular phone be set up for future messages. A series of calls and letters received by Exxon in subsequent weeks contained enough information about the circumstances of Reso's disappearance to convince investigators that they were dealing with the real abductors.

For his part, Prosecutor Murphy saw no reason for joy that the seven-week-old mystery had been solved at last. Murphy said, "This should be a cause for celebration, but it isn't because we haven't achieved our goal—the safe return of Mr. Reso."

Gary L. Penrith, the agent in charge of the Newark FBI office, agreed entirely with this assessment. He pointed out that the suspects had not given any information regarding what they had done with Sidney Reso and where he might be. He requested that anybody who may have seen the Seales or Reso over the last six weeks call a series of hotlines set up at Exxon headquarters to receive such reports.

Later in the day on Friday, June 19th Arthur and Irene Seale, both manacled, hobbled by leg irons, and wearing black prison jumpsuits, were brought before Federal Magistrate G. Donald Haneke. The magistrate held them without bail for further court proceedings scheduled for Monday, June 22nd.

The jurist told the suspects they faced life imprisonment and $1 million in fines if they were convicted of the four felony charges against them: kidnapping, conspiracy, and two counts of extortion. The papers filed in federal court accused them of conspiring with each other "and others." However, federal agents noted that they knew of no one else who was involved in the crime.

One lawmen who had spent a lot of time on the case commented, "Their organization is husband and wife."

As the court proceedings unraveled, Arthur Seale smiled at his wife. Irene answered by mouthing the words, "I love you." The husband's voice was firm when he answered yes to Judge Haneke's question as to whether the suspects understood their rights. Irene's voice showed a marked quaver as she fought back tears.

Any hope that the Seales would lead authorities to their kidnapping victim quickly proved false as the pair stone-walled it during weekend interrogations. The only new development in the case was the emergence of an as yet sketchy profile of the pair.

It was learned that the recent failure of a business venture the couple had sponsored, compounded by

51

the loss of their home and by a serious accident Arthur Seale had suffered some years ago, had left them with crippling financial problems that had followed them from New Jersey to the posh resorts of Hilton Head, South Carolina, and Vail, Colorado.

A friend said that one week before their arrest, the Seales had been at Hilton Head. It was at that time that the FBI had received a cellular phone call from Pooler, Georgia, located about 30 miles west of Hilton Head.

Other friends and acquaintances of the couple noted that Arthur Seale had grown up in Hillside, New Jersey.

After graduation from Hillside High School in the mid 1960s, Arthur Seale had worked briefly as a lifeguard. He was subsequently employed by Exxon as a security officer, guarding Exxon executives. It was speculated that during his association with the company, possibly as a chauffeur, he obtained a copy of the 1985 home address directory of Exxon executives which was to be found in the Mercedes his wife was driving when she was caught.

In late 1987, Seale moved his family to Hilton Head Island where he bought an outdoor furniture business called "Insiders." The store was situated near the entrance to the Palmetto Dunes Resort. The Seale family also purchased a home on Willett Road in the Sea Pines Plantation, one of several resort communities on the southern end of the island.

A local advertising executive noted, "They lived the good life down here. But I guess they went too far into debt and it all got overwhelming for them."

In 1988, the Seales pulled up stakes, taking off so

suddenly that they left their furniture behind and their telephone still connected. They also stiffed the advertising man for a $30,000 fee he'd earned.

One close neighbor of the Seales at Hilton Head recalled them fondly. "They were decent people who worked very, very hard. But they had to liquidate everything. If you had invested your life's savings and lost it all, and lost your house in the process, it would obviously be very emotionally devastating. And that's what happened to them."

Irene Seale's early life had been far more privileged than that of her husband Arthur. Members of her family had operated a profitable liquor store since the mid 1930s. They had also invested in other Hillside businesses and real estate in the New Jersey community.

A real estate agent who had known Irene "Jackie" Seale since her childhood commented, "Jackie didn't want for anything."

Others described Irene Seale as a vivacious, happy, outgoing person.

Irene's family lived only five blocks away from the house in which Arthur Seale grew up. It seemed natural that the slim blonde should be attracted to the dashing Admiral Farragut Academy midshipman. Resplendent in his naval officer's style uniform, Arthur Seale cut quite a figure both at the academy and in Hillside.

A current faculty member of the school who had been two years ahead of Seale recalled him as a popular, well-rounded student who played varsity football, was a member of the school's track team, and maintained a B-average "that could have been better if he tried harder. He was smart, athletic and handsome," the educator stated. "He was not only popular among the students, but also with the teachers."

After graduating from the academy, Arthur Seale spent one year at Drew University in Madison, New Jersey, but had dropped out.

The Seales were married in September 1967, and rented an apartment in Hillside. The first chinks in the idyllic portrait the couple projected showed up quickly, however.

The lack of financial responsibility on the Seales' part became public when they fled Hilton Head Island, to which they had migrated in 1977. It had been after their sudden departure from the posh South Carolina resort that it became known that they left a trail of civil lawsuits behind. Papers placed by various creditors charged the Seales with failing to pay $715,000 worth of obligations. Included in this figure was a $71,248 mortgage on a boat that Arthur had purchased. No trace of the vessel had been found.

The family move to Vail, Colorado, rather than resulting in a hoped-for fresh start, only served to compound their troubles. Despite the fact that neither Arthur nor Irene was able to secure work in the internationally renowned ski resort, they somehow managed to move into a $500,000 townhouse there. By now the Seales' troubles were not confined to financial matters. Family violence had become the concern of Vail police.

A former investigator for Eagle County, Colorado, reported that the family's home situation brought them to the attention of the police when one of their daughters ran away from the lush Vail home.

Noted the Colorado investigator, "I got the feeling that I wasn't getting the whole story from them. They were a couple with a secret, and I was the third man out. They were social wanderers who were trying to pull off a lifestyle they couldn't afford."

Sergeant Rick Anardado of the Vail police also became acquainted with the family in his official capacity. "We received three runaway reports regarding their daughter," he said. On another occasion, police units were called to the Seale home due to a domestic disturbance involving a male child.

All of the evaluations suggested that the Seales' marriage was much less harmonious than it first appeared. This hypothesis led those in charge of the probe to speculate that the couple's attitudes toward each other could provide sleuths with an opening in the on-going search for Sidney Reso.

With this in mind, arrangements were made to lodge the suspects in two separate institutions where they would be completely isolated from each other's influence. Arthur Seale was remanded to the Passaic County Jail and Irene Seale was placed in the Union County Jail.

A number of investigators felt that if a break were to come, it was likely to originate with the slender, middle-aged Irene who found herself facing charges that threatened to keep her behind bars the rest of her life.

In the weekend immediately following the Seales' arrest, FBI agents were hard at work going through a mass of documents found at the couple's Hillside home. The importance of their findings would electrify the courtroom of Federal Magistrate Haneke on Monday, June 23rd.

It was then that United States Attorney for New Jersey Michael Chertoff, in opposing any bail for the suspects, informed the court that the Searles had been amassing a store of information on hiding money in overseas banks long before they set out to kidnap Reso.

Chertoff announced that FBI agents had searched the home where the couple was staying in Lebanon Township. And they had found a list of banks in Switzerland, India, and Pakistan, with telephone and telex numbers, a book that promised to reveal "the dark world" of money laundering and capital flight, and a new passport that Arthur Seale had obtained.

According to the authorities, 10 or 11 handguns and other weapons had been seized from the premises. Among other items brought back by the searchers were newspapers and journals about kidnappings and a security company manual titled "Executive Protection Program: Kidnapping and Extortion."

Chertoff said lawmen had received several telephone calls since the suspects' arrest. The contacts came from people who claimed to be holding Reso or to know something about his whereabouts. The prosecutor noted that investigators were trying to determine whether the proffered information was from people "who have genuine control of Mr. Reso or those who are trying to commit a fraud or a hoax." He added that other evidence obtained by agents was being held in confidence as a means of testing the value of the calls received.

Sources close to the case were now more pessimistic than ever as they considered the possibilities of bringing murder charges against the suspects. One investigator felt it would be possible to bring murder charges in such a case without knowing the whereabouts of the body, "but it would be extremely difficult." The officials said prosecutors would need "trace evidence" of the death, such as a bloodstained piece of clothing or statements from those involved in the killing.

Arthur Seale, clad in an orange jail uniform, and Irene, dressed in a blue one, showed no emotion during the 50-minute proceedings. From time to time the couple did exchange glances.

As had been expected, Judge Haneke denied bail, citing the violence of the crime of which they were accused and the high risk that they might try to flee the country. In ordering the pair held for trial, the jurist commented, "It's not even a close question."

Once again, the days began to slip by with no meaningful clues arising as to whether Sidney Reso was alive or dead or where he might be hidden. Federal officials revealed they still had no solid information that the missing Exxon International president had been taken out of New Jersey by his abductors. However, they were still awaiting results of tests on possible bloodstains discovered in a van the Seales had rented.

While federal and state officials were noncommittal as to Reso's condition, a Newark FBI spokesman said the agency remained "optimistic" about finding him alive.

This feeling was no longer shared by a number of

Exxon executives. They noted that Reso suffered from a heart condition, having experienced a coronary attack three years before, and that he had probably died in captivity.

Meanwhile, activity in federal court was moving inexorably forward. On June 25th, Dick Leventhal, a spokesman for the U.S. Attorney's Office in Newark, revealed that a federal grand jury had indicted the suspects on two counts of conspiracy, kidnapping, extortion, using the mail to transmit ransom letters, and interstate travel in aid of extortion.

On Friday afternoon, June 26th, a sudden flurry of activity among federal agents prompted speculation that some major development in the case was breaking. FBI Agent Gary Penrith, in charge of the bureau's Newark office, and his assistant, Jeremiah Doyle, rushed from their office to the Gateway complex at Pennsylvania Station. The grim-faced agents maintained a cloak of silence concerning what was going on.

At 8:00 a.m. on Saturday, July 27th, Penrith and 40 law enforcement officers from seven different agencies assembled in the dense underbrush of the Bass River State Forest in Burlington County, New Jersey. The most ominous indicator of the turn the Reso kidnapping case had taken was the presence of a handsome German shepherd named "Buffy." The animal was no ordinary police canine. Because of his special training and talent, he had been brought in by New Jersey State Police to perform his special function—following to its source the noxious odor of putrifying human flesh.

For 12 long hours, the grim 40-person posse followed close on the heels of the "cadaver dog" until it made its way to a remote, tick-infested area off Exit 58 on the Garden State Parkway, about 20 miles north of Atlantic City.

There, in a shallow grave, in a state of advanced decomposition, lay a man's body which would later be positively identified as the remains of Sidney Reso. The 60-day search for the man who had risen through the ranks to head one of the world's largest companies at last had reached its end.

At first, federal and state officials maintained tight security about details of the corpse's discovery. They would not say who or what had led them to this inaccessible wooded spot off an unmarked dirt road in the vast Pine Barrens of southern New Jersey. Most of all, they refused to be drawn into any discussion of what, if any, role Irene Seale had played in the recovery of the missing man.

In a television interview from New Orleans, a nun reported that one of Reso's close relatives had told her that Irene Seale had "confessed" to the kidnapping and that Reso had "died of natural causes."

U.S. Attorney Chertoff was incensed at the "natural causes" report. Declared the prosecutor, "Nobody can say that a man who dies in captivity . . . died of natural causes. I cannot imagine causes that are less natural. The loss of Mr. Reso's life was unnatural."

Chertoff also warned reporters that it "is perilous to rely on unofficial people."

At a press conference held in Newark on the day following the recovery of Reso's cadaver, Agent Penrith was still visibly shaken from the discoveries of Saturday. He stated, "It remains unbelievable that individuals driven solely by greed could end the life of a man fifty-seven years old."

The veteran FBI agent added, "The burial site was an unbelievable setting with nests of ticks all over the place, a place unsuitable for camping and unlikely to be found accidentally. It was probably the worst place I have ever been."

The vast Pine Barrens have a history of supernatural folk lore. Spreading over 3,000 square miles, it occupies one fifth of the Garden State. The territory features sandy soil interlaced with many streams and bordered by swampland, berry bogs, and extensive pine stands. This forbidding area covers parts of Atlantic, Cumberland, Ocean, and Burlington Counties.

Legend has it that the isolated territory is the home of "The New Jersey Devil," a mythical monster with cloven feet, and "Pineys," hermits who seek refuge from the outside world.

On a more realistic note, it served as home for the illicit stills of prohibition-era bootleggers.

As Prosecutor Chertoff and Agent Penrith conducted their Sunday news conference, Dr. Robert Goode, New Jersey's medical examiner, began the arduous autopsy that would provide investigators with the final word as to how the victim had died.

There was speculation that Reso might have suffered a fatal heart attack. This theory remained in doubt because, as Penrith pointed out, while Reso had a history of heart problems, he had not been required to take prescription medicine for the condition, but had merely taken a daily aspirin tablet to head off a recurrence.

Not only were close family members mourning the loss of a loving and beloved member, but those in high places at the Exxon Corporation, where Reso had served a lifetime, were in deep bereavement. In a statement, Exxon's chairman said, "Mr. Reso made an invaluable contribution to the company in his thirty-five year career. Sid was one of the finest men I have known who combined outstanding professional competence with humanity and warmth."

Some details about the early moments of Reso's captivity were provided by the owner of the car-leasing firm who had inadvertently leased vehicles to the suspects. The information came shortly after a forensic determination showed that the stains in a van rented by Irene Seale on April 29th, the day on which Reso vanished, were blood.

The owner recalled that the vehicle was returned at 3:30, eight hours after the Exxon official had taken off for his office, only to disappear. Upon checking the van in, the owner noticed that the vehicle's interior was filthy and reeked of dried blood. Hosing the car down and using ammonia to clean up the residue of the filth, the owner recalled saying, "What did they do, pick up a dirty old road kill on the way?" Describing the situation, the owner stated, "It smelled dirty. It looked like it was splattered with dried blood, like somebody had dragged a deer into it or something, or I thought maybe she had gone hunting. I remembered saying, 'Oh, my God! I can't rent this thing out like this. Why would these people put road kills in here?' "

During the period between April 12th and June 18th, the firm rented four vehicles to Irene Seale.

61

Seale had identified herself to the owner as a crafts entrepreneur and said she needed a plain van for attending fairs.

The owner stated, "She said she wanted to sell crafts out of the van. She wanted to make sure I had the right kind because this was her business and she didn't want any names on the side."

On April 13th, Seale returned the van to the lot. "She said it worked out beautifully," the dealer noted.

On April 26th, Seale picked up another van and returned it 24 hours later. Between April 29th and June 19th, the night on which the Seales were arrested, Irene Seale rented the van on at least 10 occasions.

On May 3rd, Seale called again seeking a van. The owner told her that no vans were available. Irene Seale had no choice but to settle for a large car with four doors and wound up driving a 1991 Chevy Lumina off the lot. She brought the car back on May 5th, spotlessly clean and with a full tank of gas.

The dates were of particular significance since reports were circulating that Irene Seale had told detectives that the victim had died on May 3rd.

On June 18th, Irene Seale made her final pickup. This time it was a white 1992 Oldsmobile. It was on the evening of June 18th that the desperate game of phoned instructions, complicated drops, and the confrontation between FBI agents and the suspects played itself out.

After agents had run a make on the Olds being driven by Arthur Seale and traced it to the car rental firm, they contacted the owner. The owner is not likely to soon forget the developments that followed.

"At eleven p.m., I got a phone call," the owner said. "When the cops picked me up with the lights and the sirens, I thought, 'Oh, my God!' "

The owner and a half-dozen agents gathered in the firm's back office, examining Irene Seale's rental records. Other federal cops began to pour in. The next to show up was Arthur Seale, to the surprise of everyone. He was driving the white Olds his wife had leased. The time was now 1:30 a.m. Friday morning, and at that moment Irene Seale drove up in the couple's Mercedes to pick up her husband.

The owner commented, "The cops didn't know the Seales were going to drop the Olds off at that time. Everything was so coincidental."

Summing up the bizarre experience, the owner recalled Irene Seale as being such a nice person. "She was somebody I positively would have invited to dinner. You wouldn't think about it twice."

Speculation that Irene Seale had led federal agents to Sidney Reso's grave intensified in the days immediately following his body's discovery. However, spokesmen for the various law enforcement organizations participating in the unraveling of the kidnapping mystery refused to confirm the details. They were focusing on Tuesday, June 30th, when the couple was due to make their next appearance in federal court to plead in arraignment proceedings.

Just one week after she had mouthed the words, "I love you" to her husband, Irene Seale was now prepared to tell the court an entirely different tale. She accused Arthur Seale of 25 years of abusing and manipulating her, which led into the scheme to kidnap

Reso and caused the executive's subsequent death.

In her 35-minute arraignment before Judge Garrett Brown Jr. of federal district court, Irene Seale gave a graphic description of the horrifying events of April 29th and the days and nights that followed. Dressed as she took the stand in a white blouse trimmed in red, a blue blazer, and a white-pleated skirt, Irene Seale pleaded guilty to two counts of extortion.

Under oath, the 45-year-old woman told the court that she and Arthur had been the ones to abduct Reso. As Reso had prepared to leave his home for work, according to her testimony, Irene, dressed in jogging clothes, had returned to the white van where her husband waited. As Reso stopped his Mercedes at the mouth of the driveway and stepped out to pick up his newspaper, Seale maneuvered the van so that it blocked off access to the road. There was a struggle between the two men when Arthur Seale attempted to push Reso into the white van where Irene now sat behind the steering wheel, ready to gun the vehicle's engine. There was a shot as Reso and Seale continued to argue and scuffle inside the van. Wounded in the arm, Reso began to bleed. Still bleeding, Reso was taken to a rental storage locker the size of a small room not far from where the Seales were living.

There, the Exxon executive was gagged with duct tape, had his wrists handcuffed behind his back, and was bound hand and foot. He was left in the sweltering prison by the Seales as they began the extortion phase of their scheme.

Irene Seale told the court that the couple tried to

treat their captive's arm wound, but he was discovered dead in his prison, now-turned-tomb, on May 3rd.

Following Irene's testimony, Chertoff and Murphy, the federal and county prosecutors respectively, filed with the court a plea agreement dated June 26th, the day before Irene had led the 40-person posse to Reso's body. Under the agreement, Irene could go to prison for up to 40 years, but, the prosecutors said later that term could be reduced if she cooperated fully in her husband's trial, which had been set tentatively for September 9, 1992. One prosecutor estimated that Irene could be released in 13 years.

FBI Agent Penrith said it was Irene Seale who had initiated negotiations to plead guilty to the two counts, and the federal government agreed to drop all other federal charges against her.

For his part, Prosecutor Murphy said the state would drop all but one kidnapping charge and that any sentence given Irene Seale would run concurrently with the federal term. Murphy pointed out that he was satisfied with the plea bargain in return for Irene Seale's cooperation, which included leading lawmen to Reso's body. "There is no way we would have ever recovered Mr. Reso's remains, and it was crucial to us and the Reso family that he be given a proper burial," said the county attorney.

Murphy reported that he planned within a week to file against Seale a felony murder charge, which carries a penalty of 30 years to life. The technical side of the agreement between the federal government and Irene Seale represented a major victory for the prosecution. Under a ruling by the United States Supreme Court, issued 10 years earlier, that spouses could testify voluntarily against each other in a criminal conspiracy, there was no way that Arthur Seale could prevent Irene from taking the stand against him.

The ruling did not apply to New Jersey law, according to Murphy. Arthur Seale would be able to prevent his wife from taking the stand against him in state court by "asserting the marital privilege."

Experts in forensic medicine, apprised of the condition of Reso's body and the type of imprisonment to which he had been subjected before his death, attested that he had suffered five days of excruciating torture before dying.

One former New York City medical examiner put it this way: "You go into shock [from the bleeding], and your temperature would gradually fall. You become mentally hazy and confused, and gradually you pass out.

"The mental anguish is worse because the wound could be minimal. Being enclosed—my God—it's mental torture."

If Reso suffocated, he might not have felt any physical pain until the oxygen in the storage room ran out, according to this source. At that point, the victim would have been gasping desperately for air—with none available.

"That's what they call asphyxia by enclosure," the medical expert explained. "If there's no way for air to get in, eventually the air is used up."

The emotional stress of Reso's situation must have been beyond bearing, experts said. Sources close to the situation talked about the horror of being bound hand and foot and gagged in a crypt-like space. Even if Reso had been able to scream for help, there would have been nobody to hear. This was because the facility was unattended. Users rent their space and came and went on their own. There was no employee of any kind assigned to the premises.

On Thursday, July 2nd, relatives, friends, and associates of the fallen executive jammed into Holy Name of Jesus Church at Loyola University, New Orleans, as a former Roman Catholic archbishop told them that Reso's kidnapping and death culminated in a tragedy that defied all logic.

"Evil is a mystery, and especially in a case of such vicious evil," he told the assemblage.

A reverend asked, "Why is it that bad things happen to good people? When we experience the ravages of the violence of war, of evil that touches us in a personal way, we can be disconcerted by the power of evil."

After the Mass, Reso was buried in Lake Lawn Cemetery in the New Orleans suburb of Metairie. The Mass and burial climaxed two solid days of mourning that began on July 1st at the Lake Lawn Funeral Home. It was there where huge crowds streamed through, passing among the thousands of flowers surrounding Reso's coffin. They paid their last respects to the man who during his lifetime had earned universal love and honors.

With the federal trial for Arthur Seale scheduled to commence on September 10th, prosecutors worked tirelessly through the summer to prepare for the showdown with the remaining suspect. For his part, Seale gave no indication that he would retreat from the "not guilty" plea he had made in federal court on the very day his wife of 25 years had plea bargained her way to the possibility of leniency by giving him up as the mastermind of the plot.

But on Tuesday, September 8th, just two days before the trial was to get underway, Seale pulled the second major surprise in the saga of a crime which had gained international attention. Standing before Judge Brown, Seale matter-of-factly confessed that he was guilty on all seven federal counts pending against him.

Seale outlined how he and his wife went ahead with their plan to collect $18.5 million in ransom from Exxon even after the president of Exxon International had died. He said that Reso, who had been shot and wounded on the day of his abduction and held in the rented storage facility without food and water, had finally died of his wound. Arthur Seale called it "deterioration"—asphyxiation, infection, dehydration from four days without food or water and possibly from the effects of an existing heart condition.

As Judge Brown read off the list of charges against him, Seale in most instances answered in a clear and detached voice, "Yes, your honor, we did that."

However, there were instances where the kidnapper took issue with some points of the charges. One concerned the federal contention that Reso had died inside the wooden storage box.

"No, no, your honor," Seale interjected. "He died outside the box." Reso's condition had deteriorated so the Seales had removed him from the box. Irene

68

Seale had given the captive water to drink, according to Seale's version of the happenings.

"Actually he died in my arms. We were trying to revive him," the defendant claimed. The kidnapper also insisted that the wounding of Reso during the scuffle between them had been accidental.

However, he conceded that he was armed with a .45-caliber handgun and a .357 Magnum. The shot that had wounded his victim in the left forearm was fired by the .45, Seale said.

Another concession was that it had been part of the plan to convince Exxon executives that the company official was being held by a terrorist group, when in fact there was no connection between the crime and such an organization.

Federal Prosecutor Chertoff was not impressed with Seale's courtroom performance. The federal attorney accepted Seale's guilty pleas on the seven counts but insisted that allusions the defendant had made at several points about being "under stress" did not mean that he was either unaware of what he was doing or under any duress. Chertoff told reporters after the court proceedings that while he accepted the bare bones of the Seales' story, he remained skeptical about parts of it. The prosecutor said, "The crime represents the acme of depravity and evil." He predicted that further details challenging portions of Seale's account would be given later in the year when the admitted kidnapper was slated to be sentenced.

Chertoff called Seale's seven guilty pleas "an unconditional surrender" and said that "there was no bargain, there was no deal, and there was no mercy."

After admitting to the charges, Seale found himself facing up to 95 years in prison and $1 million in fines on the federal counts. Nor would that necessarily be the maximum time he would have to serve. In state court, Seale faced charges of felony murder and kidnapping, each of which could result in life sentences.

It is unlikely, however, that New Jersey will seek the death penalty in the slaying of Reso, since neither Seale nor his wife had intended to kill him.

The court proceedings could prove to be one of the last times Arthur and Irene Seale found themselves in the same room. Irene Seale attended the event. She stared fixedly ahead as her husband testified on the witness stand. She requested that reporters not ask her questions but did take the occasion to thank law enforcement officers for "being kind, thorough, and thoughtful."

At this writing, both Arthur and Irene Seale are awaiting sentencing in federal court for their respective roles in the abduction and death of Sidney Reso.

"EVIL SCHEME OF THE GREEDY GRANDSON!"

by Charles Lynch

VANDERGRIFT, PENNSYLVANIA
MAY 16, 1983

If everyone in this Westmoreland County neighborhood didn't know Virgil Hileman and his wife, Ruth, by name, they certainly knew them by sight. But recently the elderly Hilemans hadn't been seen, or, by actual count, not seen for nine straight days. Their disappearance had become somewhat of a mystery to concerned neighbors and the Hilemans' relatives.

Things didn't look right, or feel right. What people remembered mostly about the couple was the fact that they lived a routine life. Awnings on their front porch rose and set with the summer's sun. Life at the Hileman house was placid, orderly and predictable.

Freshly washed clothes hung on the backyard line every Monday morning like clockwork. Virgil, 78, would sip coffee on the porch while Ruth, 75, would prepare breakfast. They had been married for 57 years, and lived in their present home for the past 34 years.

The Hilemans lived a scheduled lifestyle, governed by a routine they followed ever since Virgil retired from U.S. Steel 13 years earlier after working 48 years on the sheet floor. And when the couple turned up missing on July 29, 1982, everyone who knew them feared the worst. The concern would prove justified.

On that fateful morning, a Thursday, the front awnings of the Hileman home rose, as usual. A grandson arrived and took the Hilemans to a nearby shopping center. Again, nothing unusual. But the neighbors never saw the couple again.

One neighbor later told police he became suspicious the evening of the Hilemans' disappearance. "Something just wasn't right," he recalled. "They usually lower the blinds on the side of the house and close the front door, but they didn't."

Another neighbor had noticed that the back door had been left open, again an unusual occurrence for the Hilemans. Front and rear doors, and windows, left open in a home that normally locked tight at nightfall. And the awnings remained up.

Three days later, on a Sunday, the grandson showed up at his grandparents' home. He asked a neighbor if he had seen his grandparents. When the neighbor replied no, the grandson left, saying, "They're probably with my mom and dad." The Hilemans were parents of four children, grandparents of 15 and great-grandparents of four.

On Monday, neighbors alerted another relative of the Hilemans and told him they were worried that the elderly couple might have become ill and were unable to call for help. Mail and newspapers had begun to accumulate on the front porch.

The relative arrived and entered the house. Inside, he found seven apple dumplings, which apparently had been left to cool on the dining room table; they were covered with mold. A loaf of bread was going stale on the kitchen counter and several dirty coffee cups sat in the sink.

The moldy dumplings were not a reassuring sign. One neighbor commented, "If she (Ruth Hileman) was going to be gone, they'd have put them away. She will not waste a piece of string."

The relative checked further and found Mrs. Hileman's wedding rings in the kitchen and the keys to the Hileman car on the TV set. Their 1974 Oldsmobile was parked in the street. The couple's luggage was neatly stacked in a closet and their toothbrushes and Virgil Hileman's shaving equipment were still in the bathroom.

The mailman told neighbors that Virgil would always be waiting for him to deliver his pension check at the end of the month. But on July 29th, Virgil wasn't there. The search of the house did nothing to clear up the mysterious disappearance of the Hilemans. The police were notified later that day.

Vandergrift Patrolman Louis Purificato took the initial call and visited the Hileman house on Franklin Avenue. He talked to neighbors and relatives of the missing couple, including the grandson. Purificato would state later that he felt uneasy after interviewing the grandson, but the investigation continued.

Finally, on Saturday afternoon, August 7th, as part of the ongoing police investigation of the missing couple, and when "word got around" there was a stench coming from the backyard of a relative of the grandson, Virgil and Ruth Hileman were found. Or, at least their bodies were.

Virgil's decomposing body was found lying on the ground in a wooded area, and his wife's body, burned beyond recognition, was discovered nearby in a shallow grave. Mrs. Hileman's body was so badly burned that a pathologist, at the time, was only able to conclude that the remains belonged to a white woman.

Trooper Robert Luniewski of the Kiski Valley State Police Barracks would testify later that while he was checking out the yard he detected a foul odor emanating from a brush pile where charred ashes and charcoal were stored.

Luniewski said he spotted two women's shoes and some bones in the pile. Removing the brush, he found remains of a body, the largest piece of flesh being the sole of a foot. He found arm bones and a skull. Mr. Hileman was found wrapped in a multi-colored Afghan covered with brush.

Officer Purificato, who was at the scene, said it appeared that the Hilemans walked to the woods behind the house, located on Route 66 in Washington Township, and were killed there. "There was no evidence that they were dragged," Purificato explained. It was apparent that Mr. Hileman had been shot in the chest and leg with a small caliber gun.

The grisly discovery shocked the investigators. The extent of the destruction of the body of Mrs. Hileman—only charred bones and a small piece of flesh remained—made positive proof of identity almost impossible. The case pathologist was hoping that the piece of flesh could be analyzed for blood groupings, which then could be matched against Mrs. Hileman's medical records on file at a local hospital.

The police, and first assistance Westmoreland County District Attorney Robert Johnson, got together early Saturday night and decided that an arrest warrant should be issued for the couple's grandson, Robert Hartman.

The law officials felt justified in issuing the warrant because Hartman was the last person to be seen with the couple, and it was also learned that on the day of his disappearance, Virgil Hileman withdrew a $10,000 certificate of deposit. Hartman later told police that the money belonged to him and that his grandfather was holding it for him. The money ended up in Hartman's bank account.

The suspect had also been seen in the area where the bodies were found. Adding to all of that was Officer Purificato's observation that "his (Hartman) story just wasn't adding up."

Police began searching the area for Hartman, but he was not to be found. But late Saturday night, Hartman arrived at the Kiski Valley Barracks of the state police. He was then arrested on two counts of criminal homicide. Assistant District Attorney Johnston said Hartman apparently was unaware police were looking for him when he walked into the barracks. He had come there believing a relative of his was there.

Hartman was arraigned and sent to the Westmoreland County Detention Center in lieu of $100,000 bond set by Judge Daniel Ackerman in a late-night court session.

News of Hartman's arrest, on charges that he murdered his grandparents, stunned the Hilemans' neighbors. One woman said, "I can't believe it . . . he (Hartman) kissed them all the time and told them he loved them. I cannot think of how he could have done that."

Hartman was described by another neighbor as being a conscientious and devoted grandson, driving his grandparents to the supermarket, mowing their lawn and stopping by often for visits.

A police background check on Hartman revealed that he grew up around cars. When he was nine, a relative would take him to work at an auto dealership, where the young boy would run errands around the garage.

When he was older Hartman earned money by washing cars on the lot. Eventually, he worked himself up to become motorcycle sales manager at a local Honda dealer earning about $16,000 in 1982. Police also learned that Hartman, despite his modest income, had more than $72,000 in his bank account. Hartman shared a house, paying a monthly rent of $200 with a girlfriend.

The suspect was held for trial at the conclusion of his preliminary hearing held in Vandergrift on August 12, 1982, before District Justice James H. Mann. Hartman wore shackles on his arms and legs when he was taken before Mann.

Appearing at the hearing was a woman who lived near the Hartman property on Route 60, where the bodies were found. She testified that she heard gunshots and a woman screaming on July 29th, the day the Hilemans were reported missing.

The witness said she noticed a silver-colored car parked in the driveway of the Hartman property between 10:30 and 10:45 a.m. that day. She said it was not the first time she had noticed the car on the property, located on Poke Run Church Road, and owned by a relative of the suspect.

A woman wearing red clothing, with short dark hair, was in a swing on the Hartman front porch, she said. About 11:30 a.m. she said, "I heard a couple of gunshots and a terrible screaming, then a couple of gunshots again and more screams."

She said this went on "three or four minutes," whereupon she rounded up her two children and went to her mother's house nearby and called the state police from the Kiski Valley Barracks several miles away. Officers arrived to check the Hartman residence. No one was home and police took a statement from the woman.

At 1:00 p.m. that day, she said the same silver-colored car pulled into her driveway and Bobby Hartman got out. "He said he wanted to know what was going on at the Hartman house. He was very nervous and jumpy."

The woman said such traits were uncharacteristic of Hartman, whom she had known all her life. Later that day, she said she noticed the same car "coming down from the brush area a couple of times."

The following Sunday, the witness said her family returned from a weekend trip at 6:00 p.m. and she noticed Robert Hartman again in the wooded area behind the house. "I saw him digging. There was smoke coming from the tops of trees," she recalled. "He seemed to be shoveling very fast and always looking over his shoulder, towards the road . . ."

A department store clerk was called to the stand and testified that he sold a box of .22-caliber bullets to the suspect on July 29th, the day the Hilemans were last seen alive. The 23-year-old clerk stated that it was the store's policy to ask to see the driver's license of anyone purchasing ammunition and thus have the transaction on record.

He said he found Robert Hartman's signature and license number for the purchase of less than ten boxes of .22-caliber rim-fire bullets, purchased on July 29th.

Frank Galilei, a county detective, testified he used a metal detector and found six .22-caliber casings near the Hartman house and two more in the area where the bodies were found.

The purchase of the bullets was considered damaging to Hartman's defense, court observers noted, because of the discovery of spent shell casings found at the scene. An autopsy also noted that Mr. Hileman had been killed by small caliber gunshot wounds to the chest and leg.

The murder weapon was never found. Although several weapons were removed from the house on the property where the bodies were found, none matched the caliber type thought used in the killings.

Another witness at the hearing, a teller at a savings bank in Vandergrift, testified that she cashed a savings certificate for Hileman, who was accompanied by his grandson, the morning of July 29th.

She said Hartman left during the 15-minute

process and did not recall if he returned. She said the certificate was not mature and that a penalty had been subtracted from the check. The time of the transaction was at about 9:55 a.m.

Authorities claim the certificate was for $10,000 and that most of it is in Hartman's bank account.

A neighbor of the Hilemans said she saw the couple get into a car with their grandson about 10:00 a.m. on July 29th and drive off. "They looked like they always did. There was nothing unusual . . . I waved, they nodded and smiled . . . and that's the last I saw them."

The neighbor related that three days later, on August 1st, she saw Hartman sitting on his grandparents' steps and went over. She said Hartman asked her, "Have you seen my grandparents?" She replied that she hadn't seen them since they left with him three days earlier. The woman recalled that Hartman replied, "Well, I brought them to the department store and back home and then went to Greensburg."

The woman said she never recalled an argument between Robert and the Hilemans. "It was always fun and laughter, kissing and hugging," she recalled.

State Trooper Robert Luniewski of the Kiski Valley Barracks testified to the grisly discovery of the bodies. He said another trooper found the remains of a body 136-feet from the house. He said a foul odor emanated from a pile of brush where charred ashes and charcoal were piled.

Hartman's eyes were riveted to a drawing of the murder scene while Luniewski testified. "It was a rather gruesome sight," the veteran state trooper said.

Pittsburgh Pathologist Dr. Earl Davis, who performed the autopsies, explained that Mr. Hileman's degree of decomposition indicated he had been dead about a week. He was unable to determine the distance from which the bullets were fired at Mr. Hileman.

Efforts to positively identify Mrs. Hileman's remains, by using dentures found near her body, proved fruitless when investigators learned the specialist who provided the woman's false teeth kept no records.

Three hours after District Justice Mann ruled there was sufficient evidence to hold Hartman for trial, the defendant posted $100,000 bond and walked out of jail. Hartman's freedom followed an unsuccessful scramble by prosecutors to seek a bond increase.

Hartman's trial began on May 5, 1983, in Westmoreland County Common Pleas Court before Judge Charles Loughran and a jury of five women and seven men.

Earlier, in November, Hartman's attorney had asked for a change of venue because of what he called prejudicial pretrial publicity. Judge Joseph A. Hudock, however, after reviewing defense exhibits that included newspaper clippings and tapes of television news broadcasts about the Hileman slayings, ruled that the trial would remain in Westmoreland County.

In handing down his ruling, Hudock said, "Publicity in this case cannot be said to be inherently prejudicial, or so pervasive as to render the selection of a fair and impartial jury in Westmoreland County impossible."

Assistant District Attorney Robert Johnston opened the proceedings by telling the jury that in the three months before Virgil and Ruth Hileman disappeared they allegedly gave their grandson, Robert Hartman, $72,000, which he deposited in his savings account. However, Johnson told the jury, that the one-sided financial relationship ended with the disappearance and murder of the couple.

Johnston, who was seeking first-degree murder convictions, said he would prove that Hartman and his grandfather went to a Vandergrift bank on July 29th and cashed a $10,000 certificate of deposit before it had matured.

"Virgil and Ruth were two very old people," Johnston told the jury. "They lived in Vandergrift on a quiet street . . . they had a little backyard . . . they raised four kids. They were people of very modest habits and very modest means. They were just ordinary, quiet people who were living out the twilight of their lives," Johnston explained sincerely.

The D.A. said that he would produce bank records to show that Hartman had begun receiving large amounts of cash from his grandparents on October 19, 1981, when Hileman gave him a check for $7,500.

On December 16, 1981, Hartman received $5,000 from his grandparents. On February 5, 1982, Johnston said, Hartman borrowed $10,000 from a local bank and his grandparents pledged their savings account as collateral. On May 10, 1982, Virgil Hileman gave the bank $9,480 from his savings account to repay the loan. Then, Hileman gave Hartman a check for $7,500. Johnston told the jury the payments continued.

On May 20th, his grandfather gave Hartman a check for $11,500; On June 4th, $7,500. On June 28th, Hileman withdrew a $6,000 savings bond from a bank after paying a penalty for early withdrawal. That same day, Johnston said, Hileman went to another bank and cashed two certificates of deposit valued at $20,000.

Johnston said that by May 10, 1982, Hartman had a "substantial balance" in his savings account he took out large amounts of cash every few days. Only July 10th, Hartman withdrew $30,000.

"We have no idea where the money went," Johnston told the jury. When Hartman and his grandfather went to the bank July 29th, Hileman cashed a $10,000 certificate of deposit. The bank gave Hileman a check for $9,669.20. The following day, according to the D.A., the check was deposited in Hartman's account. But Johnston said that an FBI handwriting specialist would testify that Hileman's signature was forged on the check.

Vandergrift Patrolman Louis Purificato testified the investigation began after one of Hileman's relatives reported the couple missing. Purificato related how he went to the Hileman home on August 3rd and found nothing to indicate foul play. He did notice, however, on the dining room table there were some apple dumplings that were getting moldy.

The officer testified that when he talked to Hartman the following day, the defendant suggested that his grandparents had possibly been murdered. Then, Purificato said, Hartman remarked, "Gee, they're heavy, it would take three or four people to move them."

Purificato said, "He [Hartman] told me he came to Vandergrift to pick up his grandparents about 9:45 a.m. and took them to the mart because there was an oil filter on sale and his grandfather wanted to pick one up . . . he told me after the mart he brought them home."

The officer said the search for the missing couple continued, and on August 7th, they searched a home owned by the Hartman family. "As soon as we arrived, there was an odor of decomposed flesh," Purificato testified. That's when the bodies were discovered.

A neighbor of the Hilemans testified that she was returning home from the dentist on the morning of July 29th when she saw the Hilemans get into a car driven by their grandson.

"Did you see Virgil and Ruth Hileman and Bobby Hartman return home that day?" Johnston asked.

"No," the woman answered.

"Did you ever see them again?" the D.A. asked.

Answer, "No."

The witness told Defense Attorney Kenneth Burkley that Hartman and his grandparents were very close and that Hartman had visited them frequently.

"Did Ruth Hileman ever tell you how much fun it was to be with Bobby?" Burkley asked.

"Yes," the woman answered.

"Did you ever hear her describe him as being a barrel of fun?"

"Yes," the woman replied again.

83

Patricia Mayes, an FBI fingerprint expert working in Washington, D.C., testified on May 9th that a partial thumb print on a Vicks inhaler placed Robert Hartman at the scene where police found his grandparents' bodies. The prosecution also claimed the box for the inhaler was found in Hartman's car.

D.A. Johnston amassed 79 pieces of evidence and testimony from more than three dozen witnesses to build a strong case of circumstantial evidence linking Hartman to the murders. Although no one actually saw Hartman commit the murders, physical evidence, testimony from neighbors and passers-by, linked him to the scene after shots and a woman's screams were heard.

But Defense Attorney Burkley cautioned the jury at the start of the trial to be wary of circumstantial evidence. "Circumstantial evidence is like a chain," Burkley said. "It's only as strong as its weakest link."

In his closing argument, D.A. Johnston contended that the massive amount of evidence uncovered by investigators pointed to one suspect. "There's not a single piece of evidence in this entire case . . . that points to any other single person on the face of this earth," Johnston declared.

Burkley argued that there were a number of inconsistencies in the testimony presented by the prosecution's witnesses who claimed Hartman was having lunch with them in Greensburg when other witnesses said they saw him at the Hartman residence.

The murders, said Johnston, were money related. On the money motive, Burkley argued, "There is no evidence that there was any strain between Bobby Hartman and his grandparents . . ."

After deliberating for more than four and a half hours, the jury, on May 16, 1983, found Hartman guilty of two counts of first-degree murder in the death of his grandparents.

Hartman showed no emotion when he heard the decision, but after Judge Loughran revoked his $100,000 bond, the composure Hartman maintained throughout the 11-day trial began to fade and he started to sob.

The young man faces two mandatory consecutive life prison terms. The prosecutor had not sought the death penalty, but never said why. As Hartman was taken from the courtroom by three deputies to the Westmoreland County Detention Center, he began to cry.

"NEED A CAR . . . KILL A DRIVER!"

by Bruce Gibney

NATIONAL CITY, CALIF.
MARCH 1, 1983

Bill Ambrose didn't know why exactly he decided to go to Las Vegas with his new buddies, but it probably had something to do with the fact that he was bored hanging out in Long Beach and had nothing better to do with his time.

A short angular man with long brown hair and a jutting chin, Ambrose had spent most of his 22 years hanging out, bumming around the beach and picking up a job here and there. His only steady job had been as a roustabout on a carnival that passed through town. He stayed with the carnival until it hit Seattle, where he quit and hitchhiked back to California. Now he sort of wished he had stayed with the carnival a bit longer. He liked all the characters he'd met, and if the pay wasn't great, it was at least steady.

It sure beat selling dope around the pier, his only

other regular job. Ambrose couldn't pinpoint the exact date he started selling dope. It began harmlessly enough — buying a lid of weed for ten dollars then rolling the dope into joints and selling them at a buck a piece.

It had been so easy that he quickly progressed to selling quaaludes, uppers, downers, crank, coke — anything that happened to be around at the time, and that he could dispose of quickly.

In the fall of 1981, Ambrose was back in Long Beach, California, wishing he was somewhere else. He had hit town dead broke and had spent a couple of nights sleeping in parked cars and dozing in all-night laundromats before he ran into a couple of guys with a crash pad. He stayed with them for a couple of days, and kept body and soul together by selling joints near the Belmont Pier.

It was a passable existence, but not a great one, and he half hoped to catch on with another carnival, when he ran into a couple of dope dealer buddies from San Diego.

Their reunion was somewhat amusing, as Ambrose later recalled. "I asked the guy if he wanted to buy some ludes (quaaludes) and the guy just laughed and said, 'Hey, I was going to ask if you wanted to score,' " Ambrose later told the cops.

The two had more in common than dope. They had worked as roustabouts for the same carnival just a few months earlier, and both were just hanging out without much happening in their lives.

It was Ambrose's buddy who broached the idea of the trip to Vegas. "I ripped off this guy in Riverside for some hash oil," the buddy said. "We can sell the dope in Vegas and get us some action."

Action appealed to Ambrose; he could use a little for once. The bright lights of Vegas sounded a lot better than hanging out at the pier.

"You got a car?" Ambrose asked.

"An Olds," the buddy said. "Damn thing is as big as a living room. Why don't you join us. Vegas will be a gas."

Ambrose packed up his few possessions and the next day, he, his buddy and two other guys were headed for Nevada.

Somewhere between Long Beach and Vegas, Ambrose asked where they got the Olds. It was a spiffy, down-sized model with a good sound system and a nice ride.

The new buddy, whose name was Norman, said they had been hanging out at Mission Beach in San Diego a couple of nights earlier when they decided to steal a car. The car was necessary so they could drive the 100 miles to Riverside and break into the buddy's apartment and steal his hash oil and money.

They got the car but they had to kill some sailor to get it, Norman explained.

Ambrose acted dutifully impressed. "Hey, you got to do what you have to do," he said. But deep down he didn't believe it. Ambrose had heard a lot of stories in his days with the carnival and this idle boast about blowing away a sailor for his car sounded like just another whopper.

A couple of days later he would change his mind.

National City is a blue collar community of 50,000 located south of San Diego, California. It is a no frills sort of town, big on commercial development. Its rival sister city, Chula Vista, boasts about controlled growth and a new marina; National City has car dealerships and acres of industrial parks.

Weekdays were slow ones for the National City police, and Tuesday evening, September 29, 1981 had been more boring than most: a couple of domestic squabbles, a fender-bender accident on National Avenue and that was about it. Then at around 4:00 a.m., Wednesday, a patrol officer swung by the industrial park in southwest National City and began a slow inspection of the warehouses. He took 18th Street under the freeway overpass, made a left on McKinley Street and drove the length of the street. It was at the end where McKinley turned into a cul-de-sac that the patrol officer spotted something lying near a warehouse.

He applied the brakes and stepped cautiously from the cruiser. A thick fog off the bag shrouded the warehouse, but there was no mistaking the object he spotted on the asphalt was a human torso.

The victim, a young man with clipped brown hair in his twenties, lay face down in the dirt. He wore tennis shoes, dark-brown slacks and a white shirt. A large red bloodstain marred the back of the shirt.

The warehouse area is patrolled four times each shift, which meant that the victim had not been lying there for more than two hours. The officer crouched down and checked for signs of life. There were none. Actually it was a formality more than anything else because quite obviously the victim was beyond any sort of medical help.

The officer radioed his findings to the National City police dispatcher. More police arrived at the scene. They were followed by a lab team, a deputy county coroner, and a homicide investigator, Sergeant Merrill Davis.

A veteran investigator who had been called to many similar crime scenes during his career, Davis noticed a trail of blood drops leading away from the body. He followed the stains for a distance of 30 feet to a telephone pole, where the bloodstains stopped. This blood trail told the investigator that the victim had been alive when brought to the warehouse area, and that he had been shot first near the telephone pole and then apparently later after he lay sprawled on the asphalt.

Lab men searched a wide area around the telephone pole but found no slug casings, tire tracks, shoe impressions or anything else that might have some bearing on the case.

The motive for the murder appeared to be robbery. Investigators searched the body and discovered the victim's pants pockets were turned inside out and his wallet was missing. The one thing the killer or killers ignored or overlooked, was a Navy identity card that was stuffed in the victim's shirt pocket. It listed the victim as 21-year-old Gregory Lock. A call to the Navy later in the morning revealed Lock was a nuclear technician aboard the U.S. Bainbridge. He had been staying aboard the ship since it returned from a West Pacific cruise just three days earlier. However, shipmates said that he had not returned to the ship Tuesday night. A little sleuthing uncovered the fact that Lock sometimes stayed with a couple of buddies who had an apartment in Mission Beach.

Sergeant Davis located the friends and went to the apartment. It was a small place located in the mid-Mission Beach area, just a few dozen yards from the ocean.

One of the friends said Lock had spent most of

Tuesday afternoon at the beach and then had come back to the apartment to eat and watch the news on television.

"I thought he was going to spend the night here," he said. The friend was a bit surprised when he returned from his job making pizzas at a nearby pizza restaurant to find Lock was gone.

"I figured maybe it got late and he decided to stay aboard ship," the friend said. "But the more I think about it, the more unlikely that seemed. Greg was the type of guy if he said he would be some place, he would be there."

One of Lock's favorite hangouts was a trendy beach club known as Mom's Saloon. It was located in Pacific Beach about a mile from the apartment and catered to the beach types: young people in their early or late twenties. Sergeant Davis swung by the club and showed Lock's picture to the employees.

No one could place the sailor. "It doesn't mean he wasn't here," the bartender ventured. "But we get hundreds of guys in here that look just like him."

Davis was certain Lock was in the bar Tuesday night because a rubber ink mark on the back of his hand matched the stamp used by Mom's to identify patrons who had paid the admission charge.

But what Davis didn't know was when the sailor left the bar and how he ended up behind a warehouse in National City, almost 20 miles away from the bar.

He also didn't know where Lock's car was. The 21-year-old sailor owned a cream-colored Oldsmobile. The sleuth discovered the car was not in the parking slip Lock used when staying in mission Beach. And it was not in Mom's Saloon parking lot nor anywhere in a four block area of the club. Davis contacted the San Diego Police Department and learned the vehicle had not been impounded or reported involved in a traffic accident.

Davis issued an APB on the car, informing city and county law enforcement officers the car was wanted in connection with a murder investigation and anyone finding the vehicle should immediately contact the National City Police Department.

Four days later the cream-colored Olds was spotted in the parking lot of a Las Vegas, Nevada, motel. Police moved in and arrested four suspects: Kevin John Finckel 20; Michael Williams, 24; Norman Steeg, 25; and Bill Ambrose. The arrest resulted not from the APB put out by National City police, but by a telephone tip made by Ambrose.

"Get some cops out here in a hurry," Ambrose told the dispatcher that morning. "These guys are crazy. They are going to kill someone."

With his three erstwhile buddies in handcuffs, Ambrose felt free to tell all.

He detailed how he met the three men in Long Beach and agreed to accompany them to Las Vegas. "When they told me they shot this guy to get his car I just figured it was bull," Ambrose said. "But after the last couple of days, I am not so sure."

He said he first started to wonder about his new pals after they went to the Golden Nugget Casino and spotted a drunk standing at the bar.

"The guy was pretty polluted," Ambrose said. "He was real loaded and flashing $100 bills."

Ambrose said his three friends decided to get the guns they had back in the motel then lure the drunk outside and take his flash roll. The plan fizzled when a casino bouncer ordered the drunk to leave before they could get the guns.

The following afternoon they ran into a Vegas dope dealer and invited him back to the motel for drinks, Ambrose said.

"We were getting drunk and having a good time when this guy Williams starts arguing with the dealer guy."

The argument degenerated into a shouting match, with Williams threatening to get his gun and put a bullet through the dealer's head.

"And I thought he would, too," Ambrose said. "I mean the guy looked like he was serious."

The last straw came when he, Steeg and Williams set out to cruise the streets looking for someone to rob.

"They said they wanted to find a middle-aged woman who was alone and couldn't fight back," Ambrose related. "Then they were going to take her out in the desert, take her purse and then kill her so she couldn't identify them. They were really pumped up about it."

Before the plan got to the shooting stage, though, Ambrose decided to tip the police.

"I didn't want any part of killing anybody and it was only a question of time before they turned on me," Ambrose said.

Las Vegas police searched the Olds and discovered a .38 Smith and Wesson revolver and a .38 Charter Arms pistol. Also in the car was a quantity of ammunition and a small amount of marijuana and hash oil.

The weapons were of particular interest to National City police because slugs retrieved from Lock's body determined he was shot with a .38.

The weapons were test fired; ballistics determined the Smith and Wesson was the weapon that fired the fateful bullets.

With surprising quickness, the case that had baffled lawmen just days earlier had come together. Police now had the victim's car, the murder weapon, three suspects and a witness who was eager to tell anything he knew.

What they didn't know was the circumstances surrounding the murder. They also didn't know who had pulled the trigger. Sergeant Davis grilled the three young men charged with the crime, but they weren't eager to talk.

A background investigation gave the investigator an idea of the types of persons he was dealing with. There really wasn't much to learn.

Mike "Thumper" Williams had lived most of his 24 years in a comfortable middle class home in suburban San Diego. He had been a fairly normal kid until he got caught for car theft and was sent to California Youth Authority. After serving a short stretch, he returned to San Diego and gravitated to Mission Beach, where he lived a sort of hand-to-mouth existence. "He sold dope when it was around and stole when it wasn't," according to one lawman. He lived a beach bum existence, staying with beach friends or hanging out at the 700 block of Ventura Boulevard, the nerve pulse of the beach area. His best friend, said one source, was Norman Steeg. Born in the Los Angeles area, Steeg drifted to Mission Beach where he lived by quick wits and even quicker fingers. When not crashing at the beach, Steeg could be found at his girlfriend's North Park apartment. Unlike his buddy Williams, Steeg didn't have a criminal record. His name had come to the attention of police just once when he allegedly punched out his girlfriend during an altercation over a welfare check. Other than that, his record was clean.

If the information was skimpy on Williams and Steeg, it was almost nonexistent on Finckel. Born in Washington, Finckel had migrated to San Diego with his folks and had been part of the Mission Beach scene for a year. He had no visible means of support and resorted, authorities said, to "highly creative means" to make ends meet.

Of the three, it was Finckel who decided it was time to talk to police. "I didn't shoot that guy," he told Sergeant Davis. "That was Williams and Steeg's doing."

The sergeant said he believed Finckel and was interested in hearing how the murder went down if Finckel felt like telling him. His confession, which later took the form of courtroom testimony, added still more pieces to the murder puzzle.

It began the day before the murder when Williams and Steeg were casing homes in Pacific Beach. Finckel recalled he and Williams were standing in the backyard of a home when the owner stepped from the house and chased them away.

They waited until they thought it was safe, then went back to the house and knocked on the front door. "Williams told the guy that he was with the Mafia and would blow him away if he made a report to the cops."

Williams was a bit premature with his threat, because at that moment a police cruiser pulled up to the house. Williams and Finckel were arrested for trespassing and were thrown into county jail. The following morning after their release, they gravitated back to Mission Beach.

They hung out until midnight at the beach, Finckel said. "Williams said he had this buddy in Riverside who was supposed to have lots of dope and money in his house. He told us it would be easy to break in and steal the stuff if they found a car to drive up there."

As they walked down the nearly deserted Mission Boulevard looking for a car, they spotted a man pushing his car. "We offered to help push the car and then Williams asked the guy for a ride," Finckel said.

Once in the car, Steeg put a gun to the driver's head and told him to drive, Finckel said. They continued on the freeway to National City where the driver was ordered to take the exit and go to a bunch of warehouses that was visible.

"On the way Williams emptied the guy's pockets of a wallet. I think he had about $2.50 and that was all," Finckel said.

Steeg handed the gun to Williams who ordered the driver to get out of the car and go stand by a telephone pole. Finckel said he didn't know Williams was going to shoot the guy until he heard two shots. "The guy screamed and started to run. Williams shot at him again, then ran and caught up with the guy who had fallen to the ground." The gunman allegedly then finished the job by pumping two more slugs into the mortally wounded driver.

The story that spilled from Finckel's lips was consistent with the physical evidence gathered at the crime scene. It also confirmed findings of the autopsy which reported three slugs entered the victim's back when he was moving and two slugs were fired into his back "straight on" while he lay motionless on the ground.

Williams was elated when he returned to the car, Finckel said. "He said, 'Boy, that's great. I would like to do that again sometime.' "

He said the three of them spent the night with a friend in North Park before heading for Riverside to burglarize another pal. Before they went to sleep, they took the victim's identification papers and wallet and burned them behind the apartment building.

Detectives went to the North Park apartment. In the backyard they found the charred remains of a small fire. The ashes were taken to the crime lab where, by use of a chemical process, technicians were able to raise the word "Lock" and the letter "W".

When news of these revelations got back to Finckel's two pals, it did not make them happy. Their unhappiness was undoubtedly magnified when they learned that Finckel had cut a deal with the district attorney's office. According to the terms of the plea bargain agreement, he was allowed to plead guilty to second-degree murder and receive a sentence of 16 years to life in state prison. In return, Finckel agreed to testify as a state witness at the trials of Williams and Steeg.

Chief prosecutor in the lengthy case was Rupert Linley. A 12-year veteran with the DA's office, Linley had made himself a promise that after the murder trials he would take a year off from work to sail the South Pacific in his 40-foot ketch the "Corinna."

The dream became a reality, but it took awhile. Michael Williams' trial was scheduled for 1981, but numerous delays pushed the date back until November 1982, 14 months after Gregory Lock was gunned down.

Appearing well scrubbed and composed, Williams sat at the defense table and listened without emotion as Finckel and other witnesses testified against him. Williams had pleaded not guilty to the crime, but the evidence was overwhelming. A jury deliberated just six hours before finding him guilty of first-degree murder on December 18th.

During the penalty phase the theory was advanced that Williams was a fairly normal kid until his parents broke up. A teenager at the time, Williams was apparently unable to cope with their separation. He started taking drugs, hanging out with a bad crowd, and getting into trouble.

At one point the defense attempted to put forth the idea that the cold-blooded murder of Gregory Lock might have something to do with an earlier incident in Williams' life.

Had this shocking incident triggered some sort of deep-set hatred in Williams for anyone connected with the Navy? Yes, according to his attorney. "He had all this animosity towards a sailor. And you heard that moments before the shooting the Navy ID card was produced, and Williams learned that Lock was a Navy petty officer. Michael Williams is going to die in prison at this point. The issue is whether you or God choose when he dies," the defense attorney blasted.

Prosecutor Rupert Linley argued, "We are at times in the battle between good and evil required to take a life. It is morally right to send a murderer to his death if that is what is required by his deed."

The jury deliberated just four hours before reaching a verdict: Michael Williams must die in San Quentin State Prison for the murder of Gregory Lock.

The 21-year-old defendant was led from the courtroom back to his jail cell. Linley told reporters the verdict was justified. "The defendant got Lock's car and his money, and he nonetheless killed him, just for the pure pleasure of taking a human life. He showed no remorse. In fact, he bragged about it and said he looked forward to killing again."

The same parade of witnesses appeared at the trial of Norman Steeg which began in January 1983. Steeg was a "victim of circumstances" the defense told the jury. "This was not a good day for Steeg. The robbery was out of the control of my client. When he handed the gun over to Williams, it was out of his hands. He didn't know what was going to happen until the shots were fired."

The defense asked the jury to find the defendant not guilty. In his closing arguments, Linley referred to the three marauders as a "pack of animals" and asked for a conviction of first-degree murder and the finding of special circumstances. The jury had no trouble with either request, and returned a verdict of guilty on February 6th.

During the penalty phase, Linley again asked the jury to vote for the death penalty. But this time the jurors were not so agreeable and after less than a day of deliberations, voted that the defendant be condemned to life in state prison without the possibility of parole. He is currently serving his term in the state prison system.

Mike Williams' case has been appealed to the state

supreme court. Until the case has been heard, he will remain in death row in San Quentin prison.

EDITOR'S NOTE:
Bill Ambrose is fictitious and was used because there is no need for public interest in his true identity.

"A WOMAN'S GREED LAID THE DEALER LOW!"

by Charles Sasser

Osage County—once was the Osage Indian reservation, a vast sea of tall-grass prairie and wooded draws and ridges stretching from Tulsa in northeastern Oklahoma to the Kansas border. Early on a spring Sunday in May—May 8, 1988—dark buzzards soared the spring thermals high above the faint scent of sage and bluestem.

The buzzards always meant death—a deer in the brush killed by poachers or wild dogs, a coyote succumbed to old age.

This time it was not a dead deer or coyote.

Authorities from two states were massing on an oil-lease tract described as three-quarters of a mile west of Oklahoma State Highway 99 and 50 feet south into Osage land from the Kansas line. A narrow sandy road, more like a trail, ate its way through the oil lease into a wooded depression.

'Coon hunters found the body at 2:00 a.m. Osage County Sheriff George Wayman in Pawhuska, the county seat, telephoned Deputy Russell Cottle at his residence. "Go to the jail and pick up your plaster kits and get up here," the sheriff instructed his yawning deputy. "We've got a stranger murdered and dumped."

By the time the sun edged above the rolling hills, Oklahoma and Kansas deputies, supplemented by agents from the Oklahoma State Bureau of Investigation (OSBI), were measuring, photographing, collecting evidence, and speculating about who the dead man was and how he ended up dumped in this most isolated region of the state.

The corpse appeared to be a man in his mid-30s, of medium height, medium weight, with longish brown hair. Investigators had a difficult time telling the color of his eyes—one of them had been shot out, leaving a gaping cavern, and the other was severely damaged. He lay on his back, as if staring into the sun. He was dressed like any other cowboy from this part of Oklahoma—brown cowboy boots, blue jeans, and a plaid Western-type shirt.

Its deterioration indicated that the body had lain in the field for at least 36 hours, placing the time of death as sometime around Friday. The state medical examiner ruled that the victim died of three gunshot wounds to the head. The M.E. also reported traces of amphetamines and methamphetamines in the victim's bloodstream.

"Whoever did it wanted to make sure he was good and dead," commented a deputy at the crime scene. "I guess the ol' boy died with his boots on. But why?"

There was no identification on the corpse.

It took a survey to confirm that the homicide scene lay within Oklahoma's jurisdiction. Then, while Deputy John Ferguson linotyped a regionwide description of the dead man in hopes that some law enforcement agency would recognize it, Sheriff Wayman assigned Chief Criminal Deputy Bill Williams to coordinate the fledgling crime probe.

Bill Williams was a tall, rugged man with the looks of a farmhand and the wit of a big-city homicide detective. He had earned a reputation as a skillful and tenacious sleuth. It had been Williams who solved the devil-cult slaying of the county's wealthiest Indian, Victor Red Eagle, in the previous year (see *Official Detective*, February 1989). Attention to detail lay at the core of Williams' investigative successes.

The county's chief investigator organized an inch-by-inch evidence search of the area. The findings were carefully recorded: three filter cigarettes spilled to the right of the victim's head, apparently from a pack of Winstons still in the victim's shirt pocket; a jacketed bullet underneath the victim's head that had bored completely through the dead man's skull; a spent cartridge casing from a .380-caliber automatic pistol; tire tracks spinning away from the scene along the narrow ruts of the road, of which Deputy Cottle obtained a plaster cast; and other odds and ends, such as footprints, bits of scrap paper, and a Ziplock-type sandwich bag that continued to puzzle deputies until they received a reply to Deputy Ferguson's linotype.

"We have a possible abduction in Bartlesville, Oklahoma," came the linotype reply, "with victim being Morris, Clayton Orville, 33 YOA. Our victim has similar description. He is 5-foot-8, weight 160. Our victim has scar on lower abdomen. He has a colostomy and has been using sandwich bags or colostomy bags, which he tapes to his skin."

103

That, then, also explained the ugly, reddish wound, like a puckered mouth, low on the corpse's left flank. It all but cinched the dead man's identity.

Deputy Ferguson telephoned Bartlesville Detective Steve Gardella: "I'm pretty sure we have your missing man in Osage County. Clayton Morris is dead."

The crime scene lay approximately 30 miles northwest of Bartlesville, the little city made famous by the Phillips Oil Company. Detective Gardella soon verified that the dead man was indeed Clayton Orville Morris, missing from Bartlesville since Friday. With that confirmation, lawmen from Osage County swung into action with Washington County and Bartlesville detectives in an attempt to piece together what became one of northeastern Oklahoma's most bizarre criminal episodes.

"What's the world coming to?" exclaimed an observer. "Even the cowboys are becoming dope addicts!"

A homicide victim's background and recent history often supplies valuable clues as to why the victim might have been killed and who killed him. Delving into that background is an investigative priority.

According to published reports and public courtroom accounts, 33-year-old Clay Morris served a tour in Germany with the U.S. Army before returning to Bartlesville, where he became a part-time house-painter and a full-time dealer of "crank," a potent methamphetamine. Married in 1976, he produced two daughters before he divorced and took up with a second woman, who gave him a son. The unmarried couple lived in a rundown crackerbox house on South Seneca in Bartlesville. Police described the residence as a known "dopers' hangout" where dealers and users congregated and sometimes "denned up like a bunch of dogs."

Rumor had it that the victim had survived a previous gunshot wound sustained because of his "business."

The victim's entanglement with the seamy underworld of dopers, hustlers, petty dealers and thieves threatened to complicate the police investigation. As a matter of experience, police consider the people who inhabit the doper subculture to be entirely unreliable and unpredictable, resisting all law enforcement attempts to penetrate it.

"They'll lie, steal, cheat—*anything*—in order to get another fix into their veins," explained an undercover Bartlesville policemen. "Dope burns out their brains, rots them to the core. What's left is not quite human. While they'll pimp out their own mothers to stay high, they'll cover up their crimes like a cat in a sandbox."

The dead man left on the prairie with his boot toes pointing to the buzzards was also evidence that dopers could be dangerous. Investigator Bill Williams and the cowboy detectives of the Osage almost immediately aimed their sights at drug dealers in searching for a suspect. The victim's association with the illicit drug world, the methamphetamines in his bloodstream, and his execution-style slaying—all these almost excluded any motive for murder other than that involving drugs.

Possible suspects, said Williams, sprouted like new leaves on a creek-bottom willow: "It was a case in which there were *too many suspects*."

Dealers throughout northeastern Oklahoma and

into Kansas took advantage of Morris' death to use as leverage against competitors and debtors. "You'd better pay up what you owe me," went a common threat, "or I'll do to you what I done to Clayton."

A team of investigators kept busy for days running down such threats.

Although suspects surfaced like dead fish, police soon focused on a man named Leather Willis as a key to the mystery. It was Willis, an uncle of the victim's girlfriend, police said, who nervously telephoned Bartlesville authorities late on the evening of Friday, May 6th, saying he was afraid Clayton Morris had been kidnapped.

"When did it happen?" a sleuth began the routine questioning.

"This morning about six-thirty."

More than twelve hours had passed.

"Why did you wait so long to call the police?"

Willis reportedly explained that he, the victim and the girlfriend had been using "crank," and he was afraid it would get him into trouble with the law. Besides, he added, all the "yelling and shaking" he had in him failed to arouse the girl from the drug stupor she was in at the time her boyfriend was whisked away. He said he felt he had to wait until the drugs wore off before he could safely notify the police.

Willis' official statements to the police and to the courts alleged that a man forced his way into the Morris residence on South Seneca shortly after daybreak on Friday. Present in the house were Willis, Clay Morris, and the girl, who was unconscious from drug use.

"Elliott is the only name I know him by" Willis

told police, his statements here partially paraphrased from police reports. "He is approximately five-eight with dark, greasy-looking hair, stringy and down to his shoulders. He's about twenty-five years old and was wearing a red bandana tied around his head and a jean jacket."

Brandishing a silver-colored automatic pistol, the intruder disarmed Morris of a hunting knife concealed in his belt.

"Elliott grabbed a-hold of (Morris) and said that he wanted his damned billfold," Willis continued. "Clayton said he didn't have it. They argued for a while."

Elliott quickly searched the dwelling's three small rooms, apparently not finding what he sought.

"I told him," said Willis, "that I thought he should leave. Or, better yet, that I should leave, because it was none of my business and I didn't want to be involved in it. He told me to sit down and shut up. He threatened everybody in the house and said we would all be lucky if we made it out of there alive. He told me he was the Grim Reaper seeking death."

The ordeal ended when the interloper grabbed Morris by the arm and marched him out to a black Ford Torino parked at the curb. Willis said he thought Elliott was taking Morris to confront an unknown third party who had apparently accused Morris of taking Elliott's wallet.

That was the last time Willis saw Clay Morris.

That was three days ago.

Now Morris' body had turned up on the prairie hardpan with three bullets through its skull.

After broadcasting a statewide APB (All Points Bulletin) describing "Elliott" and his vehicle and asking that Elliott be detained for questioning if spotted, authorities fanned out across Osage and Washington counties in a fast-moving run to scrape up evidence and information on a possible homicide suspect. While Bartlesville Detective Steve Gardella took charge of this fork of the sprouting probe, Osage Investigator Bill Williams took another trail.

OSBI ballistic reports on the homicide bullets reportedly narrowed the murder weapon down to a selection of .380-caliber automatic pistols manufactured by one of three firearms dealers, the most likely of which was the AMF Company. Williams used this information to sort through old theft reports and pawn receipts in a long-shot effort to trace the weapon back to a killer. He also began contacting his network of informants, without which any detective is handicapped.

Long-shot though the effort was, Williams soon compiled a short list of people who either possessed or had access to a .380 AMF automatic. That list then narrowed down to a single name—Marge Redfern, an Indian woman of 35, an ex-convict and a known dope dealer whom federal and state narcotics agents had been attempting to put out of business for years.

An informant reportedly snitched to Investigator Williams that Redfern was friendly with a female addict whose boyfriend was a Nowata, Oklahoma rancher, an older man also believed to be involved in narcotics activity. A week or so before Clay Morris' kidnapping, according to the tip, Marge Redfern and the rancher's girlfriend burglarized the rancher's house and stole a small, silver-plated .380 AMF automatic pistol.

"Marge said she needed the gun so a friend could get back some money," the snitch allegedly advised Williams.

No police burglary report existed on the incident. Williams located the rancher, who verified that his house was indeed broken into and his .380 was stolen. He simply hadn't bothered to report the crime.

Pressing on, the deputy managed to recover for comparison purposes several spent cartridge casings ejected by the .380 when the rancher was target-practicing. It didn't take long for OSBI firearms experts to conclude that Bill Williams' suspicions were correct.

The firing-pin indention on the casing from the crime scene matched the indention marks on the casings Investigator Williams gathered at the rancher's house. That meant the stolen gun was the weapon used to murder Clayton Morris. That also meant Marge Redfern was somehow involved in the brutal slaying.

"She refused to cooperate," exclaimed an exasperated Bill Williams. "She wouldn't give us the correct time of day."

For the time being, at least, authorities possessed insufficient evidence to coerce the woman into talking. But the detectives expressed confidence that the situation would be quickly remedied as probe teams headed by Detective Steve Gardella and Washington County Chief Criminal Deputy Mike Shea fitted new pieces into the puzzle. The most important of these new pieces concerned the victim's association with another drug underworld figure, 24-year-old Elliott Dean Truitt. Right down to his red bandana headband, Truitt matched the "Elliott" who had apparently abducted Clayton Morris from his house on Friday morning.

Later, courtroom accounts revealed a life history for Truitt that paralleled the victim's to an astonishing degree.

Like Morris, Truitt was separated from his first wife, who had given him three children. Both men had stormy relationships with their wives because of drugs and both men were the cause of their wives' addictions. In her recorded statements, Truitt's wife said she started using drugs in September 1987 and had been "high" and without sleep during the two weeks prior to her last breakup with Truitt.

"He threw me around several times," she said, according to news reports. "One time he pointed a gun at me and said if I didn't come around with the drugs he wanted, he would kill me."

Both women allegedly stated that their husbands had short tempers, were jealous, and had been counseled several times regarding their drug addiction. In May 1988, Morris and Truitt were living in Bartlesville with girlfriends while their wives lived elsewhere.

Police quickly established that Truitt's only transportation was a 1976 Honda motorcycle, hardly the vehicle to use in a kidnapping. However, they also learned that his Bartlesville girlfriend drove a Torino like the one described by Leather Willis, the witness to Morris' abduction.

Probing, twisting deeper into the bowels of the doper subculture, skillful detectives picked up a story of a party several weeks earlier attended by both Elliott Truitt and Clayton Morris. The story had it that

Truitt left his wallet containing $500 in the car of a friend who had since then been convicted and sent to the state penitentiary on a drug-related crime. Truitt's leaving his wallet and money accessible to "that kind of a crowd was a stupid thing to do," as one of the partygoers later phrased it.

Truitt allegedly suspected Morris of having stolen his wallet and cash. He borrowed a sawed-off shotgun from an acquaintance and obtained a silver .380 pistol from somewhere else. When the owner of the shotgun asked for it back, Truitt patted the pistol in his belt.

"This," he reportedly said, "is for Clayton Morris."

Then he patted the shotgun.

"And this," he said, "is for you."

The shotgun's owner never asked about the shotgun again.

Although he couldn't prove it yet, Detective Williams said he knew where Truitt obtained the .380 pistol—from Marge Redfern. The investigation's loose ends were beginning to twist in on themselves.

Announcing that authorities had enough evidence to pick up Elliott Truitt for questioning, Osage Sheriff George Wayman issued an arrest-on-probable-cause order for the suspect while Osage District Attorney Larry Stuart reviewed the case files. The manhunt began with a cautionary note: "Suspect known dope user. Consider him armed and extremely dangerous."

Late on Monday night, May 9th, Deputies Mike Shea and Russell Cottle, along with other cowboy-booted deputies, picked up the suspected killer's spoor in the little town of Dewey, Oklahoma, where

Truitt's estranged wife was living. It was she, police reports indicate, who informed on her husband. When a caravan of Oklahoma lawmen crossed the state line into Kansas in the pre-dawn hours of May 10th, she was riding in the lead car.

Deputy Bill Williams reportedly directed the operation. A coterie of officers silently surrounded the suspect's hideout in a small house near the corner of Cement Street and Coffeyville Street in Independence, Kansas. When the wife approached the house and was admitted, a dozen loaded revolvers and shotguns covered her from the darkness. Lawmen have always said you could never get careless while arresting dopers. Resistance by the slender, stragglyhaired man inside could only end with his being pumped full of lead.

Fifteen minutes passed. The front door slowly opened. Spotlights focused on it. Elliott Dean Truitt and his wife emerged onto the porch, Truitt's hands empty and in sight. She had persuaded him to surrender without resistance. His first words to lawmen proclaimed his innocence. He reportedly insisted that he did not kill Clayton Morris and did not know who did.

By four o'clock of that balmy Tuesday morning, the suspect sat slumped in a chair at the Bartlesville PD. Later testimony by Detective Williams, who recorded Truitt's official statements, revealed that the admitted drug addict confessed to have gone to Morris' home the previous Friday and leaving with him. However, he said, he did not abduct Morris. The two merely decided to confront the woman who'd accused Morris of stealing Truitt's money.

Truitt said the two stopped off on the way to the

woman's house to buy beer at a local convenience store. There they met a "rough-looking dude" riding a flame-orange Harley Davidson motorcycle. Morris knew the biker; Truitt said he didn't.

The biker asked Morris to follow him to a residence to drop off the motorcycle, then drive him back to town. With Truitt driving his girlfriend's Torino, the two men followed the biker toward the Kansas line, where he turned off onto an oil-lease road snaking through tall grass prairie in the morning sunshine. The road led to a clearing in a grove of trees.

"So we went out there," said Truitt in his statement. "There were four other riders out there on bikes. There was a black Corvette with California plates on it, and three or four other people down there where the bikes were. They pulled Clayton out of the car and was talking to him about some money that he owed this guy.

"There was another guy up there that I knew by the name of Johnny Rose. He was doing the biggest part of the talking, and there was another guy about 300 pounds sitting on his bike, and he was just sitting there nodding. He wasn't saying a whole lot. Evidently he must have been the guy that (Morris) owed money to."

Truitt said that one of the bikers was waving around a silver-colored pistol. "He pointed it at me and told me to 'get out of here!' So I left because they told me they'd bring (Morris) back to town."

Truitt said he heard later that police found Clayton Morris dead on the oil lease, shot through the skull three times.

It was Truitt's contention that one of the bikers killed Morris. Exactly which one was up to the police to determine.

Authorities obviously did not completely buy Truitt's story. They held him in the Osage County Jail at Pawhuska for further inquiry while officers carefully checked out his alibi. After several days spent chasing down bikers, an Osage deputy shook his head wearily.

"From everything we can find out," he said, "Elliott Truitt was lying like a rug. The people Truitt said were in the clearing that day all had alibis that held up, unlike Truitt's. Besides, we couldn't find any motorcycle tire tracks in the field."

What officers did find, however, was that tire tracks plaster-preserved from the crime scene matched perfectly the tires of the Torino that Truitt admitted he was driving on May 6th. Furthermore, the case against Truitt strengthened when forensic experts recovered two spent .380-caliber cartridge casings from the car and matched them to the one from the crime scene and to those from the Nowata ranch where the AMF automatic had been stolen. Cigarette butts in the car's ash tray were of the same brand — Winstons — found on the victim's body.

"Dopers," explained Deputy Bill Williams, "are a strange breed. While they're paranoid to the point of schizophrenia, they're also arrogant and careless."

Truitt had apparently been careless in not even attempting to destroy evidence.

"Or drugged out of his mind," commented one lawman.

D.A. Larry Stuart and Detective Williams capped the prosecution's case by issuing a subpoena to force

Marge Redfern to either disclose the part she played in the bizarre slaying or face possible murder conspiracy charges. Granted immunity from prosecution in exchange for testifying against Elliott Truitt, the female drug dealer chose to talk.

She allegedly admitted that her girlfriend and she stole the .380 AMF from the Nowata rancher, just as Williams' informant described it. She said she owed Truitt money on a previous drug deal and paid off that debt with the pistol, since Truitt wanted one. She claimed not to know what Truitt intended to do with the gun.

"When I came over to Bartlesville to buy dope," she said from the witness stand, "I brought the gun with me and paid off my past bill."

On Saturday, May 7th, the day after Morris disappeared, Marge Redfern learned Truitt's dark purpose for the automatic pistol. She testified that she and a lady friend drove to Bartlesville to "buy drugs. We were gonna go get some money sales." In Bartlesville, the two women dealers encountered an Elliott Truitt so nervous that he appeared paranoid. He told the women that he had killed Morris in an argument over money. He was still armed with a shotgun and the stolen AMF.

Marge Redfern and her friend drove Truitt to Independence, Kansas, where he could hide out until things "chilled out." Enroute, Redfern testified, Truitt remained so on edge that he thought people were following him. Redfern's girlfriend was driving. When she slowed down, Truitt pointed his shotgun at her head and cried, "Don't stop or I'll kill you."

Redfern then testified that she took the murder weapon to contacts in Kansas who cut it up and melted it down. Police were never to find any part of it.

The woman reportedly ended her police statement on a note of irony. Chuckling softly, she concluded with, "He (Truitt) said he left (Morris' body) on one of Winston Thomas' oil leases. He thought that was kind of funny."

"Why was that?" Williams asked.

"Because," Marge Redfern replied, "Winston Thomas is a big drug connection for northeastern Oklahoma and Kansas."

D.A. Stuart filed charges of first-degree murder and kidnapping against Elliott Dean Truitt on May 12, 1988. Although the motive for the slaying appeared to center on Truitt's stolen wallet, Detective Williams said he thought it went much farther than that.

"I'm convinced Marge Redfern was partly behind it," he said. "I think she wanted Morris dead to put him out of business as her competitor in the drug business. I think she knew very well what the gun she stole was going to be used for."

The saga of "The Osage Doper War," as some people were calling it, was not yet ended, even with the murder suspect behind bars awaiting trial.

On Tuesday morning, April 4, 1989, the week before Truitt was scheduled to face an Osage jury, a Pawhuska rancher breakfasting in a restaurant on Kihekah Street glanced out the window in time to see his three-quarter-ton pickup truck fishtailing out of sight down the street.

"They're stealing my truck!" he bugled, initiating a half-hour high-speed automobile chase involving Pawhuska police, Osage County deputies, Oklahoma

Highway Patrol troopers, local lake patrolman, and a smattering of cowboys and ranchers in their own pickups.

Gunshots punctuated the chase as an Osage deputy pumped three bullets into the side of the truck when it rammed his patrol cruiser. Even though the stolen pickup's tires were flattened in the chase that exceeded speeds of 100 mph, it still streaked out of town on Sunset Lake Road to Okesa and along SH-123 to the little town of Barnsdall before lawmen succeeded in stopping it.

Officers discovered their auto thieves to be Elliott Dean Truitt and another Pawhuska jailbird being held on burglary charges. They'd broken jail using a homemade aluminum knife which they held to the jailer's throat.

Truitt made it back to jail in time to face his jury.

"Everyone you see in this trial was involved in drugs and drug dealing," D.A. Larry Stuart announced in his opening statements to the court. "There are no exceptions! That includes the victim as well as the accused and the witnesses."

Even a character witness who had once employed the defendant was exposed. It turned out that the Dewey, Oklahoma rancher was also the employer of a man who had been convicted of growing marijuana on the ranch and who had previously been a suspect in the notorious Mullendore murder case, still unsolved after more than 15 years.

The D.A. demanded the death penalty. Instead, on Tuesday, April 18, 1989, the Osage jury found Truitt guilty of first-degree murder and set his sentence as life in prison without parole. He is currently serving his term at the Oklahoma State Penitentiary.

Authorities say cells are waiting at Big Mac for dope dealers and other criminals exposed by the Clayton Morris homicide investigation. It's just a matter of time, they said.

EDITOR'S NOTE:
Leather Willis, Marge Redfern, Johnny Rose and Winston Thomas are not the real names of the persons so named in the foregoing story. Fictitious names have been used because there is no reason for public interest in the identities of these persons.

"RODNEY WAS HAMMERED TO DEATH FOR $14"

by Channing Corbin

GREELEY, COLORADO
OCTOBER 25, 1982

Rodney Allen Russell hailed from the farming community of Plattsville, Colorado, population — roughly 683. Plattsville was located approximately 30 miles due south of the bustling town of Greeley, site of the University of Northern Colorado, where Rod, as he was commonly known to his friends, was a student majoring in business administration. Because of sheer necessity, it was essential that the 20-year-old student work to subsidize the high costs of attaining a college degree. His parents weren't wealthy and there were no grants or scholarships to offset the expenses.

Rod hadn't really minded though, being accustomed to hard work all of his life. He'd gone out and obtained a job as a part-time attendant at a service station located on 8th Avenue in south Greeley. His schedule left him little time for leisure between classes, homework and the responsibilities of a job. He was on duty the night of Thursday, December 3,

1981 at the station. It was a chilly, blustery, Colorado winter night and business was fairly slow. If Rod experienced any anxiety concerning the possibility of his being a victim in an armed robbery, he never discussed it. Perhaps, like so many others who are obliged to work to have the things they want, he rationalized his position and accepted the inherent risk involved on the premises that the law of averages were on his side.

Rodney Russell's killer had used neither a gun nor a knife when he accosted the young service station attendant that night bent on robbery. Instead, he'd seized a heavy hammer and battered the unsuspecting student senseless. The crime was discovered by a customer who entered the station at exactly 8:58 p.m. to get change for the soda pop dispenser. When he couldn't locate the attendant on duty, he searched the rear office. He found Russell lying on the floor in a welter of blood with one arm flung across his face and breathing heavily. Another customer entered the store about then and the man who'd found the gravely injured victim called him into the back office.

They quickly called the Greeley Police Department and requested that the dispatcher also send an ambulance as the victim was still alive. Uniformed Police Officer Larry Hernandez was one of the first to arrive on the scene. He found the critically injured victim still unconscious and did what he could to make the wounded man comfortable while waiting for the arrival of the medics and ambulance.

Officer Hernandez scanned the premises as he worked, careful not to disturb anything which might be viewed as evidence related to what appeared to be a ghastly, inhumane beating administered with a heavy three pound hammer which lay on the floor near the victim. The tool, Hernandez noted, had a pointed head and its presence and appearance was consistent with the pulverized condition of the injured man's head.

Seconds later, the service station was swarming with additional police officers and the medics, who worked swiftly to prepare the victim for a code-3 run to the Weld County Hospital. Those who worked with the victim could tell that it would be a race with death as the victim's pulse was already quite slow and his breathing labored. Rodney Russell was still alive when he was rushed into the emergency room at the hospital and he fought valiantly to survive for two more hours before dying at 11:06 p.m. without regaining consciousness. A police officer had waited in vain, hoping against all odds that the mortally injured young man would come to long enough to provide information related to the fatal attack.

Greeley Police Captain Gary Leonard and others assumed key roles as lead investigators in the case. Subsequent to the removal of the victim, the back office and the station premises were processed for clues and leads. Evidence of the unbridled ferocity of the assault upon the youthful service station attendant was apparent by the blood spattered walls in the back office where the attack evidently occurred.

Doctors at the Weld County Hospital counted a total of eight head wounds, with many of them having been inflicted in the back of the skull. It was astounding that the victim had survived as long as he had in view of the lethal damage inflicted by his assailant. The three pound hammer was determined to be a tool kept on the premises.

Police contacted the station's owner who arrived shortly after Rodney Russell was carried from the establishment and whisked away to the hospital. The owner conducted a check of the premises, at the request of investigating officers, and discovered that $14 in cash was missing. Much of the business done by the station involved the use of credit cards. Police asked the station owner to check through the credit card receipts. They would provide a ready made listing of names of many of the customers who'd patronized the station prior to the arrival of the slayer.

Thanks to the diligent efforts of the ID technicians who processed the crime scene, investigating officers were able to make several conclusions. One was that Russell was initially attacked outside the rear office and near the air hose. Evidently rendered unconscious, the attendant's assailant had then dragged him into the office where he was again bludgeoned. Tracks were discovered in and around the station which indicated that a bicycle had been ridden into the bay sometime during the hours which preceded the atrocious assault.

One of the most sagacious investigative moves employed by those assigned to the homicide was to go public with an appeal to anyone who may have passed the station or, better yet, patronized it between about 8:30 and 9:00 p.m., to contact police. Response was excellent and it complemented several voluntary contacts already made plus others which police initiated from names taken from credit car receipts found in the station. With this, investigating officers were able to greatly expand the scope of their probe.

One witness was located who told police that he had entered the service station at about 8:45 p.m. for gas. As he'd driven up to the pump, he noticed a man riding away on a bicycle. The cyclist later wheeled around and returned to the station and told the customer that he was a new employee. This witness stated that he'd given the man a credit card to pay for his purchase and that he was somewhat perplexed when the self-described new-hire was unable to operate the credit card machine. The shabbily attired, self-styled attendant then, according to this witness, blithely informed the customer to return the following day to pay for his purchase and the witness left.

This witness provided police with a concise physical description of the man whom he'd encountered almost 45 minutes prior to the other customer's discovery of the battered attendant in the rear office. The individual who returned to the station on a bicycle was most definitely not Rodney Russell. He was described as being a black-haired Hispanic, 20 to 25 years old, about 5'7" tall, clean shaven and wearing boots and a dirty, light-colored jacket. Police swiftly aired this information.

In evaluating what information they had on the all-out investigation, they were able to deduce that the killer was a local. Many night-time, hit-and-run heists, such as the one they were investigating are the work of transient, mobile bandits who invariably drive off nearby I-25 to pull a fast job for whatever is in the till. Most often, they are armed.

Greeley police intensified their search for additional witnesses, hoping to identify their suspect. Thanks to the cooperation of yet another civic minded witness, sleuths were able to fit additional pieces into the jigsaw puzzle.

A woman contacted police to report that she had been in a nearby bar early during the evening of December 3rd and had noticed a man there who she later saw ride into the service station on a bike at about 8:35 p.m. She didn't know the man's name. She recalled the incident only because it was so unusual to see anyone riding around Greeley on a frigid December night.

Police questioned others at the bar but were unable to locate anyone who knew the cycling Hispanic's name. Unknown to Greeley police, a series of incidents directly related to the bludgeon slaying of the service station attendant began to unfold about December 6th, just a few days after Russell's murder.

A young man had stumbled across what appeared to be an abandoned bicycle near a lake located southeast of Greeley. He took the bike home and gave it to a younger brother. Like many, he seldom read the newspapers and listened to the news only to hear the sports scores. Neither the finder of the bicycle nor its recipient were aware that local police were avidly searching the bike used in the commission of the December 3rd murder.

The finder's brother later decided that he'd rather have the bike's worth in cash and he sold it to a Greeley resident. During the transaction, the buyer learned the history of the bicycle, and knowing of the police's interest in abandoned bicycles, he quickly contacted them about the one he'd just purchased. When he mentioned the fact that there were brownish-colored smears on the bike's frame which looked like dried blood, police assured the man they'd be out to talk with him as fast as they could get there.

They were as good as their promise and shortly afterward, Jeanne Kilmer, a serologist with the CBI (Colorado Bureau of Investigation) was able to identify the brownish-colored smears on the bicycle as being of human origin. Kilmer went out to confirm that the blood type was the same as that of Rodney Russell's blood group. She also determined that the victim's blood group was uncommon, even rare, and possessed by only seven percent of the population. There could be little doubt that police had, in a roundabout way, recovered the suspect's bicycle.

Unfortunately, there was nothing which could be used to trace the ownership of the incongruous mode of transportation. Such was also the case with a pair of men's boots discovered in a field near Greeley by Detective Don Eyer during a search conducted on December 22, 1981. When discovered, the footwear appeared to be in good condition. The only obvious reason for their having been discarded may have been because, like the abandoned bicycle, they bore stains which looked like blood.

Another CBI serologist by the name of Ted Davelis had worked extensively with blood specimens found on the three pound hammer, the cash drawer and the bicycle. He worked with the suspicious stains on the recovered boots. He was able to determine that they were of human origin but could not group or classify them further because of the extremely limited quantity involved.

It was not until December 24, 1981 that the first major break occurred. It was then that Sgt. Tom Wagoner of the Greeley Police Department had received a most enigmatic call from an inmate then incarcerated in the Weld County Jail. Officer Wagoner was aware that, coincidentally, police had previously interrogated the inmate's girlfriend in connection with the Russell homicide case. It was Wagoner's understanding that the woman had made certain incriminating allegations against the man who had called him pleading for a "jailhouse meet to discuss something heavy."

It was Christmas Eve and a time for festive gatherings with family and friends for almost everyone except those charged with the responsibility of solving a particularly heinous murder.

Wagoner was aware that the man who'd called him was being held on charges totally unrelated to murder. Before he left to keep his appointment he spent some time with his colleagues acquainting himself with exactly what was said to Ila Garcia, the girlfriend of Johnny Arguello, the man who wanted to talk to him this chilly Christmas Eve.

Somewhat to his surprise, Wagoner learned that Ila Garcia had practically confessed to having been an accessory in Russell's murder and that she had identified Arguello, her sweetheart, as being the actual killer. But there was a catch to it all, one which left police somewhat dubious regarding Garcia's true motivations. She learned that Arguello was due to spend considerable time in jail and she became imbued with a desire to be near him and to have the jail chaplain marry them. This and the fact that much of what she had told police was untrue led them to discount much of her story.

What he'd learned about Ila Garcia's role in the case did not deter Detective Wagoner's intentions to keep his appointment with Arguello. He was in for another surprise. Johnny Arguello proved to be a man totally ready to confess to the murder. Police advised him of his rights. Orally at first, and on tape, the 30-year-old suspect described how he'd spent the day of December 3, 1981, at work at a Greeley car lot. He'd ridden his bike home after work.

Later, he had pedalled down to a neighborhood tavern where he drank several beers. By his own admission, he left the bar with the intention of robbing a gas station because he needed money. The time of his departure was about 8:30 p.m. He rode his bike to the gas station located at 8th Avenue and 2nd Street. He saw the attendant busily at work sweeping the garage bay and rode his bicycle inside the shop.

Arguello told police that he asked Russell, who was unknown to him, to air the tires of his bike. The obliging, courteous attendant laid his broom aside and stooped to pick up the air hose. It was then Arguello grabbed the heavy sledge hammer which he raised high and brought crashing down on his unsuspecting victim's head twice. He then dragged the unconscious attendant into the back office. A customer arrived at this point and Arguello, according to his confession, ran outside and pushed his bike around to the rear of the station where it was out of sight.

Afterward, Arguello related, he returned to the bay area where he used rags to cover the blood stains on the floor. The customer outside was fueling his own car and when he came inside to proffer his credit card to pay for his purchase, Arguello found himself unable to operate the credit card machine and asked the man to return later to pay for the gas.

He told the surprised customer that he was new at the job. When the man left, Arguello rushed back into the rear office and pried open a cash drawer and took a ten dollar bill and four ones. He then picked up the heavy hammer and struck the unconscious man on the floor another "six or seven times," before fleeing the service station.

He climbed aboard his bicycle and rode it south until he came to a field where he removed his blood-spattered boots and threw them away. He then rode home and told Ila that he'd killed a gas station attendant. He asked her to dispose of the bicycle and some of his clothing which she did. That was the extent of her involvement in the slaying.

Arguello's lurid, detailed confession was later reduced to writing and signed by him. He and his mistress were formally charged with first-degree murder on December 26, 1981 and Ila found herself behind bars in the Weld County Jail, separated from, but yet near the man who had calmly admitted to police that he'd taken advantage of Rodney Russell's good nature by slaying him with a heavy hammer.

Having identified a viable suspect who was now charged and behind bars, the authorities continued to work to firm up their case. Witnesses who had seen the bike-riding individual in or near the service station were requested to view the accused man for the purpose of making a positive ID. Other witnesses were located who were able to identify the bicycle.

Weld County District Attorney Stanley Peek received the investigative files on the case from Greeley police and prepared to prosecute Johnny Arguello for the brutal murder of Rodney Russell. He sensed immediately that, thanks to the expertise of the investigative officers whose efforts were supplemented by considerable scientific laboratory analysis, he had a solid case. The fact that Johnny Arguello had confessed was viewed as being secondary. D.A. Peek knew, that in accord with modern day criminal defense procedures, the defense would try to make the suspect's descriptive confession inadmissible for a variety of reasons.

One other suspect was previously charged as a suspect in the Russell slaying. He'd been apprehended while emerging from a broken window of a store shortly after the shocking murder of the youthful service station attendant. At the time of this suspect's arrest, certain evidence tended to indicate that he and an accomplice might well have been involved in the brutal hammer-slaying. It hadn't helped matters any from a police investigative standpoint when this suspect also made certain incriminating statements related to Russell's murder while being questioned. These charges, however, were ultimately dismissed prior to Arguello's arrest.

A motion to bar the press and the public by A.M. Dominguez, Arguello's defense counsel, was filed during pre-trial hearings on the premise that it would enhance the defendant's right to a fair trial. District Court Judge Jonathan Hays declined to grant the motion, stressing that the public, in a democratic society, should have the right to know what goes on in our courtrooms.

On Thursday, January 21, 1982, Johnny Arguello was ordered bound over to stand trial on a first-degree murder charge. Ila Garcia was also held to stand trial on accessory to murder charges. The court heard testimony from a relative of Ila's, several

Greeley police officers and the Weld County coroner during the pre-trial hearing. Defense counsel requested and was granted a motion to have Arguello subjected to sanity examinations before entering a plea.

Arguello's murder trial got underway during the last week of June, 1982, with the tedious process of selecting a jury. During the fifth day of this arduous task, the defendant tried to escape. As he was being escorted from the courtroom by two deputies who were returning him to his cell in the county jail just 200 feet away, he stopped to chat with two women. They later, after requesting that they not be identified, told police that the unmanacled defendant told them, "I'll have some excitement for you soon."

Seconds later, a startled Deputy Pat Richardson and Lt. Rich Cole, saw their prisoner sprint away and then break into a full run. They immediately pursued him accompanied by District Attorney Peek who'd witnessed the incident from inside the courtroom and then joined in the chase. Arguello made his way out of the courthouse and into the crowded street where he crossed over to Lincoln Park. The sidewalks were thronged with shoppers which hindered both the pursued and the pursuers. The chase proved to be of a short duration, however, as the fleeing murder defendant was apprehended within two blocks of the courthouse. He offered no resistance and was cuffed and led back to his cell. His attorney's attempts to portray him as a cooperative, repentant individual were shattered. The excitement he'd promised was minimal.

To be sure, deputies assigned to escort the defendant to and from his cell remained more alert during the remainder of the lengthy trial. With the jury selection finally complete Arguello's attorney dropped a veritable bombshell when he stood and introduced his client to the court during his opening remarks. With his hand on Arguello's shoulder, Dominguez told the jury that the man who stood accused of the vicious murder of Rodney Russell was one of 12 children who'd dropped out of high school to go to work. Then, the attorney waved papers at the jury, exclaiming that they were Arguello's confession.

"We wouldn't be here today if he (Arguello) hadn't confessed," he told the court after which he then proceeded to admit that the defendant had, indeed, used a hammer to end the victim's life.

Defense counsel then asked the jurors a question and also provided the answer, "You're probably wondering why we are here today if Johnny confessed to the murder—we are here so that Johnny Arguello will not be executed." This brief, one-minute opening statement prompted an objection on the part of D.A. Stan Peek, the prosecutor who'd aided in running the defendant down after his bid for freedom several days earlier.

"We're here because Johnny pleaded not guilty to the charges," Peek admonished. The judge overruled his objection.

Afterward, the defense submitted a list of "uncontested facts," accompanied by the stipulation that they did not constitute a guilty plea. It was all very confusing. The listed facts which the defense agreed to accept as unrefuted were: the date and location of the murder, that the death weapon was the heavy hammer introduced as evidence, that the actions of the accused caused Russell's death, that the death was caused by head injuries and that the decedent died at 11:15 p.m. December 3, 1981 and lastly, that the death of Russell occurred during the course of a robbery.

Dominguez stressed that his client would continue to plead innocent to the charge of murder. The D.A. acknowledged the fact that therefore, it would be necessary to go through the motions of presenting all available evidence.

One of the first witnesses to take the stand was the victim's father who described his murdered son as having been a "quiet, hard-working and respectful kid." Counsel for the defense objected to this testimony, calling it irrelevant and intended only to prejudice the jurors against the defendant.

Another witness to testify was an employee of WIRS (Weld Information And Referral Service) who told the court that on the day of Russell's murder, the accused had appeared at her office to request help in paying his rent. When told no aid would be forthcoming, Arguello had snapped, "You people will make me return to a life of crime."

Another woman took the witness stand to describe having seen Johnny Arguello at the bar quaffing beer shortly before he was seen riding his bicycle onto the ramp of the service station where Rodney Russell worked. The man who discovered the mortally injured victim in the back office also testified.

The 14-member jury viewed photographs of a bloodstained cabinet door, the hammer used to bludgeon the victim to death and pictures of the victim. They visited the gas station where the slaying occurred and heard lurid testimony from Dr. Myron Smith, the pathologist who'd autopsied the victim and who used diagrams of the seven head injuries to illustrate the fact that "disruption of brain tissue" was the cause of death.

The most salient and predominant theme throughout the trial was the blatant lack of even a smattering of mitigation. Existing facts established that the defendant was employed and had enough pocket change to buy several beers for himself while he formulated plans to rob a gas station. It was just another one of those murders without a wisp of justification.

As the prosecution prepared to wind up their presentation, the jury was allowed to hear Arguello's confession taken by the Greeley police 21 days after Rodney Russell's callous slaying. Everyone in the courtroom listened intently to the taped recording where Arguello was asked, "Why did you hit him again, Johnny?" and where his response was, "So he wouldn't come back to life, you know?" That and the fact that the defendant freely admitted striking the victim on the head "six or seven more times," before fleeing the station, summed it up in its entirety and the prosecution rested its case.

The jury began their deliberations at about 2:45 p.m., Wednesday, July 21, 1982. They were back in the courtroom shortly after 6:00 p.m. with their verdict of guilty as charged of the crime of first-degree murder. It was time now for the second phase of the trial to commence, the penalty phase wherein the same jurors who'd convicted the defendant would be obliged to sentence him.

On Thursday, after listening to more arguments from both the prosecution and defense, the jury again retired to deliberate whether Arguello would live or die. This time it took them only an hour and a half to decide that there were no extenuating circumstances involved and the crime warranted the death penalty. The jurors decided the brutal slaying of Rodney Russell was committed in a "heinous, cruel and depraved manner."

The findings of the ten-man, two-woman jury left Judge Hays with the obligation of passing formal sentence on the convicted slayer. On the afternoon of July 23, 1982, Arguello was again brought before the judge who intoned, "Mr. Arguello, I have the unpleasant duty to pass sentence upon you today. You have been ordered to suffer the penalty of death, and this shall be carried out during the week of October 31, 1982 to November 6, 1982." Judge Hays then stayed the date of execution pending an automatic review of the case by the Colorado State Supreme Court.

Arguello, previously having been described as able to discuss the case as if he were talking about the weather, now appeared somewhat repentant as he granted a press interview in a basement room inside the Weld County Jail. The heavily tattooed slayer who had heard himself sentenced to die in Colorado's gas chamber 15 minutes earlier told reporters, "I hate to die, to tell you the truth. But, that's the law, that's the way it is." Arguello had previously declared he thought it possible that he was insane. He based this observation on an incident which occurred when he was 21 years old and had escaped from a jail in Steamboat Springs, Colorado.

A well-placed shot fired by a pursuing police officer had flattened him and aborted his bid for freedom but left him, according to his story, with what he called "flashbacks" of the incident which might have triggered the ferocious attack on Rodney Russell. "I had the flashbacks. I thought I was shooting a gun but I was hitting him with the hammer. I kept hearing the gunshots in my head—over and over. I cried all the way home."

Ila Garcia appeared in Weld District Court on October 25, 1982, on a charge of being an accessory to first-degree murder. She was sentenced to 90 days in the Weld County Jail. This was suspended with the provision that she be placed on two years probation during which she would be involved in counseling with the Weld County Community Corrections facility.

EDITOR'S NOTE:
The name Ila Garcia is fictitious and was used because there is no reason for public interest in her true identity.

"THE KILLER DEFILED, BLUDGEONED, THEN CALLED 911"

by Harry Spiller

On Saturday, January 18, 1992, Dispatcher Bruce Graul of Illinois' Herrin Police Department was enjoying a quiet morning when the phone rang.

"Nine-one-one, emergency," Dispatcher Graul said into his mouthpiece.

"Yes, ah, there's been a rape and murder at Herrin, on the—uh, dry—in the—at the dry-cleaning place," the caller muttered.

"A rape and murder?" Graul asked.

"Yeah," the caller replied.

"Uh-huh. Whereabouts, sir?"

"I don't—I don't know the—the, uh—the address or nothing to it."

"Okay. It is at a residence or . . . ?"

"It's—it's in Herrin."

"Okay. Can you tell me where the body and everything's at?" Dispatcher Graul asked.

"Uh . . . It's in the back of the place," the caller said. "You go in there. You go through a door. Seen this, you know. It freaked me out. It looked like she was, you know, she was stripped down. But there's blood everywhere. Looked like somebody bumped her."

"It's in a gas station?"

"No. It's in—it's in the dry-cleaning place. It's right next to it."

"Okay. It's in the dry-cleaning place."

"Yeah," the caller responded.

"It's inside the building?" Graul asked.

"Yes," the caller replied.

"What is your name, sir?"

"I can't tell you. This is 911. I don't want to get—"

"I've got to have your name, sir."

"I'm sorry, buddy—it's real! Go check on it!" the caller shot back impatiently just before he slammed the receiver down.

Officer Graul immediately put a trace on the call. Sergeant Frank Vigiano and Detective Mark Brown were both in the dispatch office when the call came in. They scurried out to the dry cleaners on Park Avenue to check out the possible murder and rape.

As the lawmen pulled into the parking lot, they spotted a gold Dodge parked in front of the bay doors of what had once been a gas station, but was now converted into a dry cleaners. They quickly got out of their vehicle. Detective Brown looked through the front windows of the building while Sergeant Vigiano checked the two doors on the south side. Both doors were locked.

Vigiano continued around the building to check for other open windows or doors. When he got to the southwest corner of the building, he noticed a nylon stocking lying on the ground. He continued around the building until he met Detective Brown at the front door.

"There's a woman's stocking on the ground at the

137

back of the building," Sergeant Vigiano informed his colleague.

Both officers cautiously entered the building. The front lobby was empty. The officers moved to a door at the north side of the room. Slowly, they opened it. On the floor a few feet inside the room beyond, they saw a black purse lying there with its contents scattered all over.

The officers moved through the door but saw no one in the bay area of the building. Suddenly, however, both sleuths' stomachs tightened with knots as what had been only the possibility of a prank call now turned into the reality of murder and rape.

Near the furnace at the back of the chamber lay the body of a white female, face down. The victim was nude except for a bra. Her head was turned slightly to her left. Her arms were underneath her chest. A mass of congealed blood matted her hair and covered the left side of her face. Next to the body lay a pair of pantyhose and a pair of panties. A pale-yellow plastic garbage bag was beneath the victim's legs.

Detective Brown walked over to the body, bent down and felt her neck. There was no pulse.

"She's dead," Detective Brown said. "Let's secure the crime scene and call dispatch." His partner nodded.

Sergeant Vigiano secured the store while Detective Brown called the dispatcher. He asked that the crime scene technician from the Illinois Department of Criminal Investigation be sent to the scene. Just as the sergeant finished his request, Dispatcher Graul informed him that the 911 call had been traced to a pay phone on the corner of Cypress and Park Avenue, four blocks south of the crime scene. Brown immediately went to the phone booth and secured it.

At 9:30 a.m., crime scene technician Gary Otey from the Department of Criminal Investigation of the Illinois State Police (ISP) arrived at the crime scene. The dry-cleaners building consisted of a small sales room directly inside the front door. Upon entering, Otey noticed a small counter, a small table, and three racks for hanging clothes. On the counter top, Otey found a personal check made out to the cleaners and signed by a Milly Mason. On the table sat a partially-eaten pop tart and a half-filled cup of coffee.

Otey discovered a purse, apparently the victim's, which had been dumped in the bay area of the building. Then he moved to the south end of the bay and behind the furnace, where the nude body was lying.

Technician Otey photographed the corpse and the scene. Then he collected more than 100 pieces of evidence from the scene, including blood, hair, fingerprints, palmprints, clothing, a pair of eyeglasses, a plastic garbage bag, and a mop wringer.

After the crime scene had been processed, the coroner's assistants transported the body to a local hospital for an autopsy.

Technician Otey drove to the phone booth from which the 911 call had been made and processed it, too. He lifted two latent fingerprints off the telephone receiver.

Meanwhile, Chief of Police Tom Cunduff initiated a canvass of the four-block area around the murder scene.

A gas station attendant told officers that he'd seen a white male with short brown hair, wearing a white hat or cap, white coat, and blue jeans, talking on the phone at the booth to which the 911 call had been traced. The attendant did not see the man leave the phone booth.

A woman in the four-block area said that she saw a man running down Park Avenue around 9:00 a.m. The only thing she could remember about him was that he'd been wearing blue jeans.

Technician Otey contacted Chief Cunduff and informed him about the personal check found at the crime scene, apparently written by a Milly Mason of Herrin. The chief and Captain Tom Horn immediately obtained the address and went to the Herrin residence of Milly Mason.

Mason told the lawmen that on Saturday, January 18th, between 8:00 and 8:15 a.m., she'd gone to the dry cleaners to pick up some laundry. No one was behind the counter or in the room. So she wrote the check, picked up her clothes, and then walked to the back of the store, looking for the employee. There she encountered a brown-haired white male who was between 30 and 35 years old, 6 feet 2 inches tall, weighing 220 pounds. He was wearing a blue sock hat, blue work shirt and pants, red-plaid insulated vest, and brown lace-up boots. The man was walking towards Milly from the back of the building.

"I told him I laid a check on the counter for my clothes," she said, "and then I left. I thought he was an employee."

Chief Cunduff quickly realized that Milly Mason must have come face to face with the killer. He immediately contacted technician Otey and asked him to do a composite drawing of the suspect based on Mason's description. Copies of the composite were immediately distributed to businesses throughout the area.

In the meantime, the police found out through the owner's registration of the vehicle at the crime scene and from the manager of the dry-cleaning business that the murder victim was Kathy Anne Woodhouse, a 40-year-old mother of two children.

At 10:30 p.m. that same day, forensic pathologist John Heidingsfelder performed an autopsy on Woodhouse's body. The pathologist concluded that the victim was sexually assaulted, based on her nude condition, the bruising of her vaginal area, and the presence of dried semen stains on her skin. The doctor determined that at some point during the assault, the victim was placed on her abdomen and received a blunt-force blow to the left side of her head, just above the ear, resulting in extensive skull fractures. The pathologist concluded that the cause of death was a result of cerebral disruption and brain-stem compression, along with compound skull, orbital, maxillary, facial, and mandible fractures due to the blunt-force injury to the head.

The doctor also examined the mop wringer found at the crime scene. The wringer was bent and covered with blood. The doctor told the sleuths that the wringer was heavy enough to have been the blunt instrument that caused the victim's injuries.

The sleuths continued the probe by interviewing Tammy Edwards, who also worked at the dry cleaners. Tammy told them that she and Kathy took turns working the Saturday 8:00 a.m.-to-noon shift and that this Saturday had been Kathy's turn to work. Tammy had last seen Kathy on Friday, January 17th, at 6:00 p.m., when she'd relieved Kathy at work. At that time, Kathy told her she had received a disturbing telephone call in the afternoon. A person with a gruff male voice had asked Kathy what color toenail polish she wore.

Tammy said that the only other unusual incident Kathy told her about had occurred about three weeks earlier. That was when a white male, about six feet tall, weighing 200 pounds, with a large build and brown hair, came into the cleaners and asked to use the phone. It was raining outside and he led Tammy to believe that he needed to make an emergency call. After he dialed and began talking on the phone, Tammy realized that the call was personal. A few days later, the same man came in again to use the phone. Tammy told him that she was expecting a call, so he could not use the phone. He left and never returned. For the past several days at about noon, Tammy saw the same man walk by the store. However, she did not see him on Friday, January 17th.

A relative of the victim's told the police that Kathy had not appeared to be apprehensive about anyone. The relative said that when Kathy was living in Marion, Illinois, there were three or four occasions when she came home and heard someone leaving from the rear of the house. She never saw anyone and never found anything missing. Kathy's relative had contacted the police on two of those occasions, and then the incidents stopped.

Meanwhile, Herrin officers rounded up six people who fit the description of the suspect given by Milly Mason. The police asked the suspects to stand in a lineup. All agreed.

On January 19th, a Sunday evening, Milly Mason

attended that lineup and attempted to identify one of the men as a suspect. One of them looked similar to the man she'd seen in the dry cleaners, she told police, but she wasn't sure.

The police were quickly able to eliminate that man as a suspect, however, when they determined that he'd been at work at the time of the murder.

The probers were beginning to get frustrated and worried. They had investigated the case continuously for three weeks. Every day they checked out leads called in by citizens. Yet they weren't any closer to a suspect than they'd been on the day of the murder.

On Tuesday, February 4th, the sleuths received an anonymous call that gave them their first real lead to a suspect. The caller told them to check out Paul E. Taylor, a parolee from Louisiana who was currently living with relatives on South 16th Street in Herrin. Taylor had been released from prison around Christmas. He had been serving time for aggravated attempted sexual assault.

Detectives Mark Brown and John Allen of the Southern Illinois University Police drove to the residence on South 16th Street. A relative of Taylor's told the lawmen that on Saturday, January 18th, when she'd left for work at about 6:30 a.m., Paul had still been in bed. When she returned, about 9:30 a.m., she'd found Paul in the living room watching television or playing Nintendo.

The lawmen had found out that Paul Taylor worked at a local fast-food restaurant, so they asked the relative when the best time would be to talk with Paul. She said she was going to pick up Paul at a friend's house around 6:30 p.m. She promised the sleuths that she herself would bring Paul to the police station.

At 7:15 p.m., Detectives Brown and Allen met with Paul Taylor at the Herrin Police Department. They informed him that he was not under arrest.

"This is a voluntary interview," Detective Brown explained. "You can leave at any time."

The sleuths told Taylor that the were working on a homicide that had occurred on January 18th, and Paul's name was one of many brought up, so they were simply checking out all the names.

"Paul, we would like to run a number of tests on you. Would you consent to being fingerprinted and photographed?" Detective Brown asked.

"Sure," Taylor responded.

"We would like to get blood, saliva, head and pubic hair samples, as well," Detective Allen added.

"Okay," Taylor responded once again. Then he signed consent forms, and the lawmen took him to the local hospital for the tests. After the tests they all returned to the police station. There, the sleuths began to question Taylor.

"Paul, do you know why we asked to talk to you?" Detective Brown asked.

"Yes. Because you are investigating the murder of Kathy Woodhouse," Taylor answered.

"Did you kill Kathy Woodhouse?" Brown asked.

"No!" Taylor snapped back.

"Do you have any idea who may have killed her?"

"No. I don't know anyone around here."

The sleuths asked Taylor why he thought someone would name him as a suspect. He said he didn't know, unless it was because of his height. Taylor also told the detectives that it did not bother him that he was being questioned about the murder, but he did

144

hope that there were other people being questioned too.

"Why would someone want to kill Kathy Woodhouse?" one of the sleuths asked Taylor.

"Because they are sick!" Taylor answered curtly.

"Paul, have you ever thought about doing something like this, even though you didn't go through with it?"

"No, because it is wrong and I wouldn't have the nerve," Taylor replied.

"What do you think should happen to the person that did this?" Allen asked.

"Fry him!" Taylor shot back.

"What did you do on the morning of the murder?" Taylor said that he was home until approximately 8:45 a.m. Then he left the house, went to a local grocery store to buy a pack of cigarettes, and returned home about 9:15 a.m.

"Is there any reason you would have for killing Kathy?" one of the lawmen asked.

"No," Taylor replied.

"Have you ever been in the dry cleaners where the murder took place?"

"No."

"Have you ever been questioned about doing something like this before?"

"No!" Taylor fired back.

"Would you be willing to take a polygraph examination?"

"Yes," Taylor responded.

With that, the sleuths ended their interview with Taylor. They were suspicious of him and felt sure that he had lied about his past sexual offenses.

The next morning, the investigators went to the

dry cleaners to review customer receipts. They discovered that someone from the restaurant where Taylor worked had recently taken some shirts to the dry cleaners. The sleuths called the restaurant and asked if Taylor had been the person who'd delivered those shirts. The manager told them that Taylor had worked for the eatery for about three weeks, that he had indeed taken shirts to the dry cleaners, and that he had just turned in his resignation, saying he was going back to Louisiana.

In the meantime, the sleuths heard from the crime lab, which had conducted tests on the saliva standard taken from Taylor. The results showed that Taylor was a nonsecretor. Interestingly the person who'd raped and murdered Kathy Woodhouse was also a nonsecretor. However, the lab did not have enough head and pubic hair standards for testing. The sleuths would therefore have to bring Taylor back for additional samples.

Detectives Allen and Brown went to the 16th Street residence and asked Taylor's relative if they could talk with Taylor. Then Taylor himself came to the back door. The detectives told him that the crime lab had requested more head and pubic hair samples from him to carry out the proper testing.

"I don't know — maybe I should talk to an attorney," Taylor said.

The relative urged Taylor to cooperate with the police, but Taylor stood silently staring at the detectives.

"Do you plan on leaving town?" one of the sleuths asked him.

"No. I just got off work," Taylor replied.

"No, you didn't, Paul — you just quit your job and

told the boss you were moving to Louisiana," Detective Allen told him pointedly.

"What's going on?" the relative asked Taylor.

At that point, the detectives asked the suspect's relative if she would give them permission to search the house. She agreed. Then the sleuths asked Taylor if he would grant them permission to search his room. He also agreed.

After Taylor and his relative signed permission-to-search forms, the sleuths went to Taylor's room. There they found a pair of stone-washed blue jeans lying on Taylor's bed. The blue jeans appeared to have some small bloodstains on them. Taylor said that those were the jeans he'd been wearing on January 18th. In the closet, the sleuths also discovered a white-and-black sweatshirt that Taylor had worn on the morning of the murder. When Detective Brown lifted the end of the mattress at the foot of the bed, he found a pair of pantyhose with one leg missing lying on top of two porno magazines. The sleuths found another pair of bloodstained blue jeans in a dresser. They found no other evidence in Taylor's bedroom.

The probers continued to search the rest of the house and, while doing so, they asked Taylor's relative if Taylor had a hat. She said that he did and went to another bedroom where she pulled a blue hat from a dresser drawer. Handing it to the sleuths, she said Taylor did not like to wear the hat.

With the search ended and no other evidence found, the lawmen asked Taylor if he would go to the hospital and give them more hair samples. He agreed.

At the hospital while the samples were being

taken, Detective Eric Frattini of the Williamson County Sheriff's Department came into the examining room and asked Taylor if he would come down to the police department for further questioning. Taylor told the detective that he preferred to go home because he was going to a rock concert and wanted to get cleaned up.

Taylor was free to leave the hospital and Detective Allen gave him a ride back to the 16th Street residence.

Meanwhile, the sleuths put a surveillance team on Taylor, even as other lawmen took the evidence to the crime lab for analysis.

Taylor left his residence and went to the Southern Illinois University Arena for the concert. The surveillance team followed.

On Wednesday evening, February 5th, Detective Frattini contacted the crime lab. Serologist Grace Johnson told the detective that Paul Taylor's blood standards showed a P.G.M. of $(1+)$. (P.G.M. refers to phospho-glucomutase, a protein that serves as a "genetic marker" and is useful on a more detailed level of blood-typing.) Johnson explained that these results, coupled with the earlier results showing Taylor to be a nonsecretor, increased the chance of his being Kathy Woodhouse's murderer.

Detective Frattini then spoke with Glenn Schubert from the microscopy section. Schubert told the sleuth that the stocking taken from Taylor's bedroom was similar not only in color, but also in fabric, to the one found near the crime scene. Schubert had also compared pubic hairs from the scene with those taken from Taylor. The hairs were similar.

When Frattini spoke with latent fingerprint technician Mike Pittman, he learned that the fingerprints found on the telephone matched Taylor's.

The case investigators immediately contacted Williamson County State's Attorney Chuck Garnati to make sure they had enough evidence to show probable cause for an arrest. Garnati advised them to wait until Taylor was back within Williamson County jurisdiction, and then make the arrest.

That same evening, Illinois State Trooper Daren Lindsey and Sergeant Bob McCluskey drove to the Williamson County line and waited for the suspect. Taylor left the rock concert and crossed the county line at 10:30 p.m. Trooper Lindsey and Sergeant McCluskey pulled Taylor's vehicle over and arrested him for the rape-murder of Kathy Woodhouse.

At 11:54 p.m., the detectives read Taylor his Miranda rights. Taylor waived them and agreed to talk with the police. He told the investigators that on Saturday, January 18th, at about 8:00 a.m., he walked from his home to the dry cleaners. When he got there he walked in and told the attendant, Kathy Woodhouse, that he was going to rob her. Then he took her to the bay area of the building. At the rear of the chamber, he picked up a mop wringer, hit Kathy twice in the head, and then left.

"When did you take Kathy's clothes off?" Detective Frattini asked.

"She was fully clothed when I left," Taylor replied.

Now the sleuths told Taylor about the physical evidence found at the scene. Taylor looked down at the floor for a few seconds, then he looked up, directly at the detective. "I raped her," he said.

"Okay, Paul, now tell me exactly what happened," Frattini prompted.

Taylor said that after walking the victim to the rear of the building, he ordered her to take off her clothes and lie down on the floor. Kathy lay down on her back. Then, Taylor said, he pulled his pants halfway down, got on top of the victim, and had sexual intercourse with her. He said that he told the victim he was having an orgasm.

Then, he said, Kathy asked him, "Did you hear that car pull up?"

Taylor told her that he didn't hear anything. He got up and told Kathy to turn over on her stomach. Then he walked toward the front of the store, where he saw a woman standing at the counter. She told him that she was there to pick up her laundry and to leave a check in payment.

"Fine!" Taylor told her curtly.

The customer then walked out.

Taylor said he walked back to the rear of the building and picked up a mop wringer on the way. He hit the victim twice over the head with it. Then he went to the front of the bay, took $4 from the victim's purse and dumped the rest of its contents on the floor.

After that, Taylor said, he walked down Main Street south of the cleaners. He found a pay phone and called 911 to report that there had been a murder and rape at the cleaners. Taylor said that the officer on the line sounded as though he didn't believe him, so Taylor told him, "It's real! Go check it out!" Taylor then hung up the phone and went home.

On Friday, April 10, 1992, Paul Taylor pled guilty to the murder and rape of Kathy Anne Woodhouse. On Thursday, October 15, 1992, a 12-person jury sentenced him to death.

EDITOR'S NOTE:
Milly Mason and Tammy Edwards are not the real names of the persons so named in the foregoing story. Fictitious names have been used because there is no reason for public interest in the identities of these persons.

"HOW MANY VICTIMS FOR THE GREEDY GOLDEN GIRL?"

by Jack Heise

ST. LOUIS, MISSOURI
APRIL 15, 1985

The murder trial in East Alton, Missouri, was billed by the news media as being the best show to hit town in years. It lived up to the advance notices.

It had an Alfred Hitchcock plot, with intrigues within intrigues, and a star-studded cast that included the flamboyant nationally famous defense attorney, F. Lee Bailey.

Bailey lived up to his press notices, clad in an expensive three-piece pin-striped suit and highly polished cowboy boots, as he bounced out of his chair to shout objections or challenge a witness. He paced almost constantly with theatrics that included twisting the leg of a testifying pathologist and acting out the murder scene with an assistant.

His counterpart, Prosecutor Robert Trone, was an entirely different type of character, but equally as talented. He wore a slightly rumpled suit with lace-up shoes with a flat black shine. He spent much of his time slumped in his chair as he deliberately and methodically presented his case in a slow drawl.

The leading lady was an attractive blonde, known as the "Golden Girl."

There were plenty of villains in the cast, including three who had been convicted of multiple murders, with one of them waiting to be executed.

There were 90 bit players waiting in the wings to take their place on stage in the witness stand. A number of them were investigators who had developed the plot over a period of eight years.

And like any smash Broadway hit, the audience came early, queuing up hours before the courtroom doors opened for a seat on one of the 14 benches for spectators or to stand shoulder-to-shoulder along the paneled wall.

Those who were unable to get inside waited patiently in the hallway hoping someone might have to go to the bathroom and one of the cherished spaces would become available. Few left, however, not even for the lunch break, having brought sandwiches with them so they would not have to leave.

The real drama began on November 3, 1977, with the murders of Arthur and Venita Gueswelle at their farm home in Edwardsville. The wealthy, elderly couple were found sprawled on the living room floor. Both were fully clothed and had not been bound or gagged. There were no signs of a struggle. The couple apparently had lain face down on the floor; then Venita had been shot three times in the back of the head and two shots had been fired into the back of Arthur's head.

Detectives were baffled when they came to investigate the slayings. There were no indications of a forced entry, so the victims must have let the killer or killers into their home. There were no witnesses and neighbors on adjoining farms could not recall having seen anyone come to or leave the house on the night of the murders.

Nothing of value appeared to have been taken, not even the wallet from Arthur's pocket. Burglary or robbery was ruled out as a motive.

Investigators checked with relatives, friends and persons who had known the couple for many years in the farming community. Not one could come up with anything to suggest a motive for the seemingly senseless crime.

With little more to work with than the small-caliber slugs that had claimed the victims' lives, the case was eventually put on the back burner to wait for some kind of a break.

A strange twist in the case developed 17 months later when Ronald Gueswelle, the son of the slain couple, failed to return to his St. Louis home from his work with an oil company in Wood River on the night of March 31, 1979.

A missing person report was filed with the police the following day. Foul play was immediately suspected because the father of three children was a good family man, a steady worker and would have no reason to voluntarily disappear.

Four days later police found his body sprawled on the backseat of his car in a parking lot near a motel in East St. Louis. The left side of his head had been crushed with a blow from a blunt instrument, and he'd been shot in the chest.

Investigators determined that he had not been slain in the car. From the amount of blood and other physical evidence, they reasoned that he had been slain somewhere and then dumped onto the backseat and driven to where the car had been found.

The slaying fit a pattern of a robbery murder. But as the detectives checked further, they became doubtful about the motive.

They learned that Gueswelle had worked late at his office in Wood River on the night he had been slain. Had he driven straight home, he would have arrived around 11 o'clock.

Persons who knew Ronald Gueswelle well said that he was not in the habit of picking up hitchhikers, in fact he had often said that anyone was foolish to take a stranger into their car, particularly at night.

There was the possibility, however, that someone could have stopped him with some kind of a ruse or jumped into the car while it was stopped at a traffic signal. A close friend of the slain man told the detectives that he knew Gueswelle was in the habit of locking all the doors of his car before driving and that he had been with him on several occasions when he followed that routine.

The investigators working on the slaying of Ronald Gueswelle checked with the investigators who had worked on the murders of his parents in an attempt to learn if there could be a possible connection.

Detectives who had checked out every possible lead for some motive for the murders of Arthur and Venita Gueswelle said they had drawn a complete blank. They said the elderly couple had left a sizeable estate and their son Ronald had inherited a sum in the neighborhood of $500,000.

The detectives learned that in addition to his inherited money and his own estate, Ronald Gueswelle carried 14 insurance policies for a total of $193,000. It meant that his widow Barbara was a very wealthy widow.

The investigators had to consider the possibility that the murder had been one for profit.

But when they questioned persons who had known the couple intimately, it appeared highly unlikely that Barbara could have slain or hired someone to kill her husband. They were told that she was considered to be an ideal mother to her three children. There had never been a hint of an extramarital affair and sleuths were told she, her husband and their children were the ideal American family.

Barbara had everything she needed or wanted that money could buy and there would be no point in killing her husband for the $500,000 estate.

The investigation went nowhere for more than two years, despite the best efforts of the detectives. They were unable to locate where Ronald Gueswelle had been slain and they could not come up with any motive for the murder of his parents.

Barbara remarried and moved with her new spouse and children to Glen Carbon. It appeared that the baffling mystery of the three murders would eventually reach the unsolved files.

Then came a surprising development.

Andre Jones, a 29-year-old man, who had been convicted of two murders in St. Louis and was waiting an appeal from the death sentence, confessed that he had killed Ronald Gueswelle.

He swore that his girlfriend, a prostitute, had picked up Gueswelle and they had gone to a motel for sex. He broke into the room to rob the man and Gueswelle had put up a struggle.

He said he had struck Gueswelle alongside the head and when he continued to struggle had shot him in the chest. He had put the body in the back-seat of Gueswelle's car and driven it to where it had been found.

It appeared that at least one of the mysterious murders had been solved.

But the detectives who had put in so much time on the Ronald Gueswelle case weren't completely satisfied.

"I don't know what the hell is going on," one of the detectives said. "But it don't add up. Ronald Gueswelle wasn't the kind of guy who would pick up with some hooker on his way home from work."

They checked on the confession given by Jones. Maids who had been on duty at the motel on the morning following the slaying were questioned. They could not recall having cleaned up any blood in any of the rooms.

The motel clerk could not recall having seen anyone fitting the description of Ronald Gueswelle. There were no auto licenses on the register that matched that of Gueswelle's car.

Jones had said that he had thrown the gun used in the murder into the river, but was vague as to the exact location so a search for it would be futile.

The detectives eventually located the prostitute Jones claimed had lured Gueswelle into the motel. She denied having been with Gueswelle or knowing anything about the murder, which would be a natural reaction, since she could have been charged as an accessory.

The detectives, however, were inclined to believe her statement. She said she had no idea why Jones would confess to a murder he did not commit or why he would implicate her in it.

One of the detectives had a possible explanation. "Somebody wants the Gueswelle case cleared," he said. "They've gotten to Jones and paid him for the confession. He's already under two death sentences and you can only execute a person once."

The question now was who had gotten to Jones and how they had managed it.

Jones was uncooperative. When told that he was suspected of having made the false confession, he said, "It's no skin off my nose. If you don't want it, you know where you can stuff it."

Persons who had visited Jones were checked out. Inmates who were in contact with him were also questioned. They were unable to come up with any information to suggest why Jones would make a false confession to the murder of Ronald Gueswelle.

The case was back to checkmate.

There appeared to be no point in prosecuting Andre Jones for the murder of Gueswelle. He was already under two death sentences and the prosecution would only cloud any additional case, in the event that the confession was false as the detectives suspected.

There was another long wait and then came a break that appeared to be the first real lead in the murders of Arthur and Venita Gueswelle.

Glennon E. Engleman, a former St. Louis dentist, along with Robert W. Handy were tried and convicted for two murders-for-profit in Missouri. Engleman received two 50-year sentences and Handy, for cooperating with the investigation, was given two sentences to run concurrently with a 17-year sentence

158

for mail fraud.

Ballistics indicated that the weapon Engleman used had fired the shots that killed Arthur and Venita Gueswelle.

The detectives questioned the persons who had known the slain couple. No one recognized Engleman or Handy as persons who had contact with the victims.

"It was a hired hit and that's why we've been stymied for so long," one of the detectives said. "And I think I know who has the answers for us."

The investigators questioned Andre Jones. When informed that they knew he could not possibly have killed Ronald Gueswelle as he had claimed in his confession, Jones recanted the confession.

"Who paid you to make that phony confession?" he was asked.

Jones insisted that he had not been paid to make the false confession. He said that he had received word that unless he confessed to the murder harm would come to his family.

"Who threatened you?" he was asked.

Jones claimed that he did not know. Word had come to him through the prison grapevine. "I didn't have anything to lose, so I went along with it," Jones explained to detectives.

The investigators told Jones that they did not believe him and that he knew who had threatened to harm his family.

"Was it a guy named Engleman or maybe Handy?" he was asked.

Jones continued to insist that he didn't know who had made the threat and wouldn't name the person or persons who passed the information to him.

"Look," he told the investigators. "The state may execute me one of these days, but it's going to take time. But if you are a snitch, it can happen in a hurry."

There was no way the detectives could force Jones to tell them who had either paid him or threatened him into making the false confession.

The investigators were certain that whoever had paid for the murders of Arthur and Venita Gueswelle had also paid for the killing of their son. The only person who could have profited from the murders was Barbara Gueswelle. She had inherited her husband's estate of over $500,000.

The detectives ran a thorough background check on Mrs. Gueswelle, Engleman and Handy, hoping that they could link her to the slaying. They were unable to locate anyone who could state positively that Mrs. Gueswelle knew either Engleman or Handy.

The investigators took their information to Prosecutor Trone. He pointed out the difficulty if they attempted to prosecute Engleman for the murders of Venita and Arthur Gueswelle.

The only evidence they had was the comparison of the slugs used to kill the persons Engleman had been convicted of shooting and the slugs that had killed the Gueswelles. The weapon that fired them had not been found.

There were no witnesses to the murders of the Gueswelles nor any witness to the contract that had been out on them. It was a cinch that if Barbara Gueswelle was involved, as the detectives suspected, she wouldn't furnish any information.

"I don't like to go to trial half-cocked," Trone said.

"Because if you lose a case, it's gone forever under double jeopardy."

"There's one possibility," a detective suggested. "That guy Handy got off light by cooperating in the two murders. We might be able to make a deal with him."

He pointed out that the 52-year-old Handy had only been convicted of a conspiracy to commit murder and not actually committing the murders.

"He'll be out in a few years the way things stand now," the detective said. "If we can convince him that if he's convicted on the Gueswelle murders he could spend the rest of his natural life in prison, he might be willing to make a deal and talk."

If Handy could provide the information they needed, it would be a matter of losing one to get two. Trone said to make a deal he would have to get court permission. He said he would see what he could do.

The court granted permission to make a deal with Handy only if Handy had not been the actual killer but had been an accessory or a party to the conspiracy to commit murder.

The investigators went to the prison where Handy was serving his time. They spelled it out for him that they knew Engleman had killed Ronald Gueswelle and his parents and he had probably been paid for the job by Barbara Gueswelle. They wanted him to be a state's witness to the murders.

"What's in it for me?" Handy asked. "You guys can't deal me out of here."

"But we can deal you in for a long time, possibly the rest of your natural life," a detective responded.

Handy shrugged. "You guys wouldn't be here if

161

you had a case," he said.

"Are you willing to gamble on that?" he was asked.

Handy thought it over. He said he would make a deal to become a state's witness on the condition that if he was convicted of conspiracy to commit murder he would not serve any additional time.

The detectives took the proposition to Pros. Trone. "It isn't a good deal," one of the detectives said. "But without it, we've got nothing."

Trone took the proposition to the court and was granted permission to make the deal with Handy that he would not be sentenced to serve time in addition to that he was doing on the condition that Handy would testify in court.

The detectives returned to the prison. Handy agreed to the terms and gave the investigators a statement which he later repeated under oath at the trial.

He said he had known Glennon Engleman for almost 30 years and they were close friends. He said that Engleman had come to him in March or April of 1976 and told him that he stood to make a large sum of money. He said he was surprised when the dentist told him that a woman wanted her husband killed and would pay to have the job done.

Handy claimed that he told Engleman to keep him out of the plot and Engleman had told him not to worry about it because it wouldn't take place right away. He had advised the woman to take out more insurance on her husband to sweeten the pot.

Handy said that Engleman told him in September that the plans had changed. He had learned that the woman's husband had wealthy parents. The new plot was to kill them first and wait until the inheritance was settled before killing him.

"You refer to a woman," a detective said. "Did you know who the woman was?"

"Not right away," Handy responded. Glen only called her the 'Golden Girl.' I don't know whether he was referring to her blonde hair or that she was going to come into a bundle of money."

Handy said that at a later time he had met with Engleman and the woman and learned that she was Barbara Gueswelle.

"What was the relationship between Engleman and Mrs. Gueswelle?" Handy was asked. "Were they intimate?"

Handy shook his head negatively. "Glen told me that when you do a professional hit job, you don't become involved with the client and you don't make contact with the person to be hit until it's time to do the job. That way you can't be connected with it."

Asked how Engleman had come in contact with Mrs. Gueswelle, Handy said he did not know. All that Engleman had told him was that she wanted her husband killed and was willing to pay well for someone to do the job.

He related that on the night of November 3, 1977, Engleman had picked him up and they went out to dinner. He said that Engleman had told him, "You're going to have to go with me. We're going to kill those two people."

"And you went along with him?" he was asked.

Handy said he went with Engleman because he knew he was a violent man and was afraid of him. He said he feared that if he did not go with him and somehow Engleman was caught, he might suspect he had squealed on him and Engleman would kill him.

163

The investigators didn't actually buy that part of Handy's story, but it was his statement and they asked him to continue.

Handy said they drove out to the rural farmhouse near Edwardsville. Engleman told him that he was going into the house posed as a representative of the farm bureau.

He said he had waited in the car while Engleman went into the house carrying a .38-caliber pearl-handled pistol. He heard some shots and Engleman came back to the car.

Handy said he had asked Engleman, "How did it go?"

"Smooth as silk," Engleman responded. "They cooperated real nice and just laid down on the floor and I blew them away."

Handy recalled that on the return trip to St. Louis Engleman had told him he hadn't taken anything or touched anything in the house and the murders could never be traced to him.

He said Engleman had bragged to him, "This is just going to be the start of my famous crimes. There's lots of insurance money out there and if you plan it and do it right you can get rich."

Handy said Engleman had apologized for getting him involved, but had told him that when the insurance money came rolling in, he'd make it right with him.

Referring to the murder of Ronald Gueswelle, Handy related that he had gone with Engleman to Wood River where Gueswelle was employed by an oil company with the plan to waylay him on his way home and kill him. They were thwarted by the fact that Gueswelle did not go to work that day.

Handy said that on the evening of March 31, 1979, Engleman came to him and said, "This is payday. We're going to kill Ronald Gueswelle."

He said they drove to a store parking lot in Fairmont City where Mrs. Gueswelle picked them up in her car and drove them to her home. She told them that her husband would be late coming home from work and they waited in the garage for him.

Gueswelle drove up around 11 o'clock and opened the garage door. "When he opened the garage door, Engleman shot him," Handy said. "Ron had a stunned look on his face. Engleman said something to him, I don't know what it was, and Ron turned to look at the house. That's when Engleman hit him alongside the head with a hammer and he fell."

Handy said Engleman then called to Mrs. Gueswelle and told her that he was ready for the towels. Mrs. Gueswelle came out with an armload of towels and began cleaning up the blood while he and Engleman dragged Gueswelle's body to his car and put it on the backseat.

He said that Mrs. Gueswelle was still cleaning up the blood when he and Engleman drove away with the corpse. They took the car with the body in it and left it in a parking lot near a motel in East St. Louis where the car and body were found four days later.

Handy claimed that he had not been paid any money for being with Engleman while the murders were being committed, but Engleman had told him that Mrs. Gueswelle had given him some money to pay his income tax and he was due to get more later when the insurance policies were paid off.

With this statement from Robert Handy, the detectives then obtained a warrant charging Barbara

165

Gueswelle with first-degree murder. The investigators drove to Glen Carbon and took her into custody. Advised of her legal rights, she chose to remain silent and be represented by counsel.

It took two weeks for the attorneys to present the testimony of 90 witnesses and 130 exhibits to a panel of six men and six women in the Madison County Court of Circuit Judge P.J. O'Neal on the counts that Barbara Gueswelle had conspired and paid for the murders of her husband and his parents.

The testimony that had kept the courtroom jammed was completed on Friday, April 12, 1985. Closing arguments from the prosecution and defense were delivered on Saturday morning.

The blonde, 42-year-old defendant appeared to be almost emotionless as the attorneys pleaded with the jurors, F. Lee Bailey asking for an acquittal and Pros. Trone demanding a conviction.

Pacing in front of the panel, Bailey asked the jurors to consider the character of the witnesses who had given the most damning testimony against his client.

"They are convicted felons ready to swear to any lie to curry favors with the law," Bailey argued. "Without their testimony, the state has no case against the defendant."

Referring to the confession that had been given by Andre Jones and then recanted, he said, "If you can't eliminate Jones, there is a reasonable doubt."

Turning the panel's attention to the testimony of Robert Handy, Bailey used a large chart to list 29 discrepancies in his testimony. "He was caught lying before your very eyes," Bailey said. "When Handy concluded his direct examination, you had to think,

166

'What a terrible woman.' But when Handy concluded his cross-examination, it was impossible not to think, 'My God, that man was not even there.' "

In his final plea, Bailey called upon the jurors to be aware of the consequences of an incorrect verdict. "There is no more horrendous thing to contemplate in a free country than to punish someone for something they have not committed."

Pros. Trone addressed the panel and told them that the state was not asking for the death penalty, only a guilty verdict on the counts filed against the defendant.

After reviewing the testimony that had been given, Trone pointed toward the defendant and said, "There is a woman who set up her own in-laws, her own husband, and boy has she done well. She came out, you might say, smelling like a rose. She came out with $598,000."

Referring to the discrepancies Bailey claimed he had found in the testimony, Trone nodded toward Bailey and paid him a left-handed compliment by warning the jurors, "He's very artful in cross-examination. You load it with a double-barrel question, drop one part and you have the wrong answer."

The closing arguments were completed at noon. The jurors were sent out to lunch. They began their deliberations at 2:15 p.m. and although it was known they would not likely reach a verdict quickly, very few of the spectators left their seats.

At 10:35 in the evening, the panel reported that they had not yet reached a verdict. Judge O'Neal ordered that they be sequestered and return in the morning to deliberate further.

While the jurors deliberated, the hallway to the court was lined with spectators eager to be present when the verdict was announced.

They waited throughout the day and it wasn't until 6:15 p.m. that the doors to the courtroom were opened with an announcement that the panel had reached a decision.

The verdict they returned found Mrs. Barbara Gueswelle guilty of the murder of her former husband, but innocent of the murders of his parents.

Tears rolled down the face of the defendant as the verdict was read by the bailiff. Bailey put an arm around his client and told her, "It isn't over yet. We will appeal."

Judge O'Neal delayed pronouncing the sentence, which could be from 20 to 40 years in prison and revoked the $1 million bond she had been freed on pending the trial.

Glennon Engleman, who is facing a trial on the three counts of having murdered the Gueswelles, by law must be considered innocent until such time as he may be judged innocent or guilty. The same law applies to Robert Handy who has been charged with conspiracy to commit murder and an agreement that if he should be found guilty, the penalty will not exceed 14 years.

"SIX SLUGS FOR THE DIXIE BOOKIE"

by John Railey

A pretty woman with a nice friendly smile, Phyllis June Chapman worked the counter at the Second Base, an illegal gambling joint in Trinity Township in rural Randolph County, North Carolina. The money beat most other jobs Phyllis could have had, and if she were caught taking bets on ball games, it was only a misdemeanor.

It was the morning of August 10, 1987, and Phyllis had just opened the door of the ugly cinderblock building for business. It was slow this Monday morning as the clock ticked past 9:00 a.m. The phone wasn't yet ringing with the short cryptic messages that are the bread and butter of the gambling trade.

Outside, the mercury was already climbing toward 90. The heat visibly shimmered above the dusty dry field that fell off to a dense stand of woods behind the building. The roar of cicadas drifted over the field from the trees. Once in a while, a car whizzed past on the steaming asphalt.

Phyllis wondered when her daughter would bring breakfast . . .

At 9:47 a.m., Phyllis' daughter arrived to find her mother lying unconscious behind the counter in a pool of blood. She grabbed the counter phone and called for help.

Randolph County sheriff's deputies raced to the scene. Emergency workers couldn't get a pulse from Phyllis Chapman.

Lieutenant James Eugene "Gene" Allred soon arrived. He'd be the detective on the case. At 55, Alfred was a country gent in a three-piece suit with thinning gray hair combed neatly on his head. His slow drawl disguised a sharp mind, as unfortunate suspects who tried to outthink him quickly found out.

Allred knew something about gambling and chance. The glints in his hard eyes behind steel-rimmed glasses were hard to read, and his usually pleasant deadpan expression gave nothing away. He usually won the hand when battling wits with suspects.

This was Allred's home county, and he cared about what went on. A winding path had brought him to this murder scene. Bob Mason, a homeboy Allred had fought with in Korea, had won the sheriff's race 14 years earlier. As one of his first acts, Sheriff Mason had persuaded Allred to leave his job as assistant manager at a local tire dealership and enter law enforcement.

Eight years before, Allred had made detective. His first year as an investigator, he'd made officer of the year. He'd made officer of the month several times after that. Allred had found his niche.

Lieutenant Allred began to work the crime scene, securing it for the lab technicians, calling in the State

Bureau of Investigation (SBI), and checking out what they had so far. Phyllis Chapman's body had been found behind the counter. Apparently, she had been shot six times in the chest and upper arms. Deputies were finding .22-caliber bullets and casings in the small building.

Deputies found a .22-caliber handgun and rifle on the scene, but, as Allred guessed, tests would later show that they belonged to the gambling den and were not used in the crime. Apparently, Chapman hadn't had a chance to shoot back.

Lieutenant Allred keeps an open mind during murder probes, but he ran a few possibilities through his head. Could it have been a disgruntled customer? A fellow employee? A higher-up in the illegal organization behind the operation?

Lieutenant Allred couldn't rule out robbery as a motive. Allred and other deputies soon determined that the victim's purse, containing about $400, was missing. Deputies found a grand in the trunk of Chapman's car parked outside. That was probably extra operating cash if she needed it.

The crime had occurred right in the heart of the gambling area. Randolph County's northwestern tip is dotted with these gambling dens, housed in small cinder-block buildings like the Second Base or in mobile homes tucked among the rolling hills. Could a territorial dispute have been behind the shooting? Or revenge?

Customers rich and poor bet on ball games or play the numbers in these joints. Participating, or even running an operation, is only a misdemeanor in North Carolina, carrying just a suspended sentence and a fine that one day's take more than pays for.

Even so, people involved in illegal business—even misdemeanor illegal business—aren't prone to settling their differences in court.

For almost 20 years, Randolph deputies have been finding shot and beaten corpses, sometimes stuffed in car trunks, and officials have linked many of those murders to the gambling trade. Many of the murders have been professionally planned and executed, and many have gone unsolved. Territorial disputes sometimes erupt into car and house burnings and bombings.

The gambling operators are cagey. An FBI probe of the operations a few years back had come up mostly lame—a few charges, fines, no long sentences. Overworked deputies periodically raid the joints but don't have the time or money to go undercover in the operations.

There are apparently no direct links between the Dixie gambling dens and outside, organized crime, but rumors of just such links are hard to quell. The late Thomas Thompson had this to say about such Southern gangs in his 1976 nonfiction book, *Blood and Money:*

"Certainly there was no formal syndicate, and no blood oath . . . nor were there territories to divide with organized rackets. The only glue that bonded several hundred outlaws in the Dallas area was the camaraderie of pursuing the same kind of work."

Reduce the number of thugs to fewer than a hundred, and the same would hold true for the Randolph County gambling operators.

Lieutenant Allred didn't have much to go on in the Chapman slaying. There was no weapon and no witnesses. Apparently, nobody had even heard the shots. They didn't even know whether the killer had used a rifle or handgun.

Allred learned that Chapman had been scheduled to appear as a state's witness in an upcoming murder trial in the neighboring city of High Point. But he found no evidence that anybody involved in that trial could have done it.

Allred talked to a security guard who worked for Second Base. He hadn't been working on the day of the shooting and wasn't much help.

Allred heard about an old car carrying three or four people that a witness had seen leaving Second Base shortly before Phyllis Chapman's body was found. He thought he had traced the car to High Point once, but he learned he had the wrong vehicle. Allred never found the right car.

Even with the competent help of SBI Agents Charles Hatley and Tom Sturgill, the probe was going nowhere.

The dog days of August dragged on. Deputies got a judge's order and padlocked Second Base on August 26th. The gambling operators weren't fazed, though. Usually in such an occurrence, the operators just wheel a mobile home on the property and set up a new shop there.

In late September, Chapman's family and friends posted a $10,000 reward for information leading to the arrest and conviction of her killer.

Officials, citing the slayings as the reason, began to put added emphasis on gambling violations, even though they were only misdemeanors, unlike several other states where they are felonies. This was all well and good. But Allred's probe was telling him that Chapman's slaying wasn't tied to gambling. Her boss seemed as shocked about the killing as anyone else. Other gambling bosses told Lieutenant Allred they didn't know anything, and they seemed sincere. Allred suspected that some of the gamblers had contributed toward the reward money. And on the subject of that cash, if these gamblers knew anything, wouldn't they be hopping on that reward money?

Even though Allred didn't have a murder weapon, there was still the stink of the amateur about this slaying, the feeling that not a lot of planning went into it. So Allred was reasonably sure the gamblers didn't have anything to do with the murder. But he still didn't know who did.

Weeks stretched into months as leads slowed from the tiny trickle they had been to nothing at all. The file on the Phyllis Chapman homicide case that Allred kept on his neat desk at headquarters wasn't exactly growing.

It was an investigator's nightmare. The only thing to check out were rumors and dead ends. And all the time, more murder cases and other serious cases were landing on Allred's desk, taking needed time away from the Chapman probe.

But the lieutenant's luck was about to change.

In December 1988, police in High Point, a town in nearby Guilford County, responded to a report of a body in a ditch beneath a curve in a lonely stretch of road.

Veteran High Point Detectives Lindsay Royal and Jerry Grubb had quickly tied the killing to a kid named Jeffrey Edgar Tucker and two other suspects. Tucker was elusive, but the other two were easy to find.

The two suspects told Detectives Royal and Grubb

174

that they'd been getting drunk with 17-year-old Tucker when he picked a fight with a man on a moped. Tucker had threatened to "whip this guy's ass," and when the man swung to defend himself, they said, Tucker pulled out a .22-caliber handgun and blasted the moped rider three times.

Afterwards, the suspects said, Tucker dragged the victim's body to a ditch and left it there. Grubb and Royal learned that the unarmed victim, 32-year-old Donald Ray Logan of High Point, was a family man and working stiff who'd been on his way to his third-shift job.

Meanness like that, especially from a kid so young, was enough to turn even a veteran sleuth's stomach.

Royal and Grubb had a hard time finding Jeffrey Tucker. He wasn't at the High Point house where he lived with his parents. The investigators tried to pass a message by back channels to Tucker, telling him to turn himself in through a go-between—a lawyer or a preacher—before he got hurt. The detectives knew he had a gun, and they made sure he knew they would protect themselves.

Their message elicited no response. Detectives Grubb and Royal got Tucker's mug on the six o'clock news and in the papers. Still nothing.

Then, on New Year's Day 1989, the probers learned that one of Tucker's relatives had driven him to a Savannah, Georgia, apartment. It turned out that the relative had been hiding Tucker out. She had even cut Tucker's jet black hair and dyed it orange to help him elude capture.

Detectives Grubb and Royal made a couple of calls. Soon, a Georgia SWAT team surrounded the apartment complex where Tucker was hiding out. He surrendered without incident. Within a few weeks, Tucker was extradited and being held in the High Point Jail for the murder of Donald Logan.

Meanwhile, Grubb and Royal had noticed three .22-caliber rifles on a wall on one of their visits to Tucker's home. On a hunch, Royal asked one of Tucker's relatives if they could take a look at the guns. The relative brought the guns down to High Point police headquarters.

Grubb and Royal took the guns to the SBI laboratory outside the state capital of Raleigh. They asked the lab technicians to see if the guns matched any of the bullets collected from crimes in the High Point area.

Valentine's Day usually isn't a big event for cops, but it was special for Lieutenant Allred. On February 14, 1989, he got back SBI test results showing that one of the rifles had fired the shots that killed Phyllis Chapman.

Allred, Grubb, and Royal were blown away. Jeffrey Tucker's name hadn't even come up in the Chapman case until then.

Allred got another lucky break. Grubb and Royal had never found the gun that Tucker had used in the Logan murder, even though they had divers search for it in local rivers and lakes. But Allred noted with pleasure that an autopsy and other evidence showed a .22 had been used to kill Donald Logan as well. Tucker would have been just shy of his 16th birthday when—or if—he did kill Chapman, Allred figured.

Armed with the positive test results and information from Detectives Grubb and Royal, Allred began a series of interviews. He started with two of Tucker's relatives. The first one, Stacy Barnes, said she drove him to Second Base the day Phyllis Chapman was killed there. They needed money for drugs, Barnes said, and were planning to rob the gambling den for it.

Barnes said that she, Margie Simms, Tucker, and another boy drove over to the Second Base twice that morning. The first time, they saw a white pickup truck, and they left. They then dropped the other boy off and went back. Their plan was for Margie to go in and ask to use the phone. If she didn't come out in a couple of minutes, that meant that nobody but the clerk was inside and Jeff was to come in and rob the joint.

Barnes said they planned the robbery to go off without injury. Allred took this information with a large grain of salt. It turned out that Chapman knew Tucker and could have identified him, so it made more sense that Tucker would have wanted her dead.

Next, Allred talked to Margie Simms. He talked to her twice. She gave a little bit more each time. She said the plan was going smoothly. She went in and Chapman let her use the phone. About two minutes later, Tucker walked in wearing a long Army coat in the August heat to conceal his rifle.

Chapman looked at the teenager in surprise, a look that seemed to ask what he was doing there.

Tucker demanded cash. But before Chapman could oblige him, Tucker pulled out his semiautomatic. Chapman pulled her hands up.

"All of a sudden, Jeff started shooting the girl," Simms said. "Jeff just kept shooting and shooting. He would not stop. I just stood there. I could not believe it."

Tucker then bounded over the counter and grabbed Chapman's purse. He hit her in the head with his gun butt to make sure she was out.

Simms stood motionless, shocked. Tucker grabbed her hand and told her to hurry, that they had to get out. They hopped in the car with Barnes and peeled out of the parking lot. They stopped at a service station for gas and cigarettes. Back at Barnes' mobile home, the conspirators counted the money out and divided it.

Witnesses told Lieutenant Allred that the trio split a grand. The best he could figure, though, it was only about $400. It was a sorry price for a woman's life.

Simms continued her story. Tucker burned Chapman's purse. He said that if he hadn't shot Chapman, she could have identified him and Simms. He said killing her hadn't bothered him. Lieutenant Allred had learned that Tucker hadn't seemed bothered by the Logan killing in High Point either.

A friend of Tucker's came in the mobile home and asked where they had gotten all the money. Simms said she, Tucker, and Barnes looked at each other and didn't say anything.

Allred located the friend and interviewed him. The friend said that he and Tucker left the mobile home and went riding around. Tucker told him that Chapman looked at him curiously, so he shot her six times.

The friend said Tucker also told him how he'd climbed over the counter and grabbed the cash. Tucker told the friend that the gun was just meant to scare Chapman, that he hadn't meant to shoot her.

Allred interviewed the security guard from Second

Base again. The man said he knew Tucker, and that Tucker had asked him about the ins and outs of the gambling dens before the slaying. He remembered that after the slaying, Tucker asked him if anybody had been charged. Tucker had seemed nervous, the security guard said, sitting on his hands and rocking back and forth.

Lieutenant Allred located an inmate in an area jail who claimed that Tucker had told him he didn't like Chapman and Chapman hadn't liked him.

Allred came on easy with Tucker, who was still in the High Point Jail, but he wouldn't tell him a thing. It would have been nice to have him talk, but Allred wasn't that worried.

The detective has what he calls his "arena" theory of murder investigations. Surround the suspect with enough evidence and you've got it made, the sleuth felt. He says it's hard work, but it makes for a good case, especially when you have a bunch of solid witnesses ready to come forward and testify.

Lieutenant Allred charged Jeffrey Tucker with the first-degree murder of Phyllis June Chapman on July 18, 1989—almost two years after the crime had occurred.

That summer, Tucker pleaded guilty to second-degree murder in connection with the Donald Ray Logan case. He was sentenced to 50 years in prison. Prosecutors said that Tucker had another inmate assault one of his co-defendants in an attempt to stop the co-defendant from testifying against him. The co-defendant had still been prepared to testify if Tucker had not pleaded guilty.

Tucker, a wiry kid, kept his bravado up as he awaited trial in the Chapman case. In an August 6,

1989, interview with the *High Point Enterprise*, Tucker said he'd found religion for the second time, after years of hard living.

He said he'd never even gotten his driver's license, that he was smoking pot at 14 before he even had his first cigarette. He said he'd also used LSD and cocaine.

"I was headed down the wrong road when I was on the outside," he said. "I was liable to get killed out there if I kept on the way I was going." He denied knowing anything about Patricia Chapman's murder.

"I don't know anything about that case," he said. "I don't even know where [the murder scene] is. They get you for one thing, they're going to try to get you for something else. Trying to clear the books."

Tucker changed his tune soon enough. On October 17, 1990, in Randolph County Superior Court, he pleaded guilty to second-degree murder in connection with Chapman's death and was sentenced to life in prison.

Lieutenant Allred had been standing by, ready to call in his witnesses if Tucker hadn't choked.

Margie Simms and Stacy Barnes pleaded guilty to accessory charges in the case and drew short prison terms. They'd also been convicted of helping Tucker in the High Point Case and had drawn suspended sentences and probation in that jurisdiction.

Lieutenant Allred had won another hand.

EDITOR'S NOTE:
Margie Simms and Stacy Barnes are not the real names of the persons so named in the foregoing

story. Fictitious names have been used because there is no reason for public interest in the identities of these persons.

"KNIFED PAUL FOR HIS GHETTO BLASTER!"

by Eric Wakin

BROOKLYN, N.Y.
OCTOBER 14, 1984

It was still early evening—not quite yet 8:00 p.m.—but already a chill night wind was whipping through the deserted asphalt lot and graffiti-covered slabs that serve as handball courts. On a warmer night, this Brooklyn neighborhood's park in Bensonhurst would be filled with people sitting and laughing and drinking. But not tonight, February 20, 1983.

Across the street, a subway train made its slow, clanking progress across the elevated tracks that follow New Utrecht Avenue on their way to Coney Island. There was no one waiting for the train at the 71st Street station. If you didn't own a car or absolutely have to go somewhere on foot, there was little reason to be outside in the freezing, late February temperatures. Unless, of course, you were a healthy young boy who had the consistent nocturnal habit of taking a walk before going to sleep.

Less than two blocks from the "El", as New Yorkers refer to the elevated train system, Paul Carbone,

14, had just finished bundling himself up, and, as he was leaving his home, he grabbed the box radio that he always carried on his nightly preambulations.

As he walked outside in his thickly padded coat, Paul Carbone couldn't have been safer from the elements. Unfortunately, it was nothing so natural as the weather that was to affect him on that cold night. What the happy teenager was about to encounter entirely against his will could only be described as the incarnation of evil.

Carbone quickly covered the two blocks to reach one of his favorite spots underneath the El where he could watch the rare passing cars and listen to his radio uninterrupted, except for an occasional passing train. He was as happy as any 14-year-old boy might be in the city.

As Carbone stood on the corner, three men were cruising down New Utrecht Avenue in a large car and spotted the young boy holding his radio. They also noticed the lack of witnesses on the street. Two of the men conferred and told the driver to pull over. Greed and mischief mingled in their faces as they stepped from the car and walked up to Paul Carbone.

The young boy may not have seen the car stop, but he did see two strange men approach him. He was curious at first. Carbone didn't recognize the strangers and wondered why they were walking up to him with a knowing glint in their eyes. Their motives became all too clear in the next few seconds.

One of the men demanded Carbone's radio. Paul refused to yield, a headstrong but often dangerous response to a mugger. The teenager hadn't grown up in the big city for nothing. He'd learned that people try to take what they want from you and, if you don't resist, they succeed.

Paul Carbone fought the two muggers with all of his young strength as they tried to rip the radio from his hands. He punched and kicked and maybe even yelled, but, sadly, no one was around to hear him. One of the cowardly muggers, not wanting to risk any more time struggling, pulled a large knife from his coat pocket and plunged it into Carbone's abdomen. The other thief grabbed the radio and, together, they ran back to the car laughing about the brutal crime. The third man drove away, happy his friends could have some fun on a normally uneventful night.

Young Carbone was left lying on the corner with a gaping wound just above his belt line. He was angry at the cruelty and pain he had suffered, but he refused to stay down. The teenager pulled himself to his feet and looked across the street at the only open and lighted store on the block. He thought he could get help there. He staggered the hundred feet into the storefront office of the 16th Avenue Car Service.

Inside, the owner, John Heyward, sat warming himself. He jumped up as the teenager lurched through his doorway gasping the words, "My father" and "Stabbed!"

Although Heyward was a friend of Carbone's family, he didn't recognize Paul at first, nor did he see the stab wound. Heyward thought the boy had run in gasping for breath and was saying that his father had been stabbed.

The car service owner rushed outside to see if a man was hurt nearby. His search was in vain, but he didn't know it yet. Heyward ran back to his business to get more information from the youth. When he got inside, he saw Paul collapsed on the office couch and noticed the massive wound and profuse bleeding.

Heyward reacted quickly to the emergency at hand. He and another driver for the car service tried to stop the bleeding using whatever clean materials they could find. It is often through the action of quick thinking citizens that an injured person's life can be saved.

While the makeshift bandages were held in place, an ambulance and the police were called.

Only minutes later, two members of the Bensonhurst Volunteer Ambulance Service arrived. The dedicated lifesavers worked feverishly to stop the flow of blood. They then placed the injured young man in the ambulance and, with sirens blaring, raced to the local hospital.

During this time, investigators from the 62nd precinct arrived. Detective Paul Frommer and Detective Louis Eppolito, two long-term veterans of the New York Police Department, took charge of the crime scene. Eppolito is the eleventh most decorated officer in the ranks today, and he and Frommer are well into their second decades as city detectives.

Somewhere in the vast metropolis of New York, three men were listening to Paul Carbone's radio. Little did they know that two dedicated sleuths would be devoting every waking hour to flushing them out and locking them up.

If the site of the brutal stabbing had been somewhere else in the sprawling borough of Brooklyn, the detectives might have been less shocked. Bedford-Stuyvestant, Brownsville, Redhook—together they could tick off the high-crime areas. But Bensonhurst just didn't fit into the mold of a dangerous neighborhood. Sure it had its fair share of burglaries and robberies, even a few more serious crimes, but this particular kind of brutality was indeed rare.

Bensonhurst is a quiet, residential neighborhood populated largely by close-knit Italian families whose respect for each other allows for a certain amount of freedom from crime uncommon in most other parts of the city.

Detectives Frommer and Eppolito both had a hunch, coming from years of police work, that the perpetrator wasn't from the neighborhood. While the two crime experts began to examine the crime scene for clues in what they assumed would be a case of assault with a deadly weapon, the situation changed drastically.

The ambulance attendants rushing young Carbone to the hospital had radioed ahead to ensure the readiness of an emergency operating room at Maimonides Hospital Center. As soon as the stabbing victim arrived, he was rushed to surgery, where doctors worked feverishly on him for almost four hours. However, despite the best efforts of several experienced surgeons, Paul Carbone, described as a "quiet, likeable boy with no enemies" by those who knew him, died shortly after midnight. What had been a case of assault was now one of murder.

In the meantime, the two detectives sealed off the corner with its stain of already dried blood and isolated the few witnesses they had. An investigation can be long, hard work, but if it is executed carefully and diligently from its inception, it will usually yield results. Night was upon Frommer and Eppolito, but they knew it would be some time before they'd be going to sleep. It turned out to be over 36 hours.

The investigators allowed their eyes to wander over the area surrounding the crime scene. The first thing to catch their attention were the train tracks on top of railroad ties supported by steel girders that make up the El. People living in the same place for a while tend to deemphasize parts of the urban landscape, but Frommer and Eppolito were trained detectives. They knew the stories from police lore of killers bringing their victims beneath the El to await the deafening noise of a train passing overhead. A victim's struggles and shouts could never be heard above the roaring noise of a passing train. The train was one of the few sounds that could muffle the blast of a gun fired out in the open. No witnesses would ever hear the murder. The only clue left behind would be a corpse with a neat round hole in its head.

The detectives suspected that Carbone had been the victim of a similar type of killing. He was standing near the El tracks, and if a train had been roaring past, his shouts and screams would probably have been muffled. And even if a train had not been passing overhead, there was little likelihood anyone had been out on the street on such a freezing night.

Detectives Frommer and Eppolito and the uniformed officers assisting them searched the area for any clues. They found no murder weapon, no tire tracks, no fingerprints and, understandably, no witnesses who saw the crime. The detectives speculated that the killer could have approached by foot or vehicle and escaped either way. He probably didn't know Carbone, but this possibility could not be ruled out entirely yet. If ever an investigation seemed to lead into some dead-ends, this was one.

Heyward and his employee could only tell the investigators what they saw after Carbone came into the car service. Heyward hadn't seen anyone outside at all. Already Detective Eppolito's words were beginning to ring true. He would later say, "We assumed it was going to be a tough one to break. After fifteen or sixteen years investigating, you get a feeling about it." Nevertheless, the two forged on.

The crime solvers knew it was a very trying time for the parents of the young man, but they had to know everything about the events leading up to his death. Only close relatives could tell the detectives about any enemies Paul had, or if they knew of any reason anyone might have for wanting to take his life.

The detectives went to the hospital to conduct an interview with the family of Carbone. Frommer and Eppolito were well-aware that the relatives of victims of violent crimes often feel the need to lash out with methods of retributive justice in response to the loss of loved ones. However, investigation and punishment are the jobs of the police and the courts. Inside, hidden from these people whose son had been so brutally murdered, the two detectives could only hope the killer would be brought to justice. They assured the family that they would do everything in their power to solve this case—for Paul, for the Carbone family, and for themselves. Too many families have been torn apart in the aftermath of crimes like this one.

The detectives pressed Paul's family to remember everything that transpired on the night he was murdered. The family recounted his bundling up and going outside carrying the radio he always had with him during nightly walks. This was something the sleuths hadn't known. If there was one thing the detectives were sure of, it was that no radio had been found at the crime scene. The relatives went on to say that Paul wouldn't let anyone take his radio, and the last words Paul was able to speak, before lapsing into unconsciousness, were to tell his family that he didn't want to give up the radio, which had been a gift to him at his last birthday.

As for any enemies Paul might have had, his relatives said the eighth-grader at Montauk Junior High School had none. He was considered well-liked by everyone they knew. The detectives understood the family's grief and asked them to please have faith in their ability to do their job. They promised to do everything in their power to catch the murderer.

Sleuths now surmised that someone had killed Carbone for his radio. This pointed to someone who had probably passed by and seen him standing there alone with his prize. Detective Eppolito would later remark: "Nothing is so important that you have to lose your life to keep it." It was obvious that Paul really had an affinity for his radio.

By this time, the night had turned into early morning and the detectives had completed the few interviews they had of people near the crime scene. Most residents had gone back to sleep after having been awakened by the screaming police and ambulance sirens and crackling radios.

By the next morning, word had reached most of the residents in Bensonhurst that young Paul Carbone had been murdered the night before. Already there was a rumor out on the streets that a bounty had been placed on the head of the murderer. The detectives had given reporters the details of the crime as well as a 24-hour telephone number which people who might have any information about the murder could call.

The detectives, still awake, began to knock on doors in a search for clues. They went from store to store on New Utrecht Avenue and its surrounding streets asking merchants and employees what they knew about Paul Carbone.

One local proprietor told detectives that the teenager had come into his store only a few days before his murder sporting a black eye. Carbone had told the owner that he had fought some kids who tried to take his radio. "Why don't you leave that thing at home?" was the storekeeper's suggestion to the youth. Unfortunately his advice went unheeded.

The untiring investigators went door to door in the residential areas of the neighborhood of white-and-red-brick houses and colored metal awnings. They searched and probed for a clue of any kind that would give them a break in the case. They walked in and out of low wrought-iron gates that fronted the homes in the area only to hear the same things about the young victim. He was a "nice, likeable kid" who was almost never seen without his radio. One resident even went so far as to describe the music box as Paul's "pride and joy."

The detectives worked on into the next night, stopping only briefly to eat. They worked on through the early morning hours and until daylight. Finally, after over 36 hours on this case, the two sleuths stopped to catch some sleep.

Later that day the pair was back on the streets again looking for leads. Detective Eppolito explained his perseverance this way: "When you've got a case involving a kid—and I've got four children of my own—and all of the leads go down the drain, it makes you try harder. You knock on more doors; you talk to more people and you really put the pressure on."

Frommer and Eppolito pounded the pavement of Bensonhurst. They went to the playgrounds and the streetcorners, the parks and the restaurants, to talk to the teenagers and the young adults. The detectives told the kids to come up with something or else there would be cops around for a long time asking questions. Few of the kids who spent their time hanging out on the street-corners and in the local parks wanted police around all the time. The detectives knew this and worked the kids to their advantage. The word was out on the street. Two cops were looking for the murderer of Paul Carbone and they were going to find him.

The many days of interviews with shopkeepers, neighbors and local youths had actually caused a lot of response. This was particularly true in the case of the youths who are normally hesitant to talk to their neighborhood police officers. Unfortunately, it was not the kind of response needed to solve the Carbone murder case. Young people called to turn in enemies with whom they had long-standing grudges. Sometimes they suggested their enemies were responsible for the boy's murder, and other times they reported on local burglaries and other petty crimes. Frommer and Eppolito turned over any valuable information about other crimes to other officers, but followed up on their own all the leads that seemed related to their case. The calls kept coming and they kept checking, but drew a blank on every occasion.

The fact that not one lead in Bensonhurst amounted to anything despite all the pressure led the detectives to deduce that the killer came from somewhere outside this close-knit neighborhood. But Brooklyn was as large place and they couldn't even draw the line there. The probers knew that somewhere in all of New York City a man sat listening to his murdered victim's radio.

The case might have been closed there, two weeks after the murder, if Detective Frommer hadn't had a brainstorm. The clever investigator had a hunch that someone, somewhere, knew about the killing and would be willing to talk about it. Frommer knew he could spend the rest of his life searching the city for an informant. He decided to bring his information to the entire city by means of a large poster offering a reward for information.

Frommer contacted the family of the murdered boy. They gladly offered to furnish the reward money. Hundreds of the 12-by-16-inch posters were printed and distributed to every police precinct in the city. The Carbone family covered their neighborhood and surrounding areas with many more.

The poster offered a $2000 reward to anyone who gave information that led to the arrest and conviction of the murderer of Paul Carbone. A picture of the boy, in his earlier, happier days, adorned the center of the poster. On the bottom was printed a 24-hour phone number where callers could reach the 62nd precinct.

After a slow start, the investigators soon had their

hands full with information from anonymous tipsters seeking the reward money. Some people were concerned about the particular murder and offered suggestions. Very few calls, though, offered leads based on concrete facts. One entire day was spent by Detectives Frommer and Eppolito looking for someone in the Wall Street area of Manhattan. It turned out to be a red herring, however. The two sleuths waited patiently for the reward offer to bring in something.

Meanwhile, in Coney Island, only a few miles from Bensonhurst, two young men were talking. Their conversation moved from one topic to another until one started boasting about various crimes. His companion looked skeptical until the bragger pulled a newspaper clipping from his wallet. On the several weeks-old newsprint was the story of Paul Carbone's death. The braggart boasted that he didn't carry the newspaper clip for nothing and offered to sell his disbelieving acquaintance a radio. The radio never exchange hands, however. Later, the skeptical youth would remember the encounter.

Some days later, the acquaintances of the braggart walked past a well-traveled corner in the area and noticed the Paul Carbone reward poster. Glancing casually at it, he was struck by the familiar picture and the mention of a stolen radio. Something clicked, and he sought out a uniformed police officer. Perhaps it was the reward offered or perhaps it was a sense of justice and rightness within him. Ultimately, his motive could only be known to himself.

Motive notwithstanding, the anonymous informant began to talk. He said he knew two brothers who hung out on 36th Street near where Mermaid and

Neptune Avenues cross it. He said he'd been talking to one of them and had seen a newspaper clip about the Carbone murder. The brother had also mentioned that he had a radio for sale that sounded a lot like the one in the poster.

The uniformed officer was no stranger to the poster. Everyone at the precinct had seen it. He pumped this source for more information. What were the brothers' names.

The informer said he didn't know, but the cops could find out if they went to 36th Street. He then described them as best he could, adding that they drove around in a large, white Lincoln Continental. After obtaining the witness's phone number and address, the officer thanked him and called the Coney Island stationhouse to pass on the information.

Back in Bensonhurst, Frommer and Eppolito had run out of leads. They were hoping that the poster idea would bring forth someone willing to talk to the police. Then the call came in from Coney Island. It looked like a good lead, but it could be just another dead-end, thought the sleuths. There was only one way to find out — an undercover operation.

There is nothing more noticeable than two men dressed in jackets and ties standing around in a neighborhood they don't belong in, acting like they're looking for someone. If these brothers were killers, they would have the criminal instinct to recognize two cops on their turf. So Frommer and Eppolito changed into casual clothes and drove to 36th and Mermaid. There, they began a vigilant wait for the suspects.

In the over-30 hours the pair was staked out, many cars and people passed by, but none quite matched the suspects' description. Exhausted and determined, they continued to wait. Then a car drove past with two similar looking men in it. It was a white Lincoln Continental.

The car pulled over and the two incognito detectives got out of their vehicle and walked slowly toward it. When they reached the auto, they identified themselves and ordered the two suspects out of their car at gunpoint. It only takes a split second for a cornered suspect to shoot or stab an arresting officer and both detectives were well aware of this as they eased the siblings out of the car.

Luckily, the brothers reacted carefully to the detectives' commands. They were ordered to stand against the side of their car with their arms and legs spread. The officers frisked them but found no weapons. They were then read their rights and handcuffed. The sleuths next called for back-up assistance and had the car impounded, while they brought the suspects back to the Bensonhurst stationhouse for interrogation.

Once the booking process was begun, the detectives found out the suspects' names. It was now possible to check their record of previous arrests. The police department file for the brothers, Jordan and Randy White of 23rd Avenue in Brooklyn, was quite long. Both had lengthy rap sheets; Jordan, for weapons and drug possession and grand theft auto; Randy, several times for weapons. Finally, something had come up the sleuths could sink their teeth into.

The two White brothers were taken into the interrogation room and the questioning began. They were told they would be asked some questions about the murder of Paul Carbone. Surprisingly, the brothers were willing to volunteer more information than had been expected.

When asked if they were on New Utrecht Avenue on February 20th, the two said they had been driving through Bensonhurst on that night. They said another man was with them. His name was Fabian Acevado, a trucker's helper. According to the White brothers' account, Acevado got out of the car and returned several minutes later with a radio. He didn't say where he'd gotten it and they didn't ask.

Despite the fact that the detectives confronted them with the events of the murder, the Whites denied having anything to do with it. They said they didn't know what had happened to the radio.

The detectives felt the two siblings had a lot more to tell but weren't talking. They were obviously ex-criminals who had had extensive contact with law enforcement officials and were prepared to lie in order to remain free.

The interrogating detectives asked for a description of Acevado. The Whites said he was a short dark-haired man of about 20. One noticeable thing about him was that he was often walking his Doberman Pinscher around 35th Street and Mermaid Avenue.

Detectives Frommer and Eppolito were finished with the questioning, they took the White brothers back to lock-up. They knew the evidence against them wasn't enough to hold them for long, so they went to talk to the assistant district attorney. He told the detectives to let the White brothers go as long as they could keep an eye on them, and concentrate on finding Acevado. It was exactly what the probers figured he'd say.

After releasing the brothers and cautioning them to stay in town in case they'd be needed again, the detectives began their search for the third suspect. This time, they knew his name. It only took two days to ferret out Acevado's whereabouts. He was picked up, without his dog, on Mermaid Avenue.

The detectives returned with him to the stationhouse and, after a 3-hour grilling session, Acevado made a full, videotaped confession.

Besides admitting to the murder of Carbone, he also implicated the Whites. Acevado told Frommer and Eppolito that he and the White brothers were driving through Bensonhurst together on February 20th. While Jordan stayed in the car, he and Randy White went out to rob the boy. Although Acevado stabbed Carbone, Jordan White ended up with the radio and eventually sold it.

With Acevado's confession permanently videotaped, the tireless sleuths could now pick up the White brothers and indict them for murder also.

Meanwhile, the Carbone family was told that a suspect was in custody and two more were being sought. They knew nothing could bring back their beloved, but were pleased that finally there was someone to atone for the killing.

One relative said, "I have not changed my position a bit. I am overjoyed that this animal is caught—and he is an animal when a twenty year old can pick on a fourteen year old for a radio."

Another relative added, "It tore the family apart . . . We talked about this every day . . . Maybe tonight it will be the first night of sleep since it happened."

Back on the streets, the two detectives were again

searching. In a few more days they had the White brothers in custody and charged with murder.

The wheels of justice began to turn inexorably to a conclusion.

Randy White was found to be in violation of a parole he was serving for weapons possession. The detectives contacted his parole officer, and he was sent back to prison immediately.

Jordan White was released on bail but never showed up for his trial. He was later discovered to have attempted suicide by slashing his wrists. He awaits a new trial while recuperating in the hospital.

Fabian Acevado's defense attorney first tried to have the incriminating videotape confession thrown out as evidence. His motion was denied. Acevado was convicted of murder and sentenced to 17 to 25 years in prison, of which he must serve at least 17.

The two investigators who worked tirelessly on the case for over two months could now rest. Detective Eppolito said with satisfaction, "It's always a pleasure to solve this kind of case. When they come back with a guilty verdict, you know you did a hell of a job."

Randy and Jordan White must be presumed innocent of the charges against them unless they can be proved otherwise in a court of law.

EDITOR'S NOTE:
John Heyward is not the real name of the person so named in the foregoing story. A fictitious name has been used because there is no reason for public interest in the identify of this person.

"SICK COKEHEAD'S ROB/RAPE RAMPAGE"

by Don Lasseter

When Deborah Converse arrived home from work on December 5, 1989, and opened the door of her apartment in Covina, California, at first she was shocked, then she was furious.

Somebody had ransacked her usually immaculate living room. Deborah stormed through the living room, dining area, and kitchen to see if anything had been stolen.

In the single bedroom, Deborah was relieved to see that her three rifles, kept in a corner rack, were still there. Nothing else appeared to be missing, despite the chaotic condition of her clothing and furniture. Back in the living room, Deborah checked her entertainment center. Her television set, stereo system, and crystalware were still there, but a square, dust-free area, framed by loose wires, on the shelf above the TV fueled Deborah's anger again. Her VCR was missing.

Deborah Converse called the police, then, while waiting for an officer to arrive, she telephoned a close relative and told her about the burglary. No, she said, her rifles had not been stolen and neither had her treasured Princess crystal glasses. But her VCR was gone, and she was angry that her privacy and property had been violated. Perhaps, the two women agreed, Deborah was lucky that she had not been there when it happened. At least, she had not been hurt.

At 5:00 p.m. that same evening, Chrystal Woods, community service officer of the Covina Police Department, received the call initiated by Deborah Converse. Woods was dispatched to respond to a p.c. 459, an apparent burglary in apartment 3 in the complex on Prospero Avenue. In Covina, a community service officer fields burglary reports when there is no suspect at the location. Chrystal Woods arrived at Deborah Converse's apartment, on the ground level of a two-story complex, a few minutes later, and took the report.

Officer Woods noted that the bedroom window was open and the screen was lying on the ground. Dresser drawers were pulled out and clothing was scattered all over the room. The angry victim had now discovered that her favorite Jane Fonda workout tape had been stolen along with the VCR. Chrystal Woods sympathized but felt that it was a good thing that Deborah Converse had not been at home when the burglar entered her apartment.

Eleven hours later, at 3:53 a.m. in the gloomy, dark hours of the morning of December 6th, Patrol Sergeant Charles Anthony Rosales received a radio call. "Possible burglary in progress . . . ," the radio crackled, "screams and sounds of glass breaking." The location was the same apartment building where Deborah Converse had been victimized the previous afternoon. Only this time, it was apartment number

4, next door to Converse.

Sergeant Rosales immediately relayed the emergency call to another patrol unit in the area to request assistance. "At a tactical situation such as a burglary in progress, particularly in the early-morning hours," Rosales would later say, "units are directed to the opposite sides of a particular building in order to contain that building."

At 3:56, with backup units in place, Sergeant Rosales approached apartment 4. There was no response at the front entrance, so he circled to the back, to a breezeway between the building and a wooden fence. He could see that a window was broken in back of apartment 4.

After making sure that no burglary suspect was in the vicinity, Sergeant Rosales leaned into the broken window far enough to poke his flashlight in and aim a beam of light into the bedroom. He stopped the dim light on a motionless form lying crumpled on the floor in the center of the room.

The body was lying face down, dead still, with the feet pointed toward the officer. Rosales alerted Officer R. Mangapane, and the two lawmen ran to the front. There, they jerked a sliding-glass window from its frame, and mindful that a suspect might still be in the apartment, climbed through and moved quickly to the bedroom door, which stood partially ajar. Cautiously, Rosales nudged the door open with his flashlight, then stepped into the bedroom. When he was sure that no one else was in the room, he treaded carefully to the prostrate figure.

Kneeling beside the body, Sergeant Rosales steeled himself to inspect the damage that someone had inflicted on the woman. "She had been stabbed numerous times," Rosales said, "as evidenced by approximately fifteen stab wounds in various portions of her body."

Placing his fingers on the side of the woman's neck, Rosales checked for a pulse in the carotid artery. There was none. "The body was warm," he reported, "but there was no life in the limbs. I determined at that point that the person had expired."

Sergeant Rosales directed Officer Mangapane to call 911 to get the paramedics on the scene, and then to notify the homicide unit of the Los Angeles County Sheriff's Department. Mangapane completed the calls, then stood guard at the broken window, while Officer B. Sutherland stood at the front door not only to secure it, but also to take names of anyone visiting the crime scene.

Within minutes, a paramedic arrived and verified that the woman on the bedroom floor was dead.

The morning sun was barely peeking over the smoggy horizon when Sergeant Robert W. Perry, homicide investigator for the Los Angeles Sheriff's Department, arrived at the apartment on Prospero Avenue in Covina. He chatted briefly with the Covina police officers on the scene, and then made his way through the neat, undisturbed living room and into the bedroom. He noted that it was "in terrible disarray," with "evidence of violence."

To get to the body, Perry had to step over a potted plant that had been tipped over and had spilled soil onto the floor. He saw that clothing was scattered, and furniture had been moved around in the obvious ransacking. There were crimson spots on the partly open closet door, on the floor, and on a chest of drawers that stood near the victim's head. Blood was "sprayed and splattered all the way to the top of the chest." There were also splotches of blood on the walls.

Shards of glass lay on the floor at the bottom of the broken window. The bedcovers on both bunk beds were disheveled and rumpled. Stuffed animals and dolls were strewn about.

Sergeant Perry wanted to know if the victim had been identified. Yes, he was told by the local police. Neighbors had said that the apartment was occupied by 24-year-old Alexandria Hickman. No purse was found in the apartment, but other personal belongings verified that the dead woman was, indeed, Alexandria Hickman.

The team of sleuths would learn that Hickman was a shy young woman who lived alone, was sweet and pleasant to everyone, and spent many evenings quietly watching television or crocheting. She certainly had no enemies or relatives that could result in her murder. She was proud of her collection of dolls and stuffed animals, which were always displayed on her upper bunk bed.

The victim was dressed in gray sweatpants and a blue plaid sport shirt. There was so much blood, it was hard to distinguish her features. Her battered face and body made it apparent to the investigators that she had put up a fierce struggle for her life.

Criminalists photographed the body from every angle before the coroner's examiner turned her over to scrutinize more stab wounds. When she was moved, a broken kitchen knife appeared beneath her head. It, too, was covered with blood.

Sergeant Perry noticed near the bed a glinting reflection from something on the floor, to the right of the victim's body. Looking more closely, he saw that it was a metal button, the kind usually used to fasten the waistline of blue jeans. It obviously had not come from the sweatpants on the victim. Perry carefully placed the button in a glassine evidence bag.

After an hour spent examining the body and the interior of the apartment, Sergeant Perry, with the help of the Covina Police Department officers, began to canvass the apartment complex for witnesses to supplement the information that some of the tenants had already volunteered. The complex was relatively small, with six apartments in each of the two buildings facing each other across a courtyard. The victim, Alexandria Hickman, lived on one end of the ground floor in apartment 3 next to Deborah Converse, who had been burglarized the previous afternoon.

Sergeant Perry went next door to apartment 3 to interview Deborah Converse. There was no answer to his knocks, however, and her black Chevy pickup was not in the carport. Perry decided to come back later, after speaking to the witness who had called the police at 3:55 a.m. to report hearing screams and breaking glass. The young woman lived in an adjacent apartment building, across a narrow alley.

The witness was an immigrant from Pakistan who spoke English with some difficulty. She told Sergeant Perry that she had been awakened while it was still very dark by "strange noises" that sounded like screaming. Then she had heard breaking glass and rushed to her window to look outside. "I went to see what happened," she explained. "I looked out the window to the small street . . . not street," she said,

204

seeming to struggle for the right word.

"Do you mean alley?" Perry asked.

"Yes, yes, the alley," she responded, excitedly. "Then, I see somebody walking . . . running fast. He was running to the walking side," the witness furrowed her brow as if groping for the correct word.

"Walking side?" Perry asked, puzzled. "Do you mean the sidewalk?"

"Yes, yes, the sidewalk," the woman responded.

"Could you see what the man looked like?" Perry asked, not very optimistically.

"Yes. He was kind of Mexican-looking. Young, maybe twenty-two or twenty-three. He had dark, wavy hair, almost down to here," the witness gestured, indicating nearly shoulder-length hair. "He was running, like a nervous person. It wasn't normal running. It was running with all the time looking around." Again, the woman was acting out her description by jerking her head to look behind her.

"What was he wearing?"

"A white shirt, maybe black and white, long sleeve, no buttons."

Sergeant Perry, dressed in plain-clothes, opened his jacket, and asked if the fleeing man was wearing a white shirt like he, Perry, was wearing.

The woman quickly responded, correcting Perry, "That is not a shirt, it is a blouse. The man was wearing a shirt — long sleeves, no buttons."

"A sweater?"

"No, no sweater. A shirt."

After a few minutes of conversation, Perry finally determined that the fleeing man was wearing a long-sleeved white sweatshirt, with some black pattern on it. The woman was also able to tell him that the runner was wearing white "sport shoes."

It was an excellent description, thought Perry, considering that the woman had seen a running man in a dark alley for just a few seconds, just after she had been awakened. She had been unusually observant, and despite her broken English, very helpful.

While Sergeant Perry was conducting interviews, Dale S. Falicon, a latent-fingerprint expert from the L.A. Sheriff's Department, was examining the interior of apartment 3 for prints. He had been called at 5:00 a.m., and was on the scene in less than one hour. Falicon was highly qualified for his job, having worked for three years with the FBI crime labs in Washington, D.C. After joining the L.A. Sheriff's Department in 1980, he had made more than 10,000 fingerprint comparisons and hundreds of identifications.

Using the old-fashioned carbon dust and transparent tape method, Falicon lifted a print from inside the sill of the bedroom window. Then he used a paint spray gun to coat the interior walls with ninhydrin, which reacts with amino acids in human perspiration. If a person has left a print, the chemical will cause it to become purple, and, thus, visible. Falicon found such a print just outside the bedroom door near the bathroom. He photographed it for preservation.

Outside, as the morning warmed up, Sergeant Robert Perry decided to try apartment 4 again, hoping that Deborah Converse was there. He knocked, but there was no response. From other neighbors, he learned that Deborah worked at a Pasadena auto dealer. Perry telephoned the employer and learned that Deborah had not yet arrived but had left word that she would be a little late that morning because she wanted to do some Christmas shopping.

Still anxious about Converse, Perry busied himself with other duties. He joined a criminalist and scrutinized every inch of ground outside the windows of the two burglary victims. They found a clear print of the sole of a sports shoe.

Shortly after midday, Sergeant Perry was becoming more concerned with the need to speak to Deborah Converse. She certainly would have heard something next door, he figured, considering that the woman who lived in the next building had heard the screams. He was becoming a little frustrated because he hadn't yet been able to interview Converse, or to find the tenants in the next unit, apartment 5.

Perry called Deborah Converse's employer again. No, she had not arrived yet. She was "a sociable and lively lady" but was dependable and would have called unless something was wrong.

As he would later put it, "My degree of suspicion was heightening, so I caused a window to be opened at the rear of the Converse apartment." When Sergeant Perry looked into the apartment bedroom, he was stunned at what he saw.

"By pulling the curtain aside slightly," he later reported, "you could see a pillow on the bed immediately inside. The pillow looked to be bloody. So I crawled through that open window, and . . . was able to see the victim."

Deborah Converse, like her neighbor, Alexandria Hickman, lay dead, face down on her bedroom floor. Unlike Hickman, Converse had been bound with a ligature. A green, webbed dog leash was tied around her wrists behind her back and stretched to

207

her ankles, which were also bound together. Blood was everywhere.

Alexandria Hickman had been fully clothed when found, but Deborah Converse was not. She wore a T-shirt, decorated with blue fish designs, but her shorts and panties were pulled down around her ankles. There were clear indications that she had been raped.

The bloody body was in a state of rigor mortis, indicating that Converse had been killed before Hickman. While Hickman had been stabbed approximately 15 times, Deborah Converse's corpse was punctured with nearly 50 stab wounds!

Just after entering the apartment, Sergeant Perry heard some low growls, which sounded more frightened then intimidating. From a shadowy corner, a nervous, aged female Doberman emerged. Within a minute or two, the sympathetic sergeant had made friends with the terrified old dog.

Now the search started for evidence around a second murder victim. It was the most astonishing turn of events the investigation team had ever experienced. Sergeant Robert Perry had, a few years earlier, helped investigate a murder committed by one of California's most notorious serial killers, the infamous "Night Stalker" Richard Ramirez. But Perry never encountered anything like the double murder at the apartment building on Prospero Avenue.

Similar to the situation next door, the investigators found no purse in the Converse apartment. The tiny dwelling had been thoroughly ripped apart. Sheets and blankets had been pulled from the bed, and clothing was scattered on the floor. In each of the two grisly apartments, the entry door had been locked and dead bolted. The killer had apparently

208

entered and exited from windows.

One of the officers discovered a maroon telephone in the bathroom sink of the Converse apartment. Dale Falicon, the fingerprint expert, was called over to examine the phone for prints. Because it was a hard, nonporous object, he elected to put it in a bag and take it to the lab for fingerprinting by the Super Glue technique.

Another investigator discovered a bloody kitchen knife on the building's roof. It matched those found in Deborah's kitchen, in a wooden block holding five other knives. The sixth slot was empty.

In Deborah Converse's personal directory, one of the officers located the telephone number of the relative Deborah had called the previous day. The relative was brought to the crime scene to help establish if any property was missing. The first thing the woman looked for was the rifle rack where Deborah kept her three rifles. The woman tearfully recalled how relieved Deborah had been when the guns had not been stolen the previous day. Now, they were missing.

The relative further told investigators that a .35-millimeter camera and a black purse were missing. She also gave them information about the Chevy pickup that now appeared to be stolen, perhaps by the killer.

Before leaving, the relative went to the entertainment center cabinet to check on Deborah's precious Princess crystal glasses. Tears filled her eyes again when she saw that the glasses lay on the floor, smashed into countless, tiny pieces.

Sergeant Perry arranged to put out a top priority BOLO on Deborah's black 1982 Chevy S-110 pickup truck.

A major break came minutes later. At last, Sergeant Perry was able to locate the tenant in apartment 5, next to the most recently discovered victim's unit. Rosa Ruiz, a quiet woman in her early 20s, seemed slightly reluctant to talk to the police.

"Did you know the two women who lived in apartments three and four?" Perry asked.

"A little bit. We used to say 'Hi," or 'Bye' to them, or what a nice day it was."

"'We?' " Sergeant Perry inquired. "Who is *we*?"

"Oh," Rosa whispered. "My boyfriend, Marty, and me." She told the sergeant that her boyfriend occupied apartment 5 with her.

"Where is Marty?"

"The last time I saw him was last night, about ten-thirty," the witness replied. "He was in the alley, talking to his buddy. Then they went somewhere. I went to sleep and didn't wake up until about three-thirty this morning, when I heard the cops outside."

Sergeant Perry moved the name Martin Navarette to the top of the list of people he wanted to interview.

At apartment 8, Perry talked to another resident who said she heard nothing during the night. Perry then asked her if she knew Martin Navarette.

"Yeah, I know Marty," she said. "He lives in apartment five. He was over at my place yesterday drinking beer until about four in the afternoon. He must have been drinking most of the day, 'cause when he drinks, he really gets an attitude."

"What was he wearing?" Sergeant Perry asked.

"A light-colored sweatshirt that said 'Nike,' " she candidly replied.

Another young man had noticed the commotion around the apartment complex and volunteered to talk to investigators. He said that the day before at about 4:00 p.m., he had been walking his dog and went into the courtyard of the apartments to see where Marty was. Marty was just stepping out of an apartment, and the man with the dog approached him to chat for a while, then left. A little while later, maybe 5:30, he saw Marty again, and Marty had asked, "Hey man, you know where I could get rid of a VCR?"

"No," the dog-walker claimed he told Marty. "I don't really deal with that kind of stuff." Marty seemed "kind of on edge" at the time.

It had become clear to the investigators that Martin Navarette was a man they seriously needed to find. A quick check of Navarette's criminal record revealed that he had a felony drug conviction in 1988 and was currently on probation for assault with intent to commit rape, for which he had entered a guilty plea in a Pasadena court earlier in 1989. Navarette also had a history of cocaine abuse.

Sergeant Perry went again to apartment 5 and asked Rosa Ruiz if he could enter and search the place. She readily agreed. Perry and another detective looked through the messy apartment, asked Ruiz a few more questions, then kneeled to look under the bed. They spotted two purses, one black and one white.

Inside the black purse were assorted papers, identification cards, credit cards, and a bank card, all in the name of Deborah Converse.

At the L.A. Sheriff's Crime Lab in Hollywood, print expert Dale Falicon applied the Super Glue process to examine the red telephone found in the bathroom sink in Deborah Converse's apartment. "In the Super Glue process," he explained, "the item [is put] in a 'fuming tank' and Super Glue is poured in the tank with warm water. Super Glue fumes tend to adhere to the moisture left on the item [from contact with human skin]. The print will turn a light white in color, in many cases. Then it can be dusted with black powder and then photographed."

Falicon's use of the process produced results. He found a clear palm print on the phone. It was from a right hand, and it did not match the sample he had taken from Deborah Converse.

As the day wound down at the crime scene, another resident of the apartment complex gave Sergeant Perry the name of a good friend of Navarette. Joe Cardenas, the informant said, lived in East Los Angeles and might know where Martin Navarette could be found.

But someone else had seen Martin Navarette, early in the morning, within hours after the murders.

Elena Silva was startled from a deep sleep when her phone rang at 1:30 a.m., on Wednesday, December 6th. Groggy, she barely managed to whisper "hello" into the speaker.

"Hi, did I wake you up?" Martin Navarette asked the pretty 20-year-old.

Still half-asleep, Elena said, "It's okay."

Elena was not displeased to hear from Navarette. She and the handsome, dark-eyed man, who was just four years her senior, had exchanged frequent phone calls between their dates over the last year. She really liked Martin, but she became suspicious when she discovered that he had a female roommate. He had

212

casually explained that away to her, saying the woman was really just his sister.

Elena listened as Navarette asked her to get up and go out for a ride with him. He was driving a new truck he had just purchased, he told her. That was news to her since he hadn't owned a vehicle, and previously they had always used her car.

"No, it's too late, Marty," Elena finally decided. "Maybe tomorrow night." She resisted his cajoling, and when they hung up, Elena went back to sleep.

The jangling phone woke her again at 7:00 a.m. It was Navarette. Now he was more insistent. His truck, he said, had broken down near a hamburger stand close to First and Mission in East Los Angeles. Could she come over and pick him up? Elena agreed to help him.

After hurriedly dressing, Elena jumped into her two-door Toyota Celica and drove the few miles to the hamburger stand. She arrived just 20 minutes after he had called.

Glancing around the parking lot, Elena could not see Martin. Impatience started to well up in her, but then she spotted him running from across the street. Without pausing, Martin jerked the passenger door open and leaped into the backseat. That was weird, Elena thought. Even more bizarre, he immediately stretched out to lie down on the seat. He said he was very tired. He may be tired, Elena thought, but he looked a little "sprung." She would later explain that "sprung" was street vernacular for the appearance of a person who is coming down from a cocaine high.

In addition to looking tired and "sprung," Elena observed that Martin was wearing his shirt inside out, and she was sure she could see bloodstains seeping through it. There appeared to be bloodstains near the knees of his pants, as well. Elena also noticed that Martin's jeans were "unbuckled," with no button at the top.

"Marty, what happened? You have blood on you," Elena said.

Martin's evasive answer, in a strident voice, told her to back off. Elena frowned, putting a hurt expression on her face. Navarette, attempting to soften his harshness, explained to Elena that the stains were actually paint. He quickly changed the subject, asking if she would take him to a friend's house. As they drove off, Elena saw a black Chevy pickup parked near the hamburger stand.

The Toyota was nearly out of gas, so Elena pulled into a service station. Under the bright lights of the pump island, through the open sunroof, the interior of the car was clearly illuminated. Elena looked at Navarette, still reclining in the backseat, and was now sure that the stains on his clothing were from blood.

As they drove away from the station and Elena continued to question him, Martin finally admitted that the discoloration was blood. He explained that he'd been in a fight during the night. He added that he thought he would leave the city for a while, maybe join the service.

Martin had not been in a particularly good frame of mind when she picked him up, Elena thought, but his mood grew darker as they drove. "He would roll his eyes up like I was asking too many questions," she would remember.

Elena stopped the car after Martin angrily told her that she had passed his friend's house. Parked at the

214

curb, she leaned her seat back as far as it would go to face him. She wanted to talk. But his demeanor frightened her, so she leaned forward and pulled the keys from the ignition, preparing to jump out of the car and run away.

Without warning, Navarette lunged from the backseat, and slammed his fist into Elena's nose and eyes. Blood spurted from her fractured nose.

"You know, he hit me and blood came out," Elena told the sleuths, "and then he had a blanket [from the backseat] and he put it over my face."

Before Navarette pulled the blanket over her head and applied pressure with his hand to choke off her air supply, Elena threw the keys out of the car. Navarette stopped suffocating her and demanded, "Where are the keys?"

The interruption allowed Elena to wrest the car door open, leap out, and run as fast as she could. Behind her, she heard Navarette trying to start the car. She thought the car alarm would go off; the siren was set to go off 30 seconds after the keys were removed, and she was sure he would not be able to start the car. But she was wrong. Somehow, he had managed to find the keys, circumvent the alarm, and drive away in her car.

Elena called for help and was taken to the hospital where she underwent surgery to repair her fractured nose.

Darkness had settled over the Covina murder scene, and Sergeant Robert Perry, along with another officer, acting on the information that a man named Joe Cardenas might know the whereabouts of Martin Navarette, hurried to Cardenas' East Los Angeles house.

"Yeah," Cardenas told Perry, "Marty was here today. I was walking home from an errand, a little before noon, and Marty was sitting on the stairs at the front of my house."

"What was he wearing?" the investigators asked.

"Blue jeans, white tennies, and no shirt," Cardenas told them. Cardenas also said that when Navarette got up, he picked up his shirt from the step. There was blood on the shirt and on Navarette's jeans, around the thighs. Cardenas had asked what happened, and Navarette told him he had "got in a fight with three guys."

Martin Navarette stayed with Cardenas until about 5:30 p.m. He borrowed some clothes, and Cardenas gave him a ride and let him off downtown.

"Did he leave the clothes he was wearing?" Perry asked.

"Yeah, man," Cardenas replied. They were in the washroom at the back of the house. Cardenas readily gave the bloody clothing to the officers. Sergeant Perry noted that the shirt was a bloodstained short-sleeved sport shirt, not a white sweatshirt imprinted with the word "Nike" as witnesses had described. Perhaps the sweatshirt would turn up later. Cardenas also gave the officers the address of a relative of Navarette, near Covina, where the fugitive might have gone.

Sergeant Perry and other deputies arrived at the Covina address at 8:00 p.m. — almost simultaneously with Martin Navarette! The suspect surrendered meekly, was handcuffed, and transported to jail, where he was booked on suspicion of murder. Mug photos were taken, along with shots of his scratched hands and a deep gash at the base of his left thumb.

216

These injuries, the investigators figured, were made by Alexandria Hickman during the desperate fight for her life.

On the following day, Eugene Carpenter performed autopsies on the bodies of Alexandria Hickman and Deborah Converse while Sergeant Perry observed. Carpenter verified that the cause of death for both women was multiple stab wounds. He also concluded that the knife found on the apartment roof was probably the murder weapon used on both women. The knife discovered under the head of Alexandria Hickman, the investigators speculated, had been in the hands of the unfortunate victim when she was trying to defend herself.

Sheriff's deputies found the black pickup truck belonging to Deborah Converse near the hamburger stand where Navarette had abandoned it. It was towed to an impound station where blood samples from the interior were collected and sent to the crime lab.

In the L.A. County Sheriff's Crime Lab, Elizabeth Kornblum, senior criminalist, examined the bloodstains on the shirt and jeans recovered from the home of Joe Cardenas. Through carefully developed procedures, she compared the blood to samples taken from the two victims' bodies and from Martin Navarette. She concluded that stains just above the right knee of Navarette's jeans were "consistent with having come from Alexandria Hickman." She also was able to determine that the bloodstain found in the pickup could not have come from the victims, but was "consistent with having come from Navarette" himself. It was hard evidence proving that Navarette had been in the vehicle.

Two weeks after Martin Navarette's arrest, the woman who lived in apartment 8 at the murder scene, the woman who had described the Nike sweatshirt, telephoned Sergeant Perry. She told him that Rosa Ruiz, Navarette's roommate in apartment 5, was moving out. The witness was watching from her second-story balcony and saw a little boy take some bags of trash from apartment 5 and throw them in the dumpster. Among the things thrown in the trash was a white plastic supermarket bag that had some clothes in it, and the witness was curious, so she sent a neighbor boy to retrieve the bag.

"What was in it?" Perry asked, correctly anticipating the answer.

"That sweatshirt that Marty was wearing," the woman responded, "the one with 'Nike' on it. And it has blood all over it."

Sergeant Perry wasted no time in retrieving the sweatshirt and placing it in the hands of Elizabeth Kornblum, the serologist specialist. Kornblum duplicated the same tests she had previously conducted on Navarette's other clothing. Kornblum found that a bloodstain on the left sleeve of the sweatshirt, near the cuff, was "consistent with having come from Deborah Converse."

There was now strong evidence that Martin Navarette had killed both victims.

Because there had been a burglary and robbery along with the murders, Deputy District Attorney John Urgo announced that the prosecution would prove the "special circumstances" necessary in California law to seek the death penalty.

John Urgo had been with the district attorney's office since he had taken his law degree in 1980 in Los

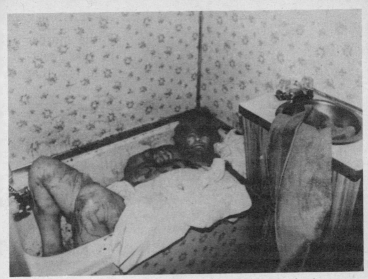

Benjamin Hernandez, butchered in the bathtub
of his trailer in rural Oregon.

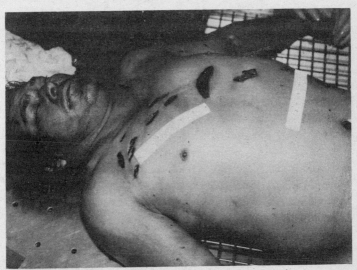

A fraction of the numerous stab wounds
are visible in this morgue photo.

Robert Dotts.

James Cudaback.

Exxon executive Sidney Reso.

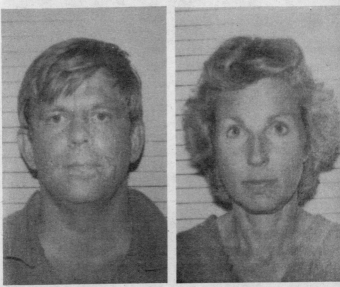

Arthur and Irene Seale, Reso's kidnapper/killers.

Paul Taylor murdered Kathy Ann Woodhouse, then called 911.

This blood-smeared mop wringer was Taylor's fatal bludgeon.

Bookie Phyllis June Chapman was found dead in an illegal gambling den.

Jeff Tucker pleaded guilty to killing Chapman.

Arrow points to the slashed body
of Alexandria Hickman.

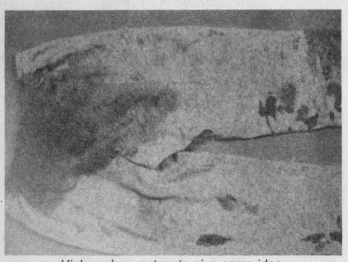

Hickman's sweatpants give some idea
of the amount of blood at the scene.

Hickman's killer,
Martin Navarette,
had already killed
that night.

Knife rack furnished
Navarette with his
first murder weapon.

The nude body of Bernard James Oberbrockling III
was found in a field in Amarillo, Texas.

Thomas Schumacher, Oberbrockling's killer.

The murder weapon, a .25-caliber automatic.

James Barnes being brought into custody.

Blood on the kitchen floor shows where Barnes attacked 92-year-old Molly Hawk.

Tellers Helen Barnard and Diana Jackson were brutally slain by bank robber David Holland—who was caught on the bank's security camera.

Belinda Jo Stark,
one of Robert Maury's
three victims.

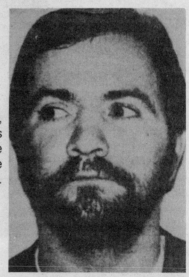

Robert Maury,
who offered cops
clues to the
killings—for the
reward money.

Angeles. The 36-year-old attorney had prosecuted 12 murder cases, but this was to be the first case in which he would seek the death penalty.

The murder trial got under way in early April 1991, in Superior Court Judge Theodore Piatt's courtroom in Pomona. Henry A. Bastien, the deputy public defender assigned to handle the defense case for Martin Navarette, argued that the defendant was too drunk and stoned on cocaine to have been capable of premeditating the killings. A defense witness testified that he and Navarette had shared some rock cocaine in the laundry room of the apartment on the day of the crimes.

But John Urgo, using four fingerprints taken from the crime scenes that matched print samples from Navarette, the shoe print made by him outside the window of one of the victims, the blood samples, and other evidence, argued that Navarette was clearly guilty of the murders. Urgo convinced the jury that Navarette knew very well what he was doing, pointing out that after stealing Converse's pickup, the defendant had even called Elena Silva for a date, "as if he was celebrating the event."

After deliberating for only six hours, the jury came in with a verdict on April 16, 1991. Even though officials firmly believed that Navarette had been the burglar who raided the Converse apartment the day before the murders, the jury found him not guilty of that burglary. On the critical indictments, multiple murder and robbery, the jurors unanimously found Navarette guilty. Eight days later, the same panel of 12 recommended that Navarette receive the death penalty.

Judge Piatt was faced with the decision whether to

accept the jury's recommendation or to reduce the sentence to life without the possibility of parole.

The judge read an emotional letter from a friend of Alexandria Hickman's. In it, the friend wrote, "It is true that Martin Navarette is a young man and that it is a tragedy to end his life. However, those he brutally murdered, without provocation, are dead—law-abiding, kind people who were hurting no one. Alex was a credit to her family, church, and community. She even tried to help Navarette's [girlfriend], a battered woman. While it may be true that Martin Navarette had previous substance abuse problems and that they may have affected his judgment, many people abuse alcohol and drugs, but do not become cold, premeditated murderers and rapists." The writer asked the judge to sentence Navarette to the maximum penalty allowable—death.

On August 14, 1991, Judge Piatt agreed with the jury and the letter writer. He sentenced Martin Navarette to die in the gas chamber, and sent him to San Quentin Prison to join the more than 330 other prisoners on California's death row.

EDITOR'S NOTE:
Rosa Ruiz, Joe Cardenas, and Elena Silva are not the real names of the persons so named in the foregoing story. Fictitious names have been used because there is no reason for public interest in the identities of these persons.

"THEY SAWED THE HOMO'S HEAD OFF FOR 73 CENTS!"

by Bruce Gibney

NEWPORT BEACH, CALIFORNIA
MARCH 12, 1982

The Inn Spot is located one block off the Coast Highway in the tourist-laden art colony of Laguna Beach, California. It is something of a neighborhood place which offers an old English pub ambiance, a small dance floor and a dimly lit atmosphere where patrons can socialize without risk of being seen.

Women stop by but rarely stay for long; the Inn Spot is a gay bar, one of many in Laguna Beach, and the men have little interest in the opposite sex.

At eight o'clock Sunday evening August 27, 1978, a realtor from Corona del Mar named Ruben Martinez slipped into the bar and shouldered his way to the front. Dressed in a red polo shirt and beige slacks, he had come from a seafood meal at a nearby restaurant and was looking for a quiet drink with the guys.

"Beer," he told the bartender. While waiting for his brew, he spun on the bar stool and sized up the crowd.

It was a typical Sunday night gathering: gray haired painters, sports jacketed businessmen, tank topped antique dealers conversing or staring at other men, most of them young and alone.

About half of the crowd was either standing at the bar or seated at small tables that lined the walls. The rest stood in small clusters or were dancing on the parquet dance floor. The music was loud but not deafening as it was on Fridays and Saturdays.

Cupping the cold beer with one hand, Ruben cut across the bar and joined two friends he noticed upon entering. He stayed to chit-chat for several minutes before moving on to another group seated several tables down.

Sometime before ten o'clock Ruben Martinez struck up a conversation with a young man standing at the bar who was new to the Inn Spot. He went by the name of Fred, was in his early twenties, and had light blond hair and a boyish face. He was apparently alone.

Friends recalled seeing Ruben talk to the young man. But no one saw him talking to the two young men who sauntered into the bar at around 10:15 p.m. Nor did they see Ruben leave with them.

Their identities, in fact, would remain a mystery for well over a year.

Ruben's real estate office was located in the business section of Corona del Mar, a short commute from his unpretentious two bedroom condo on Iris Street. Business was brisk at the office Monday morning and the other realtors began to worry when Ruben did not show up to work.

At seven that evening a buddy went by the Iris Street condo to see if Ruben was all right. As he told police, "I saw Ruben's Datsun wasn't in the driveway so I figured he might have gone somewhere. Then I went to the front door and saw it was ajar."

He rang the doorbell and yelled inside, but the only response to his announcements was a small hungry poodle that ran into the living room yelping for food.

The sight of Ruben's four-footed companion did little to assuage the friend's mounting dread. It was inconceivable that Ruben would suddenly leave home without making sure that his dog was adequately provided for.

Standing now in the living room, he sensed that something was terribly wrong. A few seconds later he found out what it was. And terrible wasn't the word for it.

At 8:15 p.m. the quiet community of Iris Street was disrupted by the wail of Newport Beach police cruisers arriving in front of Ruben's condo. The cruisers were soon complemented by cars from the Orange County Sheriff's Crime Lab and the county coroner.

The first detective on the scene was Newport Beach Detective Al Fischer. Going into the home, he noticed the small living room with its white pine paneling and Mediterranean-style furnishings was neat and in order.

The same could not be said for the master bedroom. Drawers had been yanked from bureaus and dumped upside down on the bed in what appeared to be a frantic search for money and valuables.

The ransacking, however, had produced very little loot. Ruben lived simply and kept very little jewelry and money in his home. After a relative went through the house, it was determined that nothing of value had been stolen in the gory slaying.

In fact, the 45-year-old realtor had been murdered for just 73 cents.

Neighbors described Ruben as a friendly, good-natured sort who entertained quietly at his home. One recalled a conversation in which Ruben said he had recently been spending his spare time remodeling his condo with wood paneling and didn't have much time for socializing.

"He was a good guy, but I can't say I knew him very well," the neighbor explained. "He lived his own life and kept to himself."

Fischer determined the time of death from an electric clock that had been pulled from the socket and stopping the hands at 11:43.

The murder was one of the most gruesome the veteran sleuth had investigated in his years on the force.

The 45-year-old realtor was found laying face up with his hands at his side, his battered face and head outlined in a puddle of dried blood. The initial examination indicated the victim's throat had ben cut. But additional observation revealed the slit mark across the throat extended back to the spinal column and that the head was attached to the neck by only a pencil-thin piece of tissue. The neck had not been slit; it had been sawed through.

The detectives noted that prior to the fatal injury to the throat, Ruben had been beaten in the front and top of the head with a heavy object that had broken the skin and left orange waxy deposits embedded in the scalp.

"What was he beaten with?" the detective asked himself. The condo was searched but no object with the distinctively colored wax was found. The search also failed to produce the weapon that was used to cut the throat. There was only one logical conclusion drawn from this, and that was the weapons had been taken by the killers when they left.

One of the weapons was recovered the following morning. Detective Fischer got a call at the Newport Beach station from Orange County crime technician Scott Cade who breathlessly told him: "Grab your seat, Al, because you are not going to believe this."

Cade had left the crime scene on Iris Street at four in the morning too tired to think straight and wanting only to get back to his home in Mission Viejo. Normally he would have taken the Newport Beach freeway, but on impulse decided to take the leisurely drive along Coast Highway.

Cade said he was south of Corona del Mar and was almost to the Laguna Beach city limits when the headlights picked up a bright orange object on the side of the road. The color of the object caught his attention because he had just spent several hours wondering about the waxy stuff found imbedded in Ruben's scalp.

Pulling off the road, he ran back and discovered the orange object was a pumpkin-sized candle that had apparently been tossed out on the road and had cracked upon impact. Cade didn't know what the odds were but they had to be astronomical to drive down a road he rarely took and find the murder weapon by the roadside.

But this is, in fact, what happened. The candle shards were wrapped in plastic and taken to the Orange County Crime Lab where blood and hair samples were found embedded in the wax. Additional analysis revealed the blood had the same enzyme characteristics as the victim's and that their hair follicles were also similar.

One mystery was solved. Ruben had been beaten with the massive chunk of candle wax that had come from his home. The killers had then made their escape south on the Coast Highway and tossed the weapon out on the pavement.

Unfortunately, the rest of the case did not fall into place so easily.

Three days after the murder, Ruben's Datsun B210, which had been missing from the driveway when investigators arrived, was found abandoned in Laguna Beach. There were no prints on the car, and no witnesses who remembered the driver or knew how long it had been parked there.

The car had been abandoned three blocks from the Little Shrimp restaurant where Ruben was seen eating his dinner alone. The affable realtor was later seen at the Inn Spot bar where he went to sip a few beers and check out the scene.

Detective Fischer learned from a witness at the Inn Spot about a young man with blond hair who Ruben had been chatting with before 10:00 p.m.

A police artist worked up a sketch of the man which Detective Fischer took back and showed to people in the bar.

One thought the man's name was Fred. Others shrugged. There were, after all, many young blond-haired men hanging around gay bars who matched the sketch. No one knew Fred's last name or knew where he might be found.

Detective Fischer went back to the bar on Sunday night to see if Fred would make another appearance.

But he never did and police never found him.

The investigation dragged on through September and into October. Tips phoned into police headquarters alerted detectives to several suspects who had victimized homosexuals and often hung around gay bars.

Fischer, now joined by Detective Darryl Youle, followed up on the tips. Posing as homosexuals, they toured gay bars from Newport Beach to West Hollywood, trying to get a lead, any lead, that might put them closer to finding Ruben's killer. After two months, they got to know their way around the gay bar scene, but were no closer to learning the identity of Ruben's killer than that first day of the investigation.

By Christmas, the cops had run out of clues. Ruben's name had dropped out of the newspapers, and it was business as usual at the Inn Spot and the other places the realtor used to frequent. The condo was sold, and his friendly poodle was given to relatives, and his job at the realty company was given to someone else. Except for his few close friends, his family and the two Newport Beach detectives, it was as if the victim never existed.

Then, almost a year later, Ruben's name leaped from the unsolved murder files when the detectives were contacted by the police in Costa Mesa.

On September 11, 1979, a convicted robber on parole from Nevada was arrested in Costa Mesa for public intoxication. It was a misdemeanor rap, but the ex-con didn't want to be sent back to the pen and offered police a deal: his freedom for the name of a killer.

Eager to hear his story, Detective Fischer and

Youle raced to the Costa Mesa jail.

The informant was a character named Bill Guyton. He related that in late 1978 or early 1979, he was driving along the Coast Highway near Laguna Beach when he stopped to pick up a friend of his who was hitchhiking.

The friend was John Allen Keith, 21, of San Clemente. Guyton said they had been buddies since high school days and shared a mutual interest in motorcycles.

They drove to Keith's home in San Clemente where they drank a few beers and worked on Keith's motorcycle.

"We were working on the bike when he told me he and a friend of his had killed some guy in Laguna Beach," Guyton said.

The town was wrong. But everything else Guyton remembered of the conversation fit the unsolved slaying in Newport Beach.

"Keith said he and his buddy had made friends with a guy in a homosexual bar in Laguna Beach and returned to the man's home late that evening.

"Keith said they beat the . . . out of the dude, ransacked his house and left him to die," Guyton said. "Keith said they only made 73 cents in the deal and that it was hardly worth killing over."

The two became worried that they might have left fingerprints in the house for police to find and decided to return on Keith's motorcycle to wipe the place clean.

"My buddy said they walked into the bedroom and the guy was still alive!" Guyton told detectives. "He was even trying to get up."

The two solved the problem by taking a miter box

saw from the closet and sawed the man's head off.

The detectives ran a crime check on John Keith. They learned he had spent time in the California Youth Authority in 1977 for the burglary of a motel and had been on parole for two years.

The informant said he didn't know the name of Keith's buddy who had participated in the murder, which presented the Newport Beach sleuths with something of a problem. How were they going to learn his name without tipping their hand to John Keith?

They ran crime checks on Keith's friends and inmates he had met while at the California Youth Authority. They also put Keith under surveillance, tailing him when he hitchhiked home from work, or visited a friend, and even once stopped to give him a ride.

Nothing worked. Sleuths had a list of names, a lot of crime reports, but nothing that pointed the finger at the killer's accomplice.

Then they got lucky. While checking through a list of speeding tickets, Youle discovered that Keith had been stopped for speeding in Laguna Beach at 1:30 a.m. August 28, 1977.

Youle's eyes were almost burned out from reading the computer list of tickets, but this one made him stop. He thought about the clock that had been pulled from the wall in Ruben's bedroom, freezing the hands at 11:43.

"The guy was stopped just two hours after the fight in the bedroom," the detective said to his partner.

The ticket had been issued by Laguna Beach Patrol Officer Will Yourex. Though it had been written

13 months ago, Yourex remembered the incident because Keith had made the remark, "Hey, I know you. You used to work the beach area south of here."

The patrol officer remembered Keith wore a nylon jacket and helmet and didn't remove his gloves when he signed the ticket. There was a passenger on the back of the bike, but Yourex didn't pay much attention to him. "The guy seemed about the same age as Keith and had light blond hair," was all the patrol officer could recall.

The detectives decided to use Officer Yourex as bait to trick Keith into revealing the name of the passenger. On October 26th, Yourex went to the repair shop in Mission Viejo where Keith worked, with the story that he wanted estimates for work needed done on his sister's Honda.

The detectives had supplied the patrol officer with several ploys to work the conversation around to the night the ticket was issued, but they weren't necessary.

"I remember you," Keith told the officer. "You wrote me that speeding ticket in Laguna Beach."

"That's right," Yourex said, picking up the cue. "You and that friend of yours. I forget his name."

"Dave Bics," Keith beamed. "We must have been going ninety before you stopped us. We were really flying that night."

But flying not half as high as a couple of sleuths named Fischer and Youle, who now had the name of the second suspect.

Nineteen-year-old Anthony David "Dave" Bics lived in Dana Point near San Clemente and had been a friend of Keith's since high school. Bics had been the second man arrested in the motel burglary in

230

1977 that sent Keith to the California Youth Authority.

The detectives knew who the players were in the real-life murder mystery, but they still needed more evidence before making the arrests.

They got a little help when Bill Guyton called them at the station and said he had some information they might want.

"I know the name of the second killer," Guyton said after meeting with the sleuths. "But it is going to cost you this time. I need some bread."

Detective Youle produced a mugshot of Bic and took pleasure in watching Guyton's face sag.

"Damn, you guys already know who it is," he said dejectedly.

"We can still work a deal," Detective Fischer said. "But you are going to have to go to work for us."

The lawmen knew Keith had recently lost the use of his motorcycle due to a speeding violation and was forced to hitchhike from the repair shop in Mission Viejo to his girlfriend's house in San Clemente, where he was staying.

The two decided to make Keith's misfortune work to their advantage. They rigged Guyton with a body mike and told him to pick up Keith after work hitchhiking and give him a ride back to San Clemente. During the trip, Guyton was instructed to work the conversation around to the murder, which the two had earlier discussed in Keith's garage. The conversation would be recorded, with the detectives following Guyton in an unmarked car.

Getting the 21-year-old biker to talk proved to be no problem. As they cruised down the freeway, he could barely contain his excitement as he told about the gory slaying of the 45-year-old realtor. He said the only time he was scared was when stopped by a cop in Laguna Beach for speeding. "Bics told me to just act cool and not to take off my gloves when I signed the ticket because I had blood on my hands."

A similar meeting was arranged with Dave Bics. The shaggy-haired accomplice was more reluctant to talk about the "73-cent" murder than his enthusiastic friend, but after some probing, he admitted taking part in the slaying.

With tapes in hand, Fischer and Youle went to the Orange County District Attorney's Office. Their mood was euphoric. The statements conformed to everything they knew about the case. There could be no mistake; they had the right guys.

Their euphoria was shortlived, however, when after a meeting, Deputy DA Dave Carter told them the incriminating tapes might be thrown out of court because road noise and other sounds made them inaudible or unintelligible.

"I might get a conviction," he admitted. "But it would be chancey. Before I file charges, I want better tapes."

Youle and Fischer could not hide their disappointment. They had spent a lot of man-hours on the case, only to be told their efforts weren't good enough.

Retiring to a bar after the meeting with DA Carter, the two began kicking around ideas on how to get the necessary tapes.

"If Carter wants tapes, we will give him tapes," Fischer said.

"Pictures too," Youle grumbled. "Tapes and pictures."

"Hell, while we are at it, we might as well make a movie," Fischer suggested.

The detectives suddenly became more animated than the two beers apiece would indicate. They had played plenty of roles in the 14-month murder case, but this would be the best yet; Fischer and Youle were going to become movie directors.

Concocting a scheme to get the necessary evidence, the two began searching for a motel that would serve as the location for their first movie.

After some searching, they found a modest place close to the freeway and in the suburban town of El Toro. They went to the manager and identified themselves as brothers-in-law who wanted adjoining rooms for a family reunion they had planned. They tactfully did not tell him they would be drilling a hole through the adjoining wall, or that the family reunion consisted of a couple of black sheep who had sawed off a man's head for 73 cents.

After checking out the accommodations and thumping the wall to make sure it was made of wall board and could be drilled through, the two paid for two days lodging in advance and went to work.

The hole was drilled and a one-way mirror placed over the hole in the room where Keith and Bics would be lured. The motel light bulbs were replaced with 10-watters to provide proper illumination, and microphones were installed in several locations to ensure good quality sound. The taping and recording equipment was then set up in the other room and sound and video checks were run.

After a few test runs, the badge carrying filmmakers were ready. All they needed were the actors.

Guyton was contacted and told to meet the detec-

233

tives at the motel. Upon arriving, he was told the tape made in the car was not satisfactory and a second one would have to be recorded in the motel room. They did not mention the meeting would be videotaped as they did not want their first film ruined by a self-conscious actor, who might inadvertently tip off the quarry.

Guyton was supplied with a cover story that he had been out of town and wanted to see his friends and talked over some business. After several dry runs, Guyton called Keith in San Clemente on November 19th.

"I just got into town," Guyton said. "Let's get together."

"Sure thing," Keith said.

Guyton picked up Keith and after a sandwich at a nearby coffee shop, they returned to the room.

While the video camera rolled, Guyton said he was short on money and had given some thought about "rolling queers" in Laguna Beach.

"I figured it would be a cinch," Guyton said. "There are lots of queers in Laguna Beach and I could just pick up some guy in a bar like you did a couple of years back."

The conversation was worked around to the murder of Ruben Martinez.

Keith broke into a wide smile. "It was nothing killing that guy," he said. Then, reenacting the crime, Keith showed how he took the miter box saw from the closet and sawed through the victim's neck. "It was bloody," Keith admitted. "It looked like a National Geographic film in there. I felt like taking a felt pen and write 'dead' across his forehead, but I didn't do it."

The confession took just 22 minutes. Afterwards, Guyton drove Keith to San Clemente and then called Bics.

Bics was shy about talking and the video camera was almost out of tape before he admitted to taking part in the crime.

The investigators took the tapes to the Orange County DA and held a private screening for Dave Carter. The tapes would not win any awards for directing, but there was no denying the power of the video document. After the lights were turned on, Carter shook hands with both detectives and said he would file charges immediately. "You guys did a hell of a job," he said leaving the room. He sounded almost apologetic.

John Allen Keith and Anthony David Bics were both arrested for the robbery and murder of Ruben Martinez. On December 19, 1981, Keith was found guilty of first-degree murder and received a sentence of life in prison without the possibility of parole.

On March 12, 1982, Anthony Dave Bics was found guilty of the same charges and received a sentence of 25 years to life in prison with the possibility of parole. Both are serving their sentences in the California prison system.

EDITOR'S NOTE:
Bill Guyton is not the real name of the person so named in the foregoing story. A fictitious name has been used because there is no reason for public interest in his true identity.

"GREEDY GRANDSON AND HIS DEVIL-WORSHIPPING GANG!"

by Gary Ebbels

LAS VEGAS, NEV.
NOVEMBER 5, 1985

It was shortly past high noon November 6, 1984, and a young woman was headed for one of the more fashionable areas of Las Vegas. She had been living in a trailer with her boyfriend behind the home of his grandparents. But the romance had abruptly ended, and she was on her way to the trailer to pick up her belongings. She had moved out just a day or two earlier.

She pulled her car into the driveway of the grandparents, Carl and Colleen Gordon, and shut off the engine. The grandparents had a key to the trailer and she would need to borrow it to get inside and get her things.

The Gordons generally stuck pretty close to home, so there was little doubt they would be in. But much to the woman's surprise, no one answered her knock. She tried the door and found it to be open.

This was indeed strange. The couple normally locked up the house when they left it. She went inside to see if anything was wrong.

There was no one in the living room, but she did notice there was blood at the foot of the staircase. A chill spread through the young woman's body. Something was radically wrong.

Gingerly, she walked to the door of the couple's bedroom. She opened it slowly.

A tightness gripped her throat and nausea swept over her. There, in the bedroom, were the blood-soaked bodies of Carl Gordon, 58, and his wife, Colleen, 57. The bedroom itself had been ransacked.

The woman ran from the bedroom to the kitchen and used a telephone there to call the Las Vegas Metropolitan Police Department. She told the Metro operator of her grisly discovery. The operator told her to wait at the Gordon home. Officers, detectives and identification experts would be there shortly.

The first to arrive were uniformed officers who had been patrolling in the area in a black and white unit. Next came Homicide Detectives Michael Geary and Burt Levos, and behind them came a van with a lab crew.

The uniformed officers were inside the house checking out the bedroom when the detectives arrived on the scene. One of the officers briefed the two sleuths upon their arrival.

He said it appeared both Carl and Colleen Gordon were victims of multiple gunshot wounds. Autopsies would have to be conducted to ascertain the official cause of death.

Levos briefly questioned the young woman who had found the corpses. They talked outside the house. She told him how she had stumbled onto the bodies while trying to get the key to the trailer in the backyard.

She explained she had been living with the Gordons' 20-year-old grandson, Dale Flanagan, but had recently broken ties with him. She said she was merely there to pick up her things and get out of his life once and for all.

Geary joined Levos outside the house. As the two detectives talked with the witness, another car pulled into the driveway. It was driven by Dale Flanagan.

He parked it, got out and approached one of the officers who stood in the driveway. He asked him what was going on, but the officer gave him no answer. He simply told him to ask the detectives who were in charge of the case. He pointed them out.

Flanagan walked over to the sleuths. He never acknowledged his former girlfriend. He asked one of the sleuths what brought them to the home of his grandparents.

When he was told the two had been murdered, he shrugged and walked back to his car. Then he drove on to his trailer.

When they were through questioning the young woman, the detectives walked to the trailer. Flanagan answered their knock. The two said they had some questions.

Flanagan agreed to answer them. But he turned out to be little help as a witness. When he was asked if he had heard any gunshots in the Gordon house the previous night, he responded that he had not been home. He explained that he had been out the entire night and was just now getting home. He had been gone from his trailer, he claimed, for approximately the last 24 hours.

When asked if his grandparents' home had ever

before been burglarized, Flanagan said it had not. As far as he knew, this was the first time they had ever been victims of a crime, he said.

Since the bedroom and some other rooms in the house had been ransacked, the detectives assumed the Gordons were murdered when they came upon a burglar in their home. They asked Flanagan if anything was missing from his trailer.

He replied everything in the dwelling appeared to be in order. He said the door had been locked, just the way he left it, and the interior had not been ransacked. He told the detectives the burglar must have quit after killing his grandparents and ransacking their house.

Before the sleuths left the trailer, they gave Flanagan their telephone number at headquarters, and asked him to call, should he think of something to add to his statement.

They went back to the Gordon house, where the lab crew was finishing up. The bodies had already been removed to the morgue downtown. An identification expert with the lab crew told Geary and Levos that very little physical evidence had been found in the house. He said some latent fingerprints had been lifted in the bedroom, but that was about it for crime scene evidence.

With that, the probers returned to headquarters to begin a preliminary file on the case. As they worked up the file, they realized they shared a common hunch. They were both bothered by the fact that Dale Flanagan had shown no emotion upon finding out his grandparents had been murdered.

Sometimes relatives and loved ones go into a slight state of shock upon finding out about a murder and show little emotion at the time. But at least they show some emotion. All Flanagan did was shrug and walk away.

But they knew their hunch was just that—a hunch—and that it was their job to dig up evidence that would convict the burglar who had gunned down the upper middle-class couple in their own home.

It was mid-morning, November 7th, when Geary and Levos were furnished with the autopsy report. It confirmed that the victims had died of multiple gunshot wounds. It also showed that they were killed with two different weapons. One was used on Colleen Gordon and the other had been used on Carl. The bullets removed from the bodies were booked into the police evidence vault.

While it was possible one burglar carried two weapons and had used them both on the Gordons, sleuths reasoned it was more likely that two burglars, each carrying a single weapon, had broken into the home and that each had taken on one of the Gordons—two victims, two killers.

So now the detectives found themselves searching for a pair of ruthless burglars with no clues as to their identities. The search would not be an easy one. They put the word out on the street that they were looking for two murdering burglars. The usual snitches and stool pigeons were asked to join in the search.

A week went by, and then another, and nothing turned up on the street. Still another week passed, and the trail grew ever colder.

November was nearing an end when the detectives decided to call on Dale Flanagan again. They had not heard from him since the day the bodies were discovered, so there was no reason to believe he would be able to offer them anything new. But they had nothing else with which to work at this time, so they figured they had nothing to lose by talking with him — even if it appeared they had nothing to gain, either.

Their knock on the trailer door was answered by a young woman. When they asked for Flanagan, she said he was not home. She explained she had moved in with Flanagan a couple of weeks earlier. She had known him for some time, she continued, and had decided to move in when his last girlfriend moved out.

The woman said she expected Flanagan home by the early part of the evening. She would not be there, though, because she was a dancer at a local night spot.

The detectives asked her to have Dale call them as soon as he got in.

Flanagan's call to headquarters came the following morning. He told the detectives he had nothing more to say to them. He said he would have called them sooner if anything further concerning the double homicide had popped into his mind.

There was nothing more the sleuths could do at this point in the investigation. The case would remain open, of course, but there was little cause for optimism.

November turned into December, and the windy days in the Las Vegas valley were almost as cold as the trail to the burglars who had murdered Carl and Colleen Gordon.

Geary and Levos were in their offices at headquarters on the morning of December 6th when a familiar face popped in. It was the woman who was living with Flanagan, and she was accompanied by a uniformed officer. The two walked into Levos' office. Levos immediately summoned Geary on the intercom.

The uniformed officer told the two detectives that he and the woman had been friends for years and that she had contacted him this morning with important information concerning the Gordon murder case. He then directed the woman to tell the detectives what she had told him.

She settled herself into a seat in front of the desk and told the following incredible story:

She had moved in with Flanagan only because she thought he was involved in the murder. She had always wanted to be an investigator, and this case had given her the chance to see how well she could do in the field. She had known Flanagan casually for a long time.

She knew there was no love lost for the Gordons on his part. She had never heard Dale say anything nice about the couple, and had, on many occasions, heard him speak badly of his grandparents. With this in mind, she offered to be his next live-in girlfriend.

She also knew his temperament. She knew how he could react in certain situations.

On December 5th, she managed to pull all the right strings. She picked a fight with him. She had tried this method several times since moving in, but each time the chemistry hadn't been just right. But this day it was.

In the middle of the argument Flanagan snapped,

"I killed my grandparents! What do you think of that?"

When she finished the story, the young woman was asked to wait in the lobby for a few minutes.

After she exited the office, the detectives had just one question for the uniformed officer — could she be believed?

The officer said she most certainly could. He confirmed the fact that she had always wanted to be an investigator. He also said she was a person who would not make up the story of the Flanagan confession just to make the world think her a crafty investigator.

The woman's story provided probable cause for the arrest of Dale Flanagan. A warrant was obtained, but no immediate arrest was made because Flanagan had dropped from sight. It was presumed he feared the woman had gone to the police with his confession to her.

The detectives periodically checked his trailer in the days to come. On December 12th they hit pay dirt. They found Flanagan at home. He was read his Miranda rights, handcuffed, placed in their unmarked car and driven to headquarters.

The Miranda warning gives a suspect the right to remain silent. But Flanagan chose to talk. He readily admitted he was involved in the slayings, but said he wasn't going to take the rap alone. He said five other young men joined him in the crime.

He said the others were Michael Walsh, 16, Johnny Ray Luckett, 18, Randy Moore, 20, Roy McDowell, 19, and Herb Johnson. All but McDowell were into devil worship, but the murders were not committed in the name of Satan, said Flanagan.

Flanagan admitted to only limited participation in the slayings.

Warrants were prepared for the arrest of the five men he named as accomplices. McDowell and Luckett were arrested in Las Vegas within the next few days. Johnson saved the authorities the trouble of looking for him. He turned himself in when he found out there was a warrant on file for his arrest.

By mid-December, all but Walsh and Moore had been arrested and jailed in lieu of high bail. The remaining two had apparently fled the jurisdiction, but their arrest warrants remained on file.

There was yet another young man who was named by Flanagan at the December 12th confession, but no warrant was ever prepared for him. Flanagan said this young man was with them at Moore's house when the murder was planned but did not go to the Gordon home. The young man was questioned by the detectives, and he agreed to be a witness against the other six.

He told the detectives that money was the motive for the murder, and that the house was ransacked to make it look like a burglar did it. He explained Flanagan had it in his head that he was named beneficiary in at least one of his grandfather's life insurance policies.

As it turned out, he was not named in the policies at all, nor was he named in any will.

December was in its final days when an Arizona Highway patrolman stopped an auto driven by Michael Walsh near the Nevada border. Walsh may not have realized it is routine for police officers to radio headquarters for outstanding warrants every time they pull over a motorist for a violation. Maybe he didn't realize that a warrant issued in Nevada would be broadcast to police departments in every state of the union.

Whatever the reason, Walsh waited patiently in his car while the highway patrolman returned to his vehicle to radio his headquarters. He never tried to flee.

When the patrolman was told of the warrant, he immediately placed Walsh under arrest on the murder charges. He was held in Arizona, and Geary and Levos were informed of his arrest. The young man waived extradition and was quickly brought to Las Vegas, where he was booked into the Clark County Jail.

This left only Randy Moore to apprehend.

It was late in January when Moore was arrested in Mexico. Authorities there checked him for outstanding warrants in his native United States and found out about the murder charges that had been lodged against him. He was held in a Mexican jail while Las Vegas authorities were informed of his arrest.

Mexican jails are no picnic, so Moore chose to waive extradition and be returned to the United States as soon as possible.

Once in Las Vegas, he was booked into the county jail, where he joined the other five. None were able to post the extremely high bail.

In the months to come, the case against the six defendants slowly worked its way through the judicial system. The prosecution was placed in the hands of Chief Deputy District Attorneys Dan Seaton and Mel Harmon. While they had self-serving confessions from all six, they lacked an eyewitness. They wanted the death penalty, but they knew a jury would be reluctant to hand one down, since each defendant admitted to only minimal participation, and none admitted to squeezing off the fatal shots.

A plea-bargaining agreement with the least-involved suspect appeared to be the only way out. The testimony of the young man who was at Moore's house when the killing was planned would not be enough, because he did not accompany the others to the crime scene.

It was the middle of summer, 1985, and the District Court trial for Flanagan and his gang was drawing near. Defense attorneys had exhausted all possibilities of springing their clients on a technicality, and all attempts had failed. The young men would take their chances with a jury.

The prosecutors, meanwhile, working with the detectives, went over the self-serving statements of the suspects time and time again.

While none would admit committing the actual killings, they all agreed on one thing — Johnson was the driver of the getaway car. He never left the vehicle and never went inside the house. Detectives decided to have a talk with him. And why would he refuse, if the prosecutors were willing to let him plead guilty to a mere manslaughter count, for which he would probably draw probation, in exchange for his cooperation?

As expected, Johnson was willing to tell the sleuths anything they wanted to know, and was also willing to turn state's evidence in exchange for the plea-bargaining arrangement.

He said that, as they drove away from the crime scene, Flanagan admitted to him that he shot his grandmother after grabbing her by the jaw and slamming her onto her bed. At about this time, Flanagan's grandfather came down the stairs to try to help her. Johnson went on to say that Moore boasted of gunning down the grandfather while he was still on the stairs. The man buckled when the slugs tore into his flesh, but managed to stumble into the bedroom, where he died with his wife.

An October trial was scheduled to be held in the courtroom of District Judge Donald Mosley. But before that trial date, Mosley accepted Johnson's plea of guilty to the reduced charge of manslaughter and placed him on five years' probation. As a result, he was released from the county jail.

With a week to go before the trial, Walsh got cold feet at the thought of going in front of a jury, being convicted and possibly sentenced to death. His attorney approached Seaton and Harmon about a plea-bargaining agreement. Since Walsh had not shot anyone, the prosecutors were willing to give him a deal.

But this deal would be nothing like the one Johnson got.

The prosecutors said they would allow Walsh to plead guilty to a pair of first-degree murder counts, and, in exchange, they would recommend a sentence of life in prison with the possibility of parole, the most lenient punishment there is for first-degree murder in Nevada. Since there were two counts, that would mean a double life prison sentence — Walsh would have to serve a minimum of 20 years behind bars before he gained parole eligibility.

Rather than take the chance of facing the executioner, Walsh took the deal. That same deal was then offered to Luckett and McDowell since they, too, had shot no one.

But they turned it down.

No deals were offered to Flanagan and Moore, since they had been the triggermen. The prosecutors wanted nothing less than the death penalty for them.

Flanagan, Moore, Luckett and McDowell went on trial as scheduled.

In view of the strength of the state's case, the quartet never had much of a chance for acquittal. The jury found them all guilty of first-degree murder.

It was now time for the jury to set the punishment. Under Nevada law, the convicting jury sets the punishment when the verdict is first-degree murder. This jury would have the option of sending the defendants to prison for life, with or without the possibility of parole, or to a date with the executioner.

During the penalty phase of the trial, Harmon and Seaton told the jurors they could live with it if they set the punishment for Luckett and McDowell at life without parole, but Flanagan and Moore must die for their crimes.

After deliberating a punishment for each defendant, the jurors returned to Judge Mosley's courtroom with a mixed bag.

Flanagan and Moore were sentenced to death by lethal injection. Luckett was sentenced to life in prison without the possibility of parole.

McDowell, though, somehow lucked out.

His punishment was set at life in prison with the possibility of parole. Like former co-defendant Walsh, McDowell would be eligible for parole in 20 years.

The two death penalties would be automatically

appealed. That appeal could go into the federal system, should it not succeed in the state court system. This means Flanagan and Moore will not be injected with poison for at least several years.

But those years will be spent in death row cells in the Nevada State Prison in Carson City.

EDITOR'S NOTE:
Herb Johnson is not the real name of the person so named in the foregoing story. A fictitious name has been used because there is no reason for public interest in the identity of this person.

"MANHUNT FOR THE GREEDY KILLERS IN THE RED CORVETTE!"

by Jerome Chandler

PELL CITY, ALABAMA
SEPTEMBER 25, 1984

When Ellen Johnson arrived at the home of Mrs. Franklin in Pell City, Alabama to do the housekeeping, she was puzzled that no one was home. The door was unlocked, so Ellen stepped inside. Lights were on, and she heard the sound of a television coming from the bedroom. But when she cautiously peeked through the bedroom door, the room was empty.

Ellen Johnson became concerned. She had not been told the Franklins were going away somewhere. Judy Franklin's purse was still in the house. Paul Sr.'s wallet lay in plain sight under the bed. As far as Ellen could tell, all the clothes and suitcases were in their usual places, as were two bottles of medicine Mr. Franklin took every day for a liver ailment.

Concern gave way to real worry, and Ellen decided to call police.

In the gathering dusk of a hot July evening, investigators from the St. Clair County Sheriff's Department arrived on the scene.

The lights were still on, and the TV was still playing. The family's two dogs, a big German Shepherd and a beagle cross breed, still roamed the yard. There was no evidence of burglary, robbery, or a struggle. No missing suitcases. No clothing gone. "Nothing is missing out of the house except them," said St. Clair County Chief Deputy Gene Newman.

Something was missing from the basement garage, however. Paul Franklin Sr.'s bright red 1968 model Corvette was not in its customary parking place. Beyond that, it was as if the Franklin family had vanished into thin air. "Something like this," declared Newman, "is about like what they show on the *Twilight Zone*."

Worried relatives declared emphatically that they would have been notified if the Franklins were planning a trip. Petite, pretty Judy Franklin was an avid gardener. She wouldn't have gone away without asking someone to care for her flowers.

As for Paul Franklin Sr., he had multiple health problems. It was completely out of character for him to simply pick up and go somewhere, leaving behind all his credit cards, his clothes, and even his medications.

Nor had handsome, lively ten-year-old Paul Jr. mentioned a trip to anyone.

"It's like they vanished into thin air," said Gene Newman.

Careful questioning in the area revealed that the Franklins were well liked by all of their neighbors. Judy Franklin was often seen jogging around the neighborhood, offering a smile and a friendly wave as she passed by. She was, according to one resident, "the sweetest woman that ever lived."

Her husband Paul was well known in the community, having made an unsuccessful bid for the office of coroner in the fall of 1982. In a newspaper interview given during the campaign, he described himself as a salesman who had previously worked in the insurance and investment fields. When asked about his qualifications for the coroner's position, Franklin stated: "I've had vast experience in multiple deaths," and spoke of retrieving bodies in Vietnam.

Police learned that on the evening of July sixth, a Wednesday night, Mrs. Franklin had spoken by phone with a neighbor. No one had seen or spoken with any of the Franklins since. Relatives reported trying unsuccessfully to reach the family by phone several times later that night. This seemed to narrow down the time of their disappearance from sometime after about 6:30 on July 6th.

"It's the most baffling thing in our county for a long time, or ever, for that matter," stated St. Clair County Coroner Charles Foreman.

Days passed. Careful investigation of the house and grounds by officers from the St. Clair County Sheriff's Department and the Alabama Bureau of Investigation turned up nothing new. The Franklins had not returned home, nor had they contacted anyone.

On Sunday, July 10th, the St. Clair County Sheriff's Department appealed to the public for help. Print and broadcast media were given these descriptions: Paul Franklin Sr., white male, age 34, height 5 feet, 6 inches, weight 160 pounds, brown eyes, brown hair. Judy Franklin, white female, age 34, height 5 feet 2 inches, weight 130 pounds, blue eyes, blonde hair. Paul Griffin Franklin Jr., white male, age 10, height 4 feet, weight 60 pounds, brown eyes, brown hair.

Newspapers and television were provided with a recent studio portrait of the missing family. Anyone with any information was asked to contact the St. Clair County Sheriff's Department.

Meanwhile, a massive search effort had been mobilized. Searching the rolling, wooded terrain from the air were ten National Guard helicopters, a state owned helicopter, and 20 small aircraft flown by volunteers. Investigators scouted the nearby Coosa River and Bald Rock Mountain, a local landmark, extending the search into the dense and somewhat foreboding Talladega National Forest.

"We've been over the county four times," said Chief Deputy Newman on Monday, July 11th. "Every day we get more concerned for the family."

Along with a description of the missing family, law enforcement officials had broadcast a description of the missing car. All available data on the red Corvette had also been fed into the National Crime Information Center's computer.

Six days had passed with no sign of the Franklins or the car. Their Pell City neighbors were uneasy and quite concerned, calling the situation "upsetting, difficult to accept, and just plain weird."

Early Monday morning, the phone rang in the police department of the nearby town of Childersburg. A local druggist had seen some of the publicity regarding the missing Pell City family and their car. A red Corvette, wasn't it? Well, here in his parking lot was a sometimes customer of his, a guy who every once in a while brought by a used car for him to look at. Today he was driving a bright red 'Vette. The customer said he had traded someone for the car, but something didn't feel quite right. The druggist was concerned. Childersburg police fed the car's description and tag number into the NCIC. The druggist's suspicions were justified. It was the Franklins' missing car.

Driving the candy-apple red Corvette was 26-year-old John Peoples. A native of nearby Talladega, Peoples made a living "trading cars," according to Chief Deputy Newman. He had a bill of sale for this one "a very suspicious bill of sale, scrawled on notebook paper," Newman recalled. The bill of sale gave Peoples the car, valued at about $9,000 in return for half interest in a supper club located in a small town near Childersburg.

A quick phone call to the club's owners revealed that Peoples owned no part of the club, although he did have operating rights, during some of the summer months. He had done some car trading with the club's co-owner. The trade had involved a 1977 Lincoln Continental. The man had no paperwork on the deal, but he emphatically denied ever selling or trading Peoples any ownership rights in the club.

Peoples was taken in for questioning.

"Investigators questioned him from about 3:00 p.m. until about 1:30 a.m. when he was finally charged with the theft of the vehicle," Newman said. "But as far as finding the family goes, we're no closer." Peoples was characterized by Newman as "not helpful," and Newman said there was "no useful evidence" in the car.

Speaking to the press, Newman announced, "We don't have any evidence that it's foul play or that it's not. We don't know how to treat it."

On Tuesday July 12, 1983, John Peoples was formally charged with theft by deception in Talladega Circuit Court. Bond was set at $25,000. Peoples remained in custody at the St. Clair County Jail. There was still no sign of the missing Franklin family.

The flamboyant young man with the red Corvette was a well known figure locally. Mustachioed, six-foot six inch, 275-pound John Peoples was active in the Childersburg P.T.A. The father of two small children, he "almost single-handedly" built a much needed playground for the elementary school. John was currently self-employed, running a small landscape business. He had worked several years for a Pell City construction firm and made a brief foray into grocery store ownership. The grocery stores, according to Talladega County Sheriff Jerry Studdard, had been the beginning of financial troubles for John Peoples. He "started with bad checks and could never gather back the money he made." But Peoples had no criminal record. Said Sheriff Studdard, "Most people, you write them a bad check, all they want is their money. John always made good."

Paul Franklin Sr. was part of the reason Peoples could always make good. The two had met when Peoples' landscape company did some work for Franklin at his home, and on some property owned by Franklin in Talladega County. According to Sheriff Studdard, "He and John got to be real good friends."

"I knew Franklin helped Mr. Peoples on different occasions . . . in one way or another," said Peoples' former boss at the construction company.

"He (Franklin) was good to John," Studdard recalled. "He (Peoples) tried to be a big wheel. Always wore a big hat, western boots, had a Lincoln Continental . . ."

As for the red Corvette, Peoples continued to assert that he had traded for it, fair and square. He had remarried recently, and had promised his new bride an antique Corvette for her birthday, knowing that his friend Paul Franklin had one, and hoping that Franklin might be willing to trade for it. And Franklin *had* been willing to trade for half interest in the supper club, claimed Peoples. He had a bill of sale to prove it, didn't he?

Peoples said he had picked up the car on Thursday morning. The battery was dead—he'd had to push the car out of the garage and jump start it, then nurse it along . . . No, he said, he hadn't seen Franklin that day . . .

That bill of sale was fast becoming more of a liability than an asset. It had been established that Peoples did not own half interest in the club he claimed to have traded for the car. Now, a Pell City District Attorney who had done legal work for the Franklins looked at the bill of sale and recognized the writing. It was *Judy* Franklin's. Sheriff Studdard recalled, "He recognized her writing and said, 'Something's not right here . . . Paul never let his wife sign anything. He always signed for himself.' "

On Wednesday July 13th, Peoples changed his statement. He told investigators, including A.B.I.'s Ed Traylor and Sheriff Studdard, that he had indeed gone to the Franklin house on Wednesday, July 6th, intending to trade for the Corvette. When he arrived, he said, a "Mafia connection" was already there,

256

hustling the Franklins out of their house and into a big black limousine driven by another Mafioso.

Concerned for his friend's safety, Peoples said he set out to follow the big black car, driving Paul's restored Corvette. The car gave him trouble, Peoples claimed, "stalling and choking out," making it difficult to follow the fleeing black limo.

Peoples persisted, nursing the sputtering sportscar east along Interstate 20 toward the nearby town of Lincoln. Suddenly, Peoples explained, the big black car left the Interstate and proceeded at high speed down a series of side roads off Highway 77. The Corvette continued to give trouble, said Peoples, but he somehow managed to keep the limo's taillights in sight.

Peoples said he had become confused, and was now following the kidnappers down roads he did not recognize. Suddenly, Studdard recalled Peoples as saying, the Mafia car stopped, and he heard the familiar voice of Paul Franklin Sr. calling "John . . . John . . ." Then Peoples said, according to Studdard, "I knew I didn't need to be there." Shaken and fearful, he drove away in the red Corvette. "I didn't call the law because the Mafia was involved," Peoples said, adding. "They'll kill ya."

According to Sheriff Studdard, who had known Peoples a long time, one thing bothered him about that statement. Studdard remarked to Traylor, "He says he 'don't know' where this road is. That's got to be a story. He's been all up and down these roads."

Investigators from several law enforcement agencies questioned John Peoples more closely about the stopping place of the black limousine, and he finally told them that it might have been somewhere along

257

County Road 377 South, coming back from Talladega. Area lawmen, guided by Peoples, began searching the heavily wooded areas off the two-lane blacktop.

At 6:30 p.m. on Wednesday July 13, 1983, in a pine thicket just a few feet from the road, investigators found the fully clothed bodies of Paul Franklin Sr., Judy Franklin, and Paul Franklin Jr. No apparent effort had been made to conceal the bodies, except for placing them a few feet off the road. It was hot summer, and the bodies were already beginning to decompose badly, but it looked as if they had been killed by blows to the head.

All three bodies were taken to Cooper Green Hospital in the nearby city of Birmingham, where authorities hoped an autopsy would help determine the cause of death. Talladega County Coroner Clarence Haynes placed the time of death at about midnight on Wednesday, July 6, 1983. Besides having been struck on the head with a blunt instrument, Mrs. Franklin appeared to have been shot once in the arm. That wound did not look fatal.

A shocked Pell City mourned its loss. Neighbors were saddened, outraged, frightened and perplexed by turns. What could possess someone to abduct an entire family from its home and brutally murder all the members? "A multiple murder is something that doesn't seem like it would happen around here," one neighbor said.

Another neighbor remarked, "This is the kind of thing you hear about someplace else, not the kind of thing you would expect here in Pell City, right at your back door. It's frightening to think about what has happened."

On Saturday, July 16, 1983, Paul Sr., Judy and Paul Franklin Jr. were buried in Birmingham.

Even a complete autopsy had been inconclusive in determining the cause of Paul Franklin Sr.'s death. His wife and son had died from "blunt force trauma," according to Coroner Haynes. Robbery appeared to have been the motive for the multiple slayings, said Talladega County District Attorney Robert Rumsey. Franklin "reportedly kept large sums of money in his home," he said. He declined to say if any money was missing from the Franklin home.

As to the location of the triple homicide, Talladega County Sheriff Jerry Studdard felt strongly that the killing had occurred in Talladega County. "I think the evidence is going to show it happened there, on County Road 377," said the granite-jawed veteran lawman.

On Thursday, July 14, 1983, another suspect in the Franklin murder case entered the picture. It was learned that this suspect, along with Peoples, had allegedly stolen a dump truck belonging to a relative. The man's name was Timothy Millard Gooden, and he was a third cousin of Peoples. When police questioned Gooden about the stolen dump truck, he casually volunteered the information that he had dropped Peoples off at the Franklin house on the night of July 6th, the date of their disappearance.

Law enforcement officials involved in the Franklin case asked Peoples if he would be willing to be polygraphed. Peoples agreed. Sheriff Studdard was in the car with Peoples on the ride to Gadsden, some hour and a half drive from the St. Clair County Jail where Peoples was being held. Peoples seemed calm and unafraid, chatting casually with the officers about his various brushes with the law and his friendship with the Franklin family. "You ought to have heard what all he told us," recalled Studdard, "I mean, it was . . . wild!"

For the polygraph operator in Gadsden, it was even wilder. Peoples began dictating the exact form questions should take. According to Studdard, Peoples said, "You ask me did I kill all three of them at one time. You ask me that." Informed that the person administering the polygraph would decide on both the form and the content of the questions, Peoples declared, "I'm not gonna take the polygraph."

The ride back to St. Clair County was considerably more subdued than the ride to Gadsden had been. Peoples was quiet and deep in thought. Studdard recalled saying to him, "John, if you've got anything you need to talk to me about, you let me know." Peoples made no response.

Upon his return to the St. Clair County Jail, Peoples began telling other inmates that he had powerful friends who were going to help him. Sheriff Studdard said, "He said he had some people were gonna come break him out." Concerned, St. Clair County lawmen transferred Peoples to Ashville, north of Pell City but still in St. Clair County. Once there, Peoples sent a note to the jailer requesting to speak with Studdard.

The burly lawman drove to Ashville, where Peoples told him, "I want to tell you what I really know . . . I can remember where they left Judy and them by the side of the road, I remember seeing some quilts and things that came from the Franklin house."

Investigators were dispatched to the area Peoples described. They found what appeared to be a twisted piece of a .22-caliber rifle.

A few days later, acting on a "tip," officers found the rest of the rifle in the woods near an abandoned foundry, not far from where the Franklin family's bodies had been found. A Pell City gun dealer identified the Winchester .22 caliber rifle as one Paul Franklin Sr. had purchased to deter pests, specifically free roaming dogs.

On July 19, 1983, John Peoples again requested to talk with Sheriff Studdard. Studdard and St. Clair County Sheriff Lewis Brown made the trip to Ashville. Studdard confronted Peoples, saying "John, we've checked all this out. There's no Mafia involved in this. There's just you and Timmy (Gooden)." Peoples looked thoughtful. Then, according to Studdard, he said, "I'll tell you about it if you promise you won't write anything down."

While Brown and Studdard listened, Peoples made the following statement: Paul Franklin Sr. had invested $45,000 in Mexican gold pieces. Early in the summer, he had called John Peoples to drive him to Birmingham with the gold, which he intended to sell. Peoples and Franklin sold the gold to a rare coin dealer in Birmingham for $50,000 making a profit of $5,000 on the deal. Peoples said he and Franklin were partners on the deal, all $50,000 of it. Franklin, as was his habit, received the money in cash, taking it back to Pell City in two bank bags. While Peoples watched, Franklin pried the grille off an air duct and threw the bags inside. Then he called a relative, who had loaned him the money to invest in the coins, informing that relative of the sale and offering im-

261

mediate repayment of the loan. Peoples said that he listened very carefully because "Paul promised him some of the money." The relative came and collected the $45,000 loan, leaving Franklin and Peoples with $5,000 profit, which, according to Sheriff Studdard, Peoples felt was half his. During the next week to ten days, Franklin spent about $2,000. Peoples became nervous about his cut, and on the night of July 6, 1983, went to the Franklin home with his "cousin" Timothy Gooden, to collect his share of the money.

When Franklin insisted the money was gone, Peoples began arguing with Franklin and forced him down the basement stairs. He pushed Franklin into the red Corvette, shouting to Timothy Gooden to follow in the truck with the woman and the boy. They drove to the woods near Talladega. At this point, Sheriff Studdard recalled, Peoples found himself unable to continue. "He never would say . . . he would always break down and cry when he got down to the point of hitting the woman and hitting the little boy."

Studdard said to Peoples: "John, you need to write a statement. He said, 'You write this out: I am guilty of the charge ya'll are investigating.' "

In August of 1983, a grand jury handed down indictments: John Peoples was charged with five counts of capital murder. He was also charged with robbery and kidnapping. His third cousin, Timothy Millard Gooden, was charged with kidnapping and robbery. Gooden and Peoples were to be tried separately on all counts, with Gooden slated to testify for the prosecution in Peoples' murder trial. Both men pleaded innocent to all charges.

Defense Attorney Pete Short filed several motions,

one for a change of venue, and several contending that most prosecution evidence was inadmissible, due to the fact that it was obtained while his client was being illegally held on a misdated warrant.

On Monday, November 28, 1983, a jury of ten women and four men (12 jurors, two alternates) was impaneled. Talladega County Circuit Judge Jerry Fielding had ruled not to dismiss the indictments or to move the trial to another location. He ruled favorably on a motion allowing Peoples to serve as co-counsel in his own defense, a position which would allow him to address the jury.

In opening arguments Wednesday morning, November 30th, Talladega County District Attorney Robert Rumsey told the jury they would learn that Peoples had forced Mrs. Franklin to sign a bill of sale for the car, and that he beat her and her son when his rifle failed to fire. "Probably her last movement," Rumsey told the packed courtroom, "was to grab the leg of the little boy."

In testimony given the same day, a former neighbor of John Peoples testified that she had seen Peoples driving a red Corvette at about 1:30 a.m. on July 7, 1983. "He got out of the car and said, 'How do you like my wife's early birthday present?'" the neighbor testified.

Then Ellen Johnson came to the stand. Sometime in June, she told the jury, Peoples had come to the Franklin home asking for money. "John came in and spoke: 'Paul, I need some money.' Mr. Franklin said, 'You owe me $1,500. I can't let you have anymore.'" Peoples then said, "I got to have some money somehow."

The most damning testimony against Peoples

came from Timothy Gooden. Prosecutor Rumsey explained that Gooden had agreed to be a witness in return for a recommended life sentence instead of facing the electric chair.

In three hours on the stand, the 24-year-old Gooden gave the following testimony: On July 6th, Peoples took Gooden to the Franklin home. He told Gooden to wait in the truck, explaining, "They've got a bad dog." Fifteen or twenty minutes later, Gooden testified, Peoples motioned him to come in. Paul Franklin Sr. and his wife were sitting at a table with "a bunch of papers" and a telephone "thrown down on a couch." According to Gooden, Peoples asked Franklin several times to sell him the red Corvette. Each time, Franklin refused, saying the car was for his son when he grew up. "John wanted the car bad," Gooden recalled. Peoples left the room for a moment, returning with a gun. He gagged and blindfolded the woman and the boy, then took Paul Franklin Sr. downstairs.

"I heard some commotion from the basement," Gooden said. Meanwhile, Gooden testified, he permitted Judy Franklin to use the bathroom, then took her and Paul Jr. downstairs. Franklin was lying on the floor. "I couldn't say if he was dead or alive."

Gooden said Peoples put Franklin in the Corvette, covering him with a blanket. Gooden put the woman and the boy in the truck and followed Peoples to a wooded area near Talladega County road 377. Gooden watched while Peoples dragged Franklin into the woods. Then Peoples returned to the truck. "She (Mrs. Franklin) asked him what is he going to do. He said it didn't matter," Gooden said. Then, "He led the woman and the boy into the woods . . .

The woman was asking, 'Please don't.' I heard a gun-shot and a woman screaming."

Gooden did not claim to have been an eyewitness to the actual act of killing. After that, said Gooden, he drove the truck home. Peoples came by about 2:00 a.m. and picked up the truck. He told Gooden, " 'I will fix you up later (with money).' I didn't see him no more," Gooden concluded.

In an attempt to discredit Gooden's testimony, Defense Attorney Pete Short revealed that the witness had stated something completely different during an earlier interview with police, that he dropped Peoples off at the Franklin residence and then went home to bed. Gooden, however, stuck to his present statement, "What I have said today is the truth," Gooden revealed.

On Wednesday, December 7, 1983, exactly five months to the day after the Franklin family had been reported missing, the jury declared that John Peoples had murdered them, recommending 11 to 1 in favor of the death penalty.

At the sentencing hearing on Friday, January 27, 1984, Defense Attorney Short argued that John Peoples should be sentenced proportionately with Timothy Gooden, who had admittedly assisted in the Franklins' abduction. "What kind of justice is it when one person walks down the aisle grinning?" Short asked.

Prosecutor Rumsey contended that Peoples "destined his life" when he "brutally murdered" the Franklins. "People like John Peoples lost their right to live," declared the D.A.

Judge Fielding sentenced Peoples to death in the electric chair, setting the execution date for April

13th. Peoples' face was expressionless.

Alabama state law mandates an automatic appeal.

Asked how he felt about the sentence, Short replied, "I don't have any particular reaction to the sentence. I never criticize judges."

Late in September of 1984, Timothy Millard Gooden pleaded guilty to robbery charges in the Franklin case. He was sentenced by Judge Fielding to life in prison.

EDITOR'S NOTE:
Ellen Johnson is not the real name of the person so named in the foregoing story. A fictitious name has been used because there is no reason for public interest in the identity of this person.

"SHOTGUNNED HER FOUR TIMES . . . FOR A RADIO"

by Charles Lynch

PITTSBURGH, PA.
OCTOBER 2, 1981

The seven-year-old schoolboy bounded through the front door at 2:30 p.m. and into the living room of his home located in the Beltzhoover section of the city. Besides it being cold outside on this 12th day of January, the youth was also happy just to be out of school and home.

The boy knew his mother would be at work, so he called out to his sister, who should have been home. When Brenay didn't answer, the boy thought she was playing a hiding game and he immediately began a playful search of the house.

It didn't take long for the "game" to end. Within a few minutes the spirited boy found his 22-year-old sister, Brenay Dobson, on the floor of the basement bathroom. She was sitting, slumped over, in a pool of blood with her wrists tied behind her back.

The shocked, frightened boy, realizing his sister was not playing games, ran upstairs and out the front door to a neighbor's house. He pounded on the door and when the neighbor answered, the boy exclaimed, "C'mere! Brenay is laying in the bathroom . . . everything is all red blood!"

The neighbor, noting the genuine terror in the boy's face, followed him back to the house. But before she could enter, the youth had to hold back one of the family's two Doberman pinchers which had been left to guard the house.

The woman, a close friend of the family and who had been in the house numerous times before, went directly to the basement where her fears were confirmed. She knelt on the floor and tried to feel a neck pulse. Unfortunately, Brenay was dead. The woman then went quickly upstairs to the dining room where she phoned the victim's mother at work, and then she dialed the police emergency number, 911.

The friend also phoned her husband, who is a city policeman, and asked if she should remove the ropes from the victim's wrists. The officer wisely told his wife not to touch anything and just wait for the police to arrive. The woman and the boy went out to the porch and waited the arrival of the police.

A district car from the Mt. Washington station arrived at the scene on Frampton Street and the officers then notified the homicide office. Detectives Tony Condemi and Lou Serafini took the call, ". . . a woman tied up and her throat cut . . . ," from the office at 3:22 p.m.

The investigators pulled into Frampton Street 25 minutes later and were met by the exiting medics. There was nothing the medics could do, except to pronounce the victim dead.

In the basement bathroom the officers observed

the victim, whose arms had been tied behind her back with rope, sitting on the floor with her back propped up against the bathtub. The officers noted that the tub was filled with warm water.

The victim was clothed in a brown sweater, a nightgown, two pairs of wool socks and a pair of wool slacks. The slacks were lying near the right foot and were all but off the body. A pair of panties were entangled in the slacks. The victim's hands were covered with cotton gloves.

It was found out later that there was nothing eccentric about Brenay, other than the fact that she was naturally cold most of the time. Januarys are usually among the coldest months of the year in Pittsburgh. The one in 1981 was particularly cold.

It was rather obvious to the veteran investigators that the woman had been shot, and not cut as they were previously informed. Two gaping wounds were evident in the middle of the chest, under the neckline. To the uninformed looking at the body, and particularly because the victim's head was slumped into her chest area, it would appear that the death was caused by a slit throat.

Because of the upper chest wound the woman had lost a lot of blood before her heart finally stopped pumping. The blood stained the front of her clothing and had pooled on the floor around her hips.

While checking the immediate area the detectives spotted a spent, .12 gauge shotgun shell lying on the floor outside the bathroom door just against the wall. James Cotter from the city's mobile crime unit dusted the shell for prints at the scene, but it came up clean. Nevertheless, it was retained as evidence.

Cotter swept the area for more evidence, scooping

up cigarette butts, scraps of paper and dusting for more fingerprints. He found one, of all places, on the front of the tub. Unfortunately, the print would have no bearing on the case.

Condemi and Sarafini, meanwhile, had left the basement and were checking the upper floors. It appeared all of the upstairs rooms had been ransacked, as though they had been "tossed" by a professional burglar. However, the house was in the process of being remodeled and there was a general appearance of disarray.

Because of the remodeling the front door was not locked, but Brenay's mother had two Doberman pinschers in the house to deter intruders, and to guard Brenay while she wasn't home. But when police arrived one of the dogs was outside in a backyard and the other locked in an upstairs bedroom.

The victim's mother, who had rushed home from her nearby job at a thrift store, was interviewed by Detectives Frank Amity and Joseph Stotlemyer. The 38-year-old divorcee tearfully told the officers that she had last seen her daughter at 11:45 that morning when the mother left for her job.

She said she rushed home when the neighbor phoned and told her to "get home fast . . . something is wrong with Brenay." The mother was surprised that someone could have gotten inside the house without being attacked by the dogs. The mother also informed the detectives that her children — Brenay, the boy who found her body, and a 15-year-old son — were not permitted to have guests in the house unless she was home.

There appeared to be an organized, family plan of security. One based on love and survival; but somehow, someone had cracked the seal and snatched one of the family's irreplaceable possessions — Brenay Dobson's life.

Brenay, who was described by family and close friends as slightly retarded, was a gentle person. Although in the past she held several different jobs, and was not home-bound, she was unemployed at the time of the murder. Detectives learned during background interviews that the victim, in fact, had a boyfriend. But the relationship was not serious. A girlfriend described Brenay as "a quiet, sweet girl who was lots of fun to be with."

After Amity and Stotlemyer talked to the mother of the victim, they then interviewed the victim's 15-year-old brother. The teenager confirmed what his mother had said about Brenay being careful of people, and had no idea who would want to kill his sister. When he left for school that morning at 7:30 Brenay was in bed and he didn't see her.

Other detectives ordered to the scene by Sgt. John Flannigan, head of the homicide squad, began to canvass the neighborhood for possible witnesses. They hit both sides of the street and knocked on doors, but no one saw anyone coming from the Dobson house. And no one heard any gunshots. Because of the frigid temperatures not many people were outdoors, and all of the homes, again due to the freeze, were closed up tight. In broad daylight the killer apparently walked away unnoticed.

When Flannigan went back to headquarters in the Downtown Public Safety Building in late afternoon he told reporters, "We're checking the possibility that robbery was a motive." The homicide chief said there was no forced entry at the two-story house but there was "evidence of a disturbance" in several rooms.

Before the investigators left the murder scene they told members of the victim's family, after they collected themselves, to check and see if any valuables were missing. When the question was asked earlier no one could say with certainty that anything was stolen.

But at seven that night Sgt. Flannigan received a phone call from the victim's 15-year-old brother who said his $129 cassette radio player was missing. His mother also reported that an assortment of jewelry had disappeared. Flannigan and his investigators now had a motive. The chief's earlier robbery theory was correct.

The day after the murder Detectives Ronald Freeman and Robert McCabe contacted Brenay's mother for more detailed information about the stolen radio. They visited the local discount store where the radio was brought and, by luck, the manager still had in stock several radios identical to the one stolen. A photo of the radio was taken by Cotter of the mobile crime lab, and prints were passed around to homicide squad members and district officers.

At about the same time, the autopsy on Brenay Dobson was being performed by Dr. Joshua Perper, chief forensic pathologist for the Allegheny County Coroner's Office. Perper noted immediately that the body had four entry wounds and that one wound had destroyed the woman's heart. Because of the heavy amount of blood found at the scene, the heart wound was probably the last inflicted upon the body.

Perper's pathological diagnosis noted that the body suffered "four shotgun wounds of the chest and abdomen." The doctor said the gun was fired at close range. The body examination also revealed the presence of a small amount of blood in the vagina. But the autopsy never revealed the source or reason.

The doctor also found a small amount of blood and small contusions in the anus. There was a possibility, considering the physical evidence, that Brenay had been sexually abused before she was murdered.

Since theft had been established as a motive, the officers felt they were dealing with either a robber or a burglar, one who perhaps was surprised in finding a woman in the house and killed her to keep her quiet. But the officers didn't know of any burglars who carried shotguns.

In checking the neighborhood for recent burglaries, the investigators discovered that a home near the Dobson residence had been burglarized and the thief took a pressure cooker, coffee pot, bedding and an Ithica shotgun. Brenay Dobson had been killed with a shotgun.

Some of the missing pieces of the case began falling into place, but the big break came seven days after the murder. On January 19 at 3:30 p.m. the victim's mother called the homicide office and said that her older son had seen his missing radio.

Detectives Stotlemyer and Amity went to the Dobson residence as soon as they received the call, and were informed by the youth that he had seen his radio earlier that day in the possession of another teenager near the basketball court at McKinley Park.

Within 10 minutes the two officers were at the playground. Arriving at the same time were Detectives John Leckie and Thomas McCue, who had also been sent on the detail by Flannigan. The detectives approached the youth holding the radio and asked where he got it. The boy truthfully told the detectives that he got the radio from his father as a post-Christmas present. The detectives climbed into a car, along with the teen, and went to his home.

The boy's father arrived a short time later and he told the detectives he bought the radio from a man he met at a local bar for $50. He said he knew the man only as "Tom."

The father seemed confused and evasive regarding the date he bought the radio, but his son passed on the information, "Monday, January 12." The same day Dobson was bound and murdered.

The man was taken to the Public Safety Building where he was interrogated again, he was told that he was going to be arrested for receiving stolen goods. By 8 p.m., and still facing arrest, the man decided to cooperate. He not only gave a better physical description of Tom, but said he thought he knew where Tom lived.

Detectives took a statement from the man explaining how he had possession of the radio, and in which he repeated that he bought it for his son. The man told the interrogators he knew the radio was worth more than $50, but he also insisted he didn't know it was stolen. He thought he had come across a "good deal."

Early the next morning, at 12:30 a.m. on January 20, the man took Detectives Flannigan, Rege Liberi and Glenn Hores to a building on Sylvania Avenue in Beltzhoover, where he said Tom lived, ". . . on the third floor."

No one was in the apartment, so the officers decided to wait for the suspect's return. Meanwhile, Amity and Condemi, accompanied by the man who bought the radio, cruised the area looking for Tom. They were on the road less than 10 minutes when the man pointed out Tom, who was driving a Chrysler Cordoba.

The detective car pulled up behind the car and Tom took off at a high rate of speed. A chase started, other police cars from the district were called in for assistance, and finally the Cordoba was stopped at a roadblock several miles away. The car had skirted an earlier roadblock.

The pursuing officers were upset, because they knew the dangers of high-speed auto chases. They pulled the driver from the car and asked him why he was running. The driver replied, "There are outstanding warrants out for me." Later, a check at headquarters proved this statement a lie.

The man was identified as Tommy Copeland, 31, and his troubles were only beginning. Seven hours later he was charged with criminal homicide in connection with the murder of Brenay Dobson.

Prior to Copeland being charged with homicide, detectives got a search warrant and headed for the suspect's apartment. They found part of a gun stock on the porch of the apartment building where Copeland lived.

Inside the apartment detectives found jewelry identified by the victim's mother as belonging to Brenay. They also recovered .12 gauge ammunition that matched the type used in the killing, and other items reportedly stolen in the apartment burglary along with the shotgun.

Later that day, on January 20, Detectives William Hennigan and Leckie visited the home of the man who bought the radio from Copeland. They talked to the 27-year-old woman who had been living with the man, and who remembered how the sale went down. She told detectives that a stranger, with a radio, came to the house with the boy's father on January 12 at about 3:45 p.m.

If the woman's recollection of time was correct, it would have been about the same time the homicide detectives were arriving at the scene to first view the body.

According to the witness, the father asked his son if that was the kind of radio he wanted, and when he replied yes, the father told the stranger he'd buy the radio. The woman was shown a spread of nine mug-photos and was asked to pick out the man with the radio. She fingered No. 123590—Thomas Copeland, also known as David Kay and Henry Lyles.

In an attempt to cover all bases the father who bought the stolen radio was interrogated that afternoon by police to determine whether he had been involved in the actual murder. Police announced later that a report of the polygraph test given the man indicated he was telling the truth. He may have received stolen goods, but it was clear he didn't commit a murder.

In his original statement to Stotlemyer and Amity on January 20, Copeland, a jitney driver, said he was given the radio in exchange for a jitney fare. And, he said, he didn't know the man.

Copeland explained that when it came to pay for the ride one of the men told him, "We don't have any money, but how about a radio?" According to Copeland, the man had been carrying the radio in a yellow shopping bag. Copeland said he took the radio, and in turn sold it to the father in the bar. The suspect, who maintained he never saw the men before, said the incident occurred on January 12, the day Dobson was slain.

Copeland was held for trial at a preliminary hearing on January 27 at the Allegheny County Coroner's Office by Deputy Coroner Judith Friedman. Detective Condemi testified that the sawed-off stock from a stolen shotgun was found on the porch of the apartment building where Copeland lived.

Further testimony showed the gun was stolen in a burglary two houses away from Copeland's apartment. The gun was never recovered, but experts testified that a spent shell—a Remington Peters No. 6—found in Copeland's apartment, positively compared to the firing pin impression of the spent shell found at the scene. In other words, the shell found at the death scene and the one found in Copeland's apartment were fired from the same weapon.

The suspect was sent back to jail to await his trial, but on June 4, he called the homicide office and asked to meet with homicide detectives.

Stotlemyer and Hennigan advised Copeland again of his rights, and took a second statement. This time Copeland admitted that he lied in the first statement, and told the officers that he got the radio from a man he befriended in prison some years earlier.

Copeland said the man came to him after being released from jail and asked if he could live with him, for a few weeks, until he got squared away with a lady friend. Copeland said the man stayed in his apartment for a short time and then left, but before he departed he gave Copeland the radio in gratitude. The detectives checked the jail and police dockets for the name of the man supplied by Copeland, and could not find him. The detectives could find no basis for the new alibi.

Copeland went to trial in Allegheny County Common Pleas Court on October 2, 1981, and surprised the police by pleading guilty to robbing and killing Brenay Dobson. Up until then, Copeland had denied repeatedly that he played any role in Brenay's death. Copeland, despite the story he told about being in jail, had no prior record of criminal convictions.

In return for the plea of first-degree murder, the district attorney's office agreed not to seek the death penalty. The prosecution also agreed not to prosecute Copeland on three counts of receiving stolen goods and one count of attempted rape and an earlier, unrelated burglary charge in which the gun was taken.

Judge James Clarke was preparing to begin jury selection in the case when he learned that Copeland had reached a plea bargain arrangement. Judge Clarke accepted the plea and deferred sentencing pending a pre-sentence report—an academic requirement because the mandatory life sentence has already been determined with the guilty plea.

"FLASHY WIDOW'S LUST FOR CASH MADE HER KILL"

by John Railey

The body was lying on its back on the bedroom floor, a .45-caliber Derringer clutched in its left hand. The corpse lay in a spreading pool of blood, apparently streaming from a single gunshot wound to the victim's head.

The minutes were ticking toward 2:00 a.m. on September 1, 1991, a sticky Sunday morning in the southern tip of rural Rowan County, in North Carolina's Piedmont.

The victim's wife had already identified the body for detectives as that of 31-year-old Mark Quintin Tidwell. Mrs. Tidwell had called 911 at 1:47 a.m. The dispatcher had routed the call through to the Rowan County Sheriff's Department. Deputies, detectives, and emergency workers had immediately responded to the woman's Southern Lane address, a ranch-style brick home in a middle-class subdivision just outside the city limits of Salisbury, the Rowan

County seat.

The emergency workers had already ruled the man dead.

As the Rowan sleuths studied the scene, the wife, extremely upset, was alternately crying and talking to a relative. A stocky woman with a shag haircut, Mrs. Tidwell told Patrol Lieutenant Melvin Akers and Detective Linda Hines that she and her husband, after returning home from a night of bar hopping, began to argue. She said she left the house alone and returned to find her husband lying in the bedroom. She said her husband had talked of suicide in the past, and she believed that he had finally gone through with it.

Rowan County has an unusually large number of suicides each year—about 25 to 30. By comparison, the Rowan sleuths usually probe only about four or five murders a year.

Tommy Swing, a detective and crime scene technician, shot photos of the scene, including a shot of other handguns in an open dresser drawer. Sleuths collected the Derringer. Detectives had Mark Tidwell's body sent to the local hospital, where the county medical examiner studied the body and questioned the victim's wife. Based on his examination and interview, the examiner listed suicide as the cause of Tidwell's death. Under those circumstances, an autopsy would not be needed. The bullet was left in the victim's head.

Meanwhile, detectives cleared the shooting scene. Hines filed the case under the "suicide" category.

But the following Tuesday at headquarters in Salisbury, Detective Swing went over the photos of the victim's body with Lieutenant Roy Purvis, who had also been at the scene, and Captain Rick Thibodeau, the head of the patrol and investigations division. After studying the prints, it was obvious that something was amiss.

Most significant, the corpse held the gun in its left hand. Investigators had learned that Mark Tidwell was right-handed. And even if he had been ambidextrous (which he wasn't), the sleuths felt the victim could not have fired the gun as it was held.

The barrel was under the thumb, and that would have made it very hard to pull the trigger. Moreover, sleuths noticed that the head wound did not appear to be of the contact variety commonly found when a person commits suicide, shooting at close range.

A local undertaker had also found the wound suspicious as he readied Tidwell's body for burial. He had seen stippling, or tattooing, away from the head wound, a characteristic not normally seen in suicide wounds.

The undertaker had called Rowan Sheriff Bob Martin and voiced his suspicions. Martin had passed the undertaker's concerns along to his detectives.

Lieutenant Akers told the investigating officers that something about the scene had bothered him. It wasn't consistent with other suicides he had worked, he said.

Meanwhile, family members had Mark Tidwell buried in West Lawn Cemetery in the Rowan County town of China Grove. With Tidwell in the warm Indian summer earth, the case might have seemed closed. But the sleuths were bothered by those photos. And then the citizen calls started . . .

The callers—some anonymous, some not—all wanted to talk about Tidwell's death. Those who answered the phone at the sheriff's department headquarters in Salisbury routed the calls to Detective Hines. Hines had won the case by the luck of the draw — she'd been the on-call detective the night of the shooting.

The several callers all stated that they had suspicions about how Tidwell had met his end. Hines felt there was something to their concerns. She wasn't alone. Even before the calls had started, Captain Thibodeau and Lieutenant Purvis, after conferring with Sheriff Martin, had decided to reopen the case as a murder probe.

The pressure was on. This would be Hines' first murder investigation. An attractive, outgoing, 40-year-old with long, reddish-brown hair, Hines had just made detective after four years on the 110-member department, working her way up from communications and patrol.

Purvis, 44, and Thibodeau, a dark-haired, 42-year-old Maine native of French extraction, would lend Hines their years of solid investigative experience.

The new detective, aided by her superiors and fellow detectives like Swing and Terry Agner, began in classic fashion, interviewing in depth the callers, as well as the victim's friends, family, and co-workers. Over the next several days, Hines learned that Tidwell was a gentle man who made a decent living working for an air-conditioning company. He loved his wife and two daughters and seemed happy on the day of his death, relatives said. He certainly hadn't seemed like a man who was suicidal. He owned several guns, and had recently bought the Derringer from a friend.

The victim and his wife had dated since they were 16 or 17. He'd never really dated anyone else. But lately, Tidwell and his wife of 10 years had been having problems. Angie Pinion Tidwell, 31, had left her husband several times for a boyfriend, only to return again when she was homeless and unemployed.

The victim's relatives told Hines that Angie Tidwell hadn't seemed that upset about her husband's death.

Hines checked out the victim's insurance, and found out that he had policies totalling $241,629.85, with his wife named as beneficiary. Detective Hines also learned that his wife had already been making inquiries about that insurance money.

The victim's relatives also said they'd noticed a diamond ring and watch on his hands shortly before his death, yet those items were now missing.

Hines and her fellow sleuths learned that Tidwell had wanted to have her husband cremated, saying that would have been his wish, but Mark's relatives had not allowed it.

Of course, Hines had met Angie Tidwell the night of the shooting. That night, Detective Swing had told Tidwell that he'd have to swab her hands, as well as those of her husband, to test if either had recently fired a gun. The wife had said she had to go to the bathroom immediately. Hines had accompanied her to ensure that Angie didn't wash her hands.

The victim's wife had seemed upset about the routine test. But then, who wouldn't have been under the circumstances?

Detectives had delivered the swab samples to the State Bureau of Investigations SBI lab in the capital city of Raleigh. SBI agents usually assist smaller Tarheel organizations with evidence analysis.

Several days after Mark Tidwell had been buried, investigators asked Angie Tidwell to come down to headquarters for a chat. The widow, who would be cooperative throughout the probe, agreed.

In Captain Thibodeau's office, Detective Swing told Tidwell that the powder tests done on her hands might come back positive. Tidwell then told Thibodeau and Swing that she'd left some details out of her original statement.

She now admitted that she had been in the house on the night her husband was shot, and that she had struggled with him over the weapon. She said her hands had been on the gun, and she had wiped prints from the weapon. But it was still a suicide, Angie insisted.

Based on the widow's statement, the sleuths didn't have the gun checked for prints, feeling it would be fruitless.

In changing her statement, the prime suspect was showing signs of weakness. The truth was, however, she never had anything to fear from the swab tests. SBI agent Michael L. Creasey later told detectives the tests were inconclusive: they didn't show which party fired the gun.

As autumn fell across the rolling Piedmont, Hines and her fellow investigators continued to work away at the case. Though she didn't know it, the widow was helping the sleuths hang her as she continued to run off her mouth. Most of the people Angie talked to either phoned detectives, or detectives found them.

One of the victim's neighbors told the sleuths that Angie Tidwell had been worried because her prints were all over the Derringer, and that she was afraid she was going to be arrested for murder. The neighbor told Angie that she didn't have anything to worry about if Mark had killed himself. Angie Tidwell, the neighbor said, suddenly turned pale and started trembling.

The investigators learned that the widow was saying the darndest things to relatives and people she thought were her friends. She gave those folks several different versions of what had happened: To some, she said her husband had committed suicide; to others, she said he'd been shot as they struggled over the gun; to still others, she said it was she who shot him.

One of Mark's relatives said he had flat-out accused Angie of killing her husband. The widow had walked off, saying nothing.

Witnesses said Angie Tidwell had been looking for someone "to knock off" Mark for a $10,000 cut of the insurance cash. When she couldn't find anybody to do it, she said that maybe she'd do it herself when he got drunk one Saturday night, shooting him in the head and making it look like an accident.

The witnesses told probers that Angie had expressed fears that she would be "locked up."

Witnesses said that a drunken Angie Tidwell had gone looking for her boyfriend on the night Mark was shot, saying that she thought her husband was dead. The boyfriend was passed out after a night of cards.

Investigators interviewed Angie's boyfriend. He told them that Angie had been fooling around with him as well as other men both before and after her husband's death. She'd told her boyfriend that she wanted Mark to die so that she and the boyfriend could have the insurance money, the house, and the kids.

The boyfriend said he wanted no part of her plans to kill her husband. After Mark's death, Angie had given her boyfriend three different versions of what happened.

Hines and her fellow investigators worked on through the cool fall days. They learned that Angie Tidwell had had sex with at least six different men during her marriage. While Mark would be at work, Angie had affairs in their home. In fact, on the morning of his death, Angie had sex in her home with a man who'd been working on their bathroom.

During a search of the house that the widow had consented to, investigators had found nude photos of Tidwell and her boyfriend.

Detectives learned that Angie had told one lover she met in a China Grove bar after Mark's death that she'd left her husband "out there to bleed to death."

In early November 1991, Captain Thibodeau and Lieutenant Purvis discussed the case against Angie Tidwell. They agreed it looked strong, but it was obvious they needed physical evidence from the corpse that only an autopsy could provide. On November 6th, Rowan County Superior Court Judge Judson D. DeRamus Jr. signed an order to exhume the body. On November 13th, workers exhumed Mark Tidwell's body and took it to the state medical examiner's office in nearby Chapel Hill for autopsy.

Pathologists removed the fatal .45 caliber slug from Mark's head. The pathologist ruled that the wound was not of the contact variety and had left no gunshot powder residue in the wound or on the skull. Captain Thibodeau knew that, in 98.9 percent of all suicides, a contact wound is present. Completely ruling out suicide, the pathologists said the gun had likely been fired from 6 to 8 inches away.

The pathologists said the victim had probably not died immediately, but had likely died from brain swelling and internal bleeding that created pressure which in turn caused his heart to stop. Blood tests revealed that the victim wouldn't have been able to put up much of a fight the night he died. The victim's blood-alcohol content was .16, well over the legal limit for driving a car in North Carolina. Pathologists also found 12 milligrams of Xanax, a minor tranquilizer, in his system.

Angie Tidwell had told witnesses that both she and her husband had taken Xanax the night of his death.

Hines and her fellow sleuths tied up loose ends. On November 19th, they secured a warrant charging Angie Tidwell with first-degree murder. They went to the Southern Lane home that day, but got no answer to their knocks or repeated phone calls. They were sure that the widow was hiding inside.

Hines and Purvis finally caught Tidwell when she came out into her yard that afternoon. They served their warrant and took her into custody. Tidwell was placed in the Salisbury Jail without bond. She refused to give the sleuths a statement.

More than two and a half months had passed since Mark Tidwell's death. It had been a long but thorough investigation. And the grueling probe wasn't yet over. As the detectives continued tying up loose ends in the case, Angie Tidwell continued talking to anyone but the sleuths. A witness would later say that Angie called him collect several times from the jail. Twice, he asked her if she shot her husband. The first time, she denied it. The second time, she admitted to shooting him, but said nonchalantly that it was an accident.

But an SBI test would later discredit the accident story.

Agent Eugene E. Bishop found through several firings that the Derringer did not have a hair-trigger. Forensic scientists matched the fatal bullet to the Derringer.

In January 1992, a judge reduced Tidwell's bond to $35,000. Angie made it, and the sleuths watched her, making sure she stayed in the area.

Angie hadn't any help making her bond from her husband's insurance money. Mark's relatives had gotten a freeze placed on payment of the policy pending the outcome of the trial. The victim's relatives had also noticed that the policy had lapsed and been reinstated shortly before his death.

But someone had apparently forged his signature on the reinstatement document; the signature on that document was much sloppier than Mark's.

Tidwell's trial began on Tuesday, July 14, 1992, in Rowan County Superior Court. Ariadne Symons, an assistant district attorney, was prosecuting. Angie Tidwell's family had retained Bays Shoaf, a local attorney, to represent her. The 31 state witnesses, most of whom had been unearthed by Detective Hines' exhaustive investigation, held up well under Shoaf's battering cross-examinations.

As Shoaf began her case on Thursday, Angie Tidwell took the witness stand. The flashy widow wore a black-sequined top that shimmered blue at the points where it hugged her plump body.

On the stand, Tidwell chose to tell the jury her "accident story," as opposed to the two other versions of the shooting she had told. Speaking with little emotion, Angie said the shooting had occurred after what had been a night of heavy drinking in several bars for the couple.

At one bar, Angie testified, "an old boyfriend came in and spoke to me. Mark got really teed off at me about that." The real trouble started when they got home, she told the jury.

As they got ready for bed, the defendant testified, her husband took out the Derringer and put it to his head. Angie told him to put it down and come to bed.

"He started arguing that I didn't love him and that I loved [the boyfriend]. I jumped in and took the gun. The hammer was already back. I shot in the floor, but it just went click.

"Before that, he had pointed the gun at me and said he was going to kill me. He said, 'Wait, you're not worth it,' and put the gun to his side and started crying."

The defendant said her husband told her he loved her, and to tell their children he loved them. Then, Angie Tidwell testified, Mark told her she could have her boyfriend. She said she tried to pull the gun away from his head and it discharged.

"I saw a ball of fire in front of my face and I just freaked out," Tidwell said, her voice beginning to crack. "I mean, I just lost it. I was terrified."

The defendant regained her composure and continued her testimony.

"I left the room. I tried to find my car keys and

couldn't. I walked up the street. When I came back, I tried to get my next-door neighbors up. Nobody was home.

"I think I walked back in the house then. There was a big old [blood] puddle at his head. I picked the gun up. I don't know what possessed me to do it . . . I thought, 'Oh, God. My hands was all over this gun.' I used a T-shirt to wipe the gun. I laid the gun in his hand. What came to mind was, I'd probably get blamed for it anyway."

Angie said she then went to another neighbor's and called 911. She claimed she didn't even know how the Derringer worked. "The only thing I knowed about guns was you pulled the trigger."

The widow maintained she'd never fired any of her husband's guns and had never even seen the Derringer before the night her husband died. The widow said her husband had threatened to commit suicide before and had fired shots into the ceiling and the floor on other occasions. She denied suggesting that her husband's body be cremated.

During Prosecutor Symons' cross-examination, Angie claimed that she had loved her husband, but there was "something lacking" in their relationship, and that "something" had led her to seek other men.

She admitted telling conflicting stories about the shooting. She denied that she had sought someone to kill Mark. She admitted saying in anger that she wished he would die in a work accident, but she had said the same thing about her boyfriend.

On Friday morning, Tidwell concluded her testimony by standing in the witness box and exclaiming, "As God is my witness, I did not shoot my husband!"

The jury got the case that afternoon. Superior Court Judge E. Fetzer Mills had instructed jurors they could return three possible verdicts: guilty of first-degree murder, guilty of second-degree murder, or not guilty.

After less than an hour of deliberations, the jurors came back with their verdict. Tidwell showed no emotion as the jury pronounced their decision: guilty of second-degree murder. Now it was up to Judge Mills to set sentence.

The judge considered the aggravating factors that D.A. Symons had presented, including that the crime was one of premeditation and deliberation and that it was committed for monetary gain. He weighed those factors against the mitigating factors Defense Attorney Shoaf had argued, including that Tidwell had no prior record at the time the crime was committed.

The judge found the aggravating factors outweighed the mitigating factors. He hit the seemingly nonchalant widow with the maximum sentence: life.

Mills revoked Tidwell's bond. As bailiffs led the flashy widow out of the courtroom, her sleazy life of violence and wanton sex came to a crashing halt as the door slammed behind her.

From the local jail, Angie had continued to contact her boyfriend, but the state prison system would likely put a halt to that relationship. Moreover, the man had chosen to testify against her.

After Mills recessed court, the victim's relatives praised Prosecutor Symons and Detective Hines for their long hours of work on the case, saying they were "the best."

"You would think she [Hines] had been on this

job for twenty years," one relative told a reporter. "And the D.A., we can't thank him enough."

Detective Hines had handled her first homicide probe far better than Angie Tidwell had handled her first murder.

"GREEDY KILLER LURKED IN A PINE TREE AND POUNCED!"

by Don Lasseter

After he had carefully activated the burglar alarm, Truman Jue stepped out the rear entrance of one of his two pharmacies, closed the door, and twisted a large key to slam the dead bolt into the locked position. Firmly gripping a heavy briefcase, Jue squinted through his thick glasses, surveyed the dark parking lot, and got in his van to start the 25-mile trip to his home.

The weight in the briefcase was from cash, over $30,000. On the middle and last day of each month, the 43-year-old businessman routinely withdrew large amounts of cash from his bank to facilitate cashing checks the next day in his two drugstores. Jue didn't want to leave the money at either shop, even though armed guards had been hired to protect both premises during business hours, and security devices shielded them at night. Jue had recently cut back on the guard service, and one of the stores had been burglarized, so Jue chose to continue his habit of lugging the cash-filled briefcase home with him.

At 9:00 p.m., January 31, 1989, Truman Jue, weary from working nearly 14 hours, eased his van into the southbound traffic of Southern California's 405 freeway. The commuter jams had dissolved into a fast-flowing river of bright headlights and red tail lights, and the traffic flow would enable Jue to complete the trip from Carson to his Huntington Beach home in about 30 minutes. The fatigued pharmacist knew he had been followed a couple of times in the recent past. He also knew that the large amount of money he carried in the briefcase would be an irresistible temptation to any thieves in search of an easy mark.

Shortly after 9:30, Jue turned into Sweetwater Circle, the cul-de-sac where his wife and two daughters waited in a comfortable condominium he had purchased 14 years earlier. No place could be safer, he thought. In an upscale area only three miles from the sparkling waves and white, sandy shoreline of Huntington Beach, the fenced community had suffered only one burglary in the previous eight years.

Jue edged around a station wagon that was idling with its headlights on and pulled into his driveway. Ordinarily, he would park under a tall pine tree in the parking island 30 feet away, but tonight he planned to unload some large bottles of water he had brought home. As he cut the engine, Jue saw the garage door swing open to reveal his wife standing in the flood of light. Again griping the valuable case, Jue accompanied his wife into the garage and through the service door leading into the kitchen.

After securing the case next to his desk, Jue greeted his two preteen children in the living room and returned to the kitchen. He stopped to see what his wife was cooking and told her that he was going to unload the water bottles. Jue pulled the service door halfway open with his right hand. He leaned his head and left shoulder into the gap and seemed to freeze for a moment. "Who are you?" Jue suddenly gasped. "What do you want?"

The sharp, loud report of a single gunshot exploded in the room. Truman Jue hurtled backwards, crashed against a wall, and collapsed onto the kitchen floor. Blood gushed from a gaping hole in his chest. His wife instinctively slammed the door, locked it, and bent down to help her supine husband. She screamed to the children, "Call 911!"

A Huntington Beach Police Department officer arrived moments later with an emergency medical team ambulance. While the paramedics kneeled next to the mortally wounded Truman Jue, the officer began to secure the scene. As soon as he learned that the victim was dead, he notified headquarters and requested a homicide team.

In addition to a homicide "roll-out" team consisting of six officers and a supervisor, a helicopter was dispatched to search the residential town-home community. Whirling blades battered the night air, and a searchlight sent down a cone of light to probe the surrounding greenbelts, yards, and streets. The light skipped over grave markers in nearby Good Shepherd Cemetery, casting bizarre shadows between the tombstones.

A handler from the K-9 unit arrived and unleashed his dog. The animal twisted and turned with his nose to the ground, bounding through the yards near the crime scene, trying to pick up the warm scent of a perspiring fugitive or a freshly discharged firearm.

Detectives Dale Mason and Richard "Hoop" Hooper pulled up at the Jue home at 10:30. Mason was assigned the task of overseeing the investigation. A solidly built, soft-spoken man, with thick, curly dark hair, hazel eyes, and impeccable, well-tailored clothing, Dale Mason had investigated over 60 homicides in his six years on the team. He had started his law enforcement career 17 years earlier after graduating from Los Angeles City College with an Associate of Arts degree in police science.

Richard Hooper, Mason's partner, was also an experienced veteran with 19 years on the force. Husky, and still weathering a classic flattop haircut, "Hoop" was one of the most respected detectives in the entire county. He had recently broken a case that sent a serial killing couple to death row.

Detectives Mason and Hooper examined the motionless body of Truman Jue, lying in a small pool of congealing blood, his heart pierced by a single shot. The diminutive man, with full, bushy hair and a drooping mustache, looked even smaller in death. The two investigators completed a detailed scrutiny of the body and the site of the murder, then faced the sensitive task of interviewing the family. It's one of the toughest parts of the job. Dick Hooper transported the victim's family to police headquarters where they could be comfortable and away from the traumatic scene.

When she was able to stop crying and compose herself enough to talk, Truman Jue's wife told the investigator that she had been preparing dinner and had been going in and out of the garage to do the laundry. A little after 9:30 p.m., she heard a car running outside the front of the garage.

"I heard a car motor, and it was about the time he was supposed to come home, but it didn't sound like his van. I kept hearing the motor and I thought, 'No.' Then I thought maybe it was, so I finally opened the garage door and looked out."

Detective Hooper scribbled notes as the woman continued her story. She told him that she opened the garage door because her husband did not have a remote control device in the van. She saw her husband, she said, and waited for him to enter the garage. They spoke to each other briefly and then both of them went into the house. They left the garage door open.

"We were in the house about five to eight minutes," she guessed. "He went in the other room to talk to the kids, because he had brought some notebooks one of them had been asking for." Then, she recalled, Truman started to go outside to bring in the water bottles and close the garage door. "He reached down, opened the door, and kind of kicked back in surprise. I heard a voice out there."

"Can you describe the voice?" Hooper asked.

"My first impression was that it was from a black man." But the widow couldn't distinguish what the voice had said.

"I heard one shot, and Truman fell back against the wall, then on the floor." She had been standing about seven feet from her husband, at an angle where the door blocked her view into the garage. She had not seen the assailant.

"As soon as Truman fell, I ran to the door and locked it," she cried. "Then I screamed for my daughter to call 911 and went to my husband to see what I could do to help."

"Did your husband say anything?"

"No."

When asked if she knew of anyone who had reason to harm her husband—any grudges, fights, lawsuits, arguments—the woman replied that she did not. But she volunteered that Truman had been worried about being robbed of the large sums of money he carried twice each month. She mentioned the ownership of two drug stores. "My husband had been followed several times from the store. After that, he bought a mobile phone for the van and had a relative follow him home a few times. Other times, Truman took different routes, to make sure no one could find exactly where we live."

Had the store ever been robbed? the widow was asked. Someone broke into it several years earlier, when no one was there, she told the detective. But there had never been an arrest related to the burglary.

"Have you seen any strangers around the neighborhood tonight or recently?" Hooper inquired. No, she hadn't noticed any.

"Did [the victim] normally leave the garage door open when he came in?" the detective asked.

"No," the woman sobbed. "Normally he comes through the front door, unless I hear him and open up the garage from the inside."

"You heard an engine running outside, but it didn't sound like your husband's van?" The detective was searching for any possible link to the assassinated pharmacist's killer.

"As I opened the garage door," the woman explained, "I saw tail lights leaving the cul-de-sac."

"Can you describe the car you saw leaving?"

"The only thing that I saw—paid any attention to—is that it must have been a big-size American car. But I only saw part of it as it pulled away." She hadn't been able to see the license plate. She thought the car looked "kind of beige" underneath the street lights.

When the victim's two children were interviewed, they had seen considerably more. Apparently, they had looked out the front window and had seen a station wagon stopping, starting, and idling. They gave lawmen a good description of it, but hadn't been able to read the license plates.

More important, they had seen a man outside. In the darkness, they couldn't discern much about his features, but they did notice that he wore a dark-colored baseball hat.

The detectives helping Dale Mason started the long task of waking up neighbors to see if any of them had witnessed anything. One woman corroborated the description of the station wagon.

Criminalist Jeff Thompson took photos of the victim's body from several angles. Thompson also searched for footprints and fingerprints in the garage and on the driveway, but he found nothing useful.

Apparently, whoever killed Truman Jue had made a clean escape, and had left no trace of his identity or motive. The investigators speculated that the assailant intended to steal the briefcase stuffed with money, but they had nothing to verify that theory.

The body of Truman Jue was transported to the coroner's autopsy lab, where Dr. Richard Fukumoto, probably the most renowned pathologist in Orange County, would make the formal finding that the cause of the victim's death was a bullet wound to the heart.

On the morning of Wednesday, February 1st, Detectives Mason and Hooper went to the two drugstores owned by the victim. They started with the Carson store, where Truman Jue had locked up and left just 12 hours earlier. Someone, the detectives figured, knew exactly when Jue filled his briefcase with money, knew that he took it to his home, and knew where he lived. Maybe it was someone who had been associated with one of the stores, they reasoned.

Before starting the interviews of Jue's colleagues, the detectives examined records of employees' names and addresses, including those of former employees. There was an extensive list, and the two investigators knew that they faced the arduous task of tracking down and talking to everyone on the list.

While they could not yet rule out any possibility, they decided to focus initially on two potential leads.

A couple of teenage girls, they learned, had worked in the Carson store and had boyfriends who were known street gang members. If the girls had told their gangster pals of Jue's habit of handling big money, it could very well have led to an attempted robbery and his death. Dale Mason assigned a pair of detectives to pursue that angle.

An even hotter lead, Mason hoped, was a security guard who had been terminated the Saturday before the murder. Mason and Hooper would follow up on that one. They located the guard on Friday afternoon, the third day of the investigation.

The ex-security guard, they discovered, had not been fired for sloppy work, but simply as a cost-cutting measure by Truman Jue. He was cooperative in the interview, but seemed to have something on his mind that he was reluctant to tell. At last, after saying that he just didn't want to be caught in the middle of something unpleasant, he agreed to divulge his information.

The guard related that a guy named Anthony Davis, also an ex-employee, had "caused some trouble" while he worked at the Carson store. Davis, he said, "might even be the kind of guy who would plan a robbery." The detectives thanked the helpful guard, ended the interview at midnight, and immediately initiated a criminal records check on Anthony Davis.

The record contained an ordinary list of various illegal activities, but the last entry raised Detective Mason's eyebrows. Davis was currently free on bail from an FBI arrest alleging that he had robbed a bank in Long Beach two months earlier.

When the Long Beach FBI agents arrived for work, they found Detective Dale Mason waiting for them. They readily cooperated, describing how Anthony Davis had robbed a local bank and had escaped in a car driven by another man. They had an excellent case against Davis, but they didn't think they had enough evidence to prosecute the driver. The agents agreed that Davis certainly was the kind of guy who might commit the crime against Jue. Mason added these facts and opinions to his rapidly growing notebook.

There really wasn't enough to link Anthony Davis to the killing yet, but as the investigation extended over the next few weeks, Dale Mason kept that name in mind.

The detectives made up a flier, with a photograph of the victim, and large letters saying, "Truman Jue was a businessman in your community . . . ," and describing the crime. It ended with a request for anyone having any information to contact the Huntington Beach Police Department. The flier was distributed in the neighborhoods surrounding the two stores. Local newspapers chronicled the story and carried a sketch of the baseball hat seen on a man outside Jue's home.

Despite intensive efforts and long hours of work, no new leads materialized. The detectives assigned to talk to the teenage girls who had worked at the Carson store and to their gang-member buddies conducted scores of interviews, but nothing panned out. In the condo complex, only one neighbor of Jue's, so far, had been able to contribute any information about the mysterious station wagon seen on the night of the murder.

Detective Dale Mason was a bit frustrated. He would later explain, "If you're the lead investigator on a case, you have to be in a position where all the information filters through you. The lead person must know what all the investigators know. A lot of times, if it's your case, you just can't do all of the interviews or searchers. You don't get to do a lot of the fun things, like make the arrests. You're pretty much tied down to the crime scene or the station." Mason, however, by working extraordinary hours, managed to be an active participant in the hunt for Truman Jue's killer.

In the middle of March, Detective Mason got a call from the FBI agents in Long Beach who had some startling information. Anthony Davis, still out on bail, had committed another bank robbery! A surveillance camera in the bank had photographed the perp, and the agent was able to make a positive identification. Mason was interested to hear that Davis had been wearing a black baseball cap during the robbery.

With his bail revoked, Anthony Davis was being held in the federal detention center near downtown Los Angeles. Dale Mason wasted no time paying him a visit.

Anthony Davis swaggered into the interview room where Mason and a partner waited. Putting on his tough-guy image, the con sat down and sarcastically announced that he wasn't going to talk to them.

Mason snapped back, "We don't want you to talk! We want you to listen. We know you're involved in this murder, and we're going to make [get the evidence on] you. We don't know when, maybe later today, maybe a year, maybe next week, but sooner or later, we're going to come back and charge you with murder."

"We were bluffing," Mason would later tell a reporter. Mason's intuition and the few facts he had available made him believe that Davis was not the killer, but the detective hoped that Davis knew something about the crime. And when Mason finished pulling the bluff, Davis' body language confirmed the detective's belief. "When we told him that we were going to pin the murder on him, he just slumped down in his chair and wouldn't look us in the eyes. We knew we had hit a nerve." But the meeting ended there.

The cooperative FBI helped again. They had conducted a detailed background check on Anthony Davis and found out that his live-in girlfriend worked at one of the banks that Davis was accused

303

of robbing. They speculated that she could have given him some inside information. She was never charged with a crime, but Detective Mason wondered if she might be a source of information.

"We went to see her, and she didn't enjoy that. She was really upset and began to cry." The woman reluctantly talked about her boyfriend, Davis, and mentioned a name that seemed familiar to Mason. Tyrone Edwards, the woman said, was a buddy of Davis and might be able to help the detectives. But she didn't knew where he could be found.

Detective Mason recalled that he had just seen that name a few hours earlier on a list of Davis' visitors at the detention center. Mason decided to try another long shot. He knew that many of the phones used by inmates are linked to tape recorders. Prisoners know it, too, because they are required to sign waivers when they use the phones. Mason hoped that Davis had called his pal; if the call was recorded, Mason would be able to find Tyrone Edwards.

Armed with a search warrant to review the recorded telephone conversation, Mason scored a direct hit. He found Edwards' telephone number, which led to an address.

Tyrone Edwards was not involved with any of his buddy's crimes. But he knew plenty about Anthony Davis and was more than willing to share that information with the detectives.

Edwards "speculated" that Anthony Davis was not only a bank robber, but that in January 1988, he had also helped steal $75,000 from the Long Beach Shipyard Credit Union and $40,000 from the most famous tourist site in Long Beach, the ocean liner *Queen Mary.* Davis had been part of a trio in the shipyard robbery, Tyrone Edwards thought. The other two partners in the crimes, he hinted, were Davis' friends, Frank Romero and Willey Hall.

Again, Detective Mason recognized a name. He referred to his notes and found that Lenton Willey Hall had been suspected by the FBI of being the getaway driver in the bank heist allegedly pulled by Anthony Davis.

The three men certainly appeared to be career criminals, but Mason still had nothing to tie them to the Jue murder. Maybe, he thought, he could link one of them with the mysterious station wagon seen by witnesses. He would start by finding out what kind of a car Hall drove.

A records check revealed that Lenton Willey Hall was on probation in Compton. Detective Mason contacted authorities there and arranged for Hall to be interviewed. At the end of the 20-mile trip, Mason found himself waiting, alone, at the probation officer's desk. Willey Hall was ushered in.

"Hall came in and assumed that I was his probation officer," Mason would recall. "I never bothered to tell him I wasn't and just started asking about his background." Mason was careful not to ask any questions about the Jue murder because he didn't want to get into Miranda problems.

Hall readily answered questions about his childhood, where he lived, where he had been in recent months, and other general queries. Hall said he had been in California for most of the year, including January, and was unemployed.

"What do you do for money, since you're unemployed?" Mason asked.

Hall said he was living off of his "savings."

305

Mason asked him what kind of a car he drove.

"A 1985 Fleetwood Cadillac, gray over gray," Hall proudly answered.

Detective Mason left, disappointed. It would have been more exciting if Hall had said he owned a station wagon. Another disappointment popped up a few weeks later. Apparently, the station wagon had been a false clue! Investigators had finally located someone else in the vast condominium complex who knew about the station wagon. It belonged to some tourists from New Zealand who got lost while looking for their friends in the complex on the night of the murder, driving around slowly, stopping and starting, looking for the right address. Their pause on Sweetwater Circle had been nothing but a mere coincidence.

Those things happen, Mason thought. You just have to accept them and go on. The next step, Mason decided, was to check out the other man named in the trio of alleged robbers, Frank Romero. When Mason pulled his criminal history, he found out that Romero had been in custody in Cleveland, Ohio, on a kidnap-robbery charge, when Jue was murdered. That eliminated him as a possible suspect, but Mason still wanted to talk to Romero. He called authorities in Cleveland and learned that Romero was out on bail. But they could make arrangements for a meeting if Mason wanted to fly to Ohio. Mason accepted the invitation.

It was the best decision he made during the entire investigation.

Frank Romero was in a lot of trouble. He was probably facing 20 years in the pen and was anxious to cooperate with authorities, hopeful that he might be able to avoid additional charges. Mason's timing was just right, and he caught Romero in a very talkative mood.

Yes, Frank Romero said, he knew Anthony Davis and Lenton Willey Hall. Romero acknowledged that he had been involved with them in some "deals." Eventually, he would admit that he had participated with both men in the shipyard and *Queen Mary* robberies.

"Do you know Truman Jue?" Mason asked.

Romero said he knew who Jue was. He had heard that the man had been killed.

With the skills he had learned in his 17 years of law enforcement, Detective Mason zeroed in on Frank Romero. When Romero started talking, he filled in a lot of blanks in the Truman Jue case.

"I didn't have anything to do with the killing," Romero said. "I was being extradited to Ohio at the time." But he admitted that he, Anthony Davis, and Lenton Willey Hall had planned for several months to rob Truman Jue. "We just basically wanted to get the briefcase he had. We wanted to get the money."

"We watched him and followed him," Romero said. He described how they failed in their attempts to follow Jue all the way home, so they wrote down the victim's license number and with the help of a friend, traced it to Jue's home address. They drove to Jue's home, sat in Willey's gray Cadillac, and planned the robbery.

"I didn't like it," Romero complained. "It was in a cul-de-sac and way in the back. It would be hard to get out of there."

But they continued to plan, he said. "We came back at night and watched him to see where he

307

would park, how he went into the house, things like that. He parked in an island under a big pine tree and reached down and grabbed his case, and he got out and went straight into the house. I just didn't think it was a good idea. That guy might have had a gun, and there could have been a bad confrontation.

"But Willey, he really wanted to do it. He had this idea where he would climb up in the pine tree after dark, wait for Mr. Jue to park, then drop down on him and grab the case." Romero said that he thought that was a stupid idea and refused to be a part of it.

The $75,000 the three men had stolen from the shipyard, Romero said, was divided equally among them. All three had agreed to use the money to bankroll themselves to become big-time dope dealers. Romero, after returning to Ohio, had sent Davis $17,000 of his share to buy dope. Davis claimed he bought the dope, but it was "stolen." Romero was angry and suspicious, so he and Willey decided to cut Davis out of the plan to rob Truman Jue. He wasn't too happy with Willey Hall, either. Willey had used most of his share of the money to buy a 1985 gray Cadillac.

Another comment Romero made sparked Detective Mason's interest. Romero said that he had left two of his handguns with Hall. One of them was a .357 Magnum. The slug that had killed Truman Jue came from a .357 Magnum.

"Would you be willing to come to California and give us some help on this?" Mason asked. Romero consulted with his lawyer and agreed to make the trip.

On August 23, 1989, nearly six months after Truman Jue was killed, Frank Romero sat in the Huntington Beach Police Station with a telephone attached to a recorder in his hand.

When Lenton Willey Hall answered the phone, he exchanged greetings with Romero. After some small talk, Romero asked, "Hey, what about that stuff that happened down at Truman's?"

"What? What? We can't say that on the phone!" Willey barked.

"Uh, well, just tell me who was with you," Romero urged.

Willey resisted, then answered, "Wait, wait . . . let's talk in riddles, okay? I did it like this here: I'm one man, okay? And I jumped out of the tree, okay?"

"Solo? You did it solo?"

"Yeah, solo, okay? Check it out."

"Get out of here," Romero chided.

Hall continued his riddle-talk. "That man, in this old thing, was standing up there, okay?"

"He was in his van?"

"Then the woman grabbed something, and went in the house. So I bust him, and I got scared and left."

Romero humored Hall with some more small talk, then asked about the gun.

Hall answered, "So I throwed that away, okay?"

"Now which one was that, the revolver?"

"Naw . . . yeah, that was the revolver. Then I got broke and sold the other one."

Some discussion followed about where Hall disposed of the revolver. Romero guided the conversation back to the crime. "You mean to tell me that you got the [nerve] to go there and sit up in that tree?"

"Be quiet, man," Hall again warned. "You talk

309

too much."

But Romero was persistent. He wanted to know which car Hall had used. Hall denied that he drove his Cadillac.

"You got a different one?" Romero asked. "You get a G car?"

Hall knew the street vernacular for a stolen car. "Yeah," he admitted. "A Chevy Chevette that I got in Compton."

"What the hell went wrong?" Romero asked. "I mean what's so wrong you had to pop him?"

Indignantly, Hall answered, "He reached . . . what I supposed to do, let him reach and let him get me?"

"I can understand that, man."

"I was so nervous. It was funny," Hall giggled. "But I don't it, so it ain't no big thing."

The two detectives looked at each other with grim expressions. Another 10 minutes of conversation followed, before Romero asked, "You get any cash out of it?"

"Look here," Hall again admonished. "I don't want to say nothing about this on the phone 'cause I ain't got none. *None!* That [expletive] took . . . uh . . . I panicked, and . . . it was all over, see what I'm saying?"

Romero tried again to get more details, but Hall interrupted, "Why you keep wantin' to talk about this on the phone?"

Romero knew it was time to back off. Romero made some pretense of wanting to meet Hall to talk over a "sweet deal I got for you." The two men agreed to meet the following day.

Detective Mason knew that Hall was his man, but he also knew that he needed more specific admis-

310

sions from the suspect to make a case that would stand up in court.

On the following morning, Detectives Mason and Hooper concealed a radio transmitter on Frank Romero and followed while Romero drove an unmarked 1980 Datsun to 99th and Main Street in Los Angeles to keep his rendezvous with Hall. Two other detective teams were deployed to follow, and a helicopter cruised overhead to make sure that Romero and Hall didn't get lost in traffic.

While Mason and Hooper followed, trying to listen to the crackling, broken output of the transmitter, Romero and Hall drove through the heavy L.A. traffic and talked.

When Mason had heard enough, and the commuter traffic started getting impossible, Mason called a halt to the surveillance. Romero pulled to a stop at a traffic light on Olympic and Sepulveda Boulevards, and the team of officers swooped in on the Datsun. They arrested Lenton Willey Hall for the murder of Truman Jue.

To wrap up the case, Mason and Hooper formally interviewed Frank Romero, with a tape recorder running, to fill in the details that Hall had divulged to Romero during the car ride. Romero told them everything Hall had said about the night he murdered Truman Jue.

According to Romero's account of Hall's story, Hall watched Jue leave the store, then drove "very fast" to arrive at Jue's home before the victim. Hall parked his stolen vehicle on the other side of a wall at the end of the cul-de-sac, in an adjacent neighborhood, and jumped over the gate. He then climbed the pine tree and waited for Jue to arrive. Hall was alarmed when he saw a station wagon "following" Jue, assuming that it was a relative who was trying to protect the victim. When the car left, and Jue and his wife went through the garage, Hall jumped out of the tree and accidentally dropped the gun.

After picking up the weapon, according to Romero's account, Hall pointed it at the victim and yelled, "Freeze!" Hall said that he thought Jue was reaching for a gun, so he had to shoot him. Hall then ran to the west end of the cul-de-sac, climbed over the wall to his car, and escaped.

When Romero asked what Hall had done with the .357 Magnum, Hall claimed that about a week later, he dumped it in the water off a bridge near the *Queen Mary.* Investigators never found it. Romero had provided the details that Detective Dale Mason needed to hand over the case to the district attorney. Romero returned to Ohio, was convicted, and started serving eight years for armed robbery. He will be eligible for parole in 1996.

Anthony Davis is serving a similar sentence in federal prison for bank robbery.

Deputy District Attorney Charles "Chuck" Middleton prosecuted Lenton Willey Hall in January 1992, three years after Jue's murder. One reason the case took so long to come to trial was because Hall became a jailhouse lawyer and successfully challenged two defense attorneys, having them removed from his case for various reasons. He even attempted to represent himself at his trial, but he was soon convinced of the foolishness of that effort.

Chuck Middleton presented the solid case that Detective Mason had assembled, and despite the absence of any physical evidence, he argued to the jury that only one person could have killed Truman Jue. To give the jury the details, Middleton had Frank Romero transported again to California and let him tell the full story in court.

On February 5th, after deliberating only nine hours, the jury declared that Lenton Willey Hall was guilty of first-degree murder with the special circumstances of robbery.

On April 17, 1992, Superior Court Judge John Watson sentenced Hall to spend the rest of his life in prison without the possibility of parole.

EDITOR'S NOTE:
Anthony Davis, Tyrone Edwards, and Frank Romero are not the real names of the persons so named in the foregoing story. Fictitious names have been used because there is no reason for public interest in the identities of these persons.

"NAKED RUNNER WAS TRACKED DOWN AND SHOT!"

by Bill Cox

On the warm autumn afternoon of Sunday, October 9, 1988, three young boys walking across a field in the eastern part of Amarillo, Texas, made a shocking discovery. Sprawled face up was the nude and bloody body of a man.

Scared by their unexpected encounter with violent death, the youngsters ran back to a motel on busy Interstate 40, where the mother of two of the boys worked, and reported the body. The mother placed a call to the Amarillo Police Department, then accompanied the children to the field.

At 4:41 p.m., Police Corporal Ronnie Kyle was the first uniformed officer to respond to the "possible body" call. The officer took a quick look to determine that the man was dead, then placed a call for a supervisor.

When the sergeant arrived, he radioed the dispatcher to contact members of the Potter-Randall Counties Special Crime Unit (SCU). A crack team of homicide investigators and evidence technicians, the SCU includes members from the Amarillo Police Department and the sheriff departments of Potter and

314

Randall Counties. The city of Amarillo, a Texas Panhandle metropolis of 165,000, is located within both counties.

Awaiting the SCU investigators, the uniformed officers secured the crime scene, posting patrol units on three sides of the field. The shallow T-Anchor Lake formed a natural trespass barrier on the remaining side of the area.

SCU detectives are called out on all violent deaths in which homicide is even a remote possibility. Contacted at their homes, Sergeants Sandy Morris, Ron Hudson, and Greg Soltis were the first SCU officers to reach the scene.

Morris, an assistant coordinator of the investigative unit, was in charge of field operations and took charge of the probe from the uniformed personnel on hand. The sleuths parked their cars a safe distance from where the corpse lay and walked gingerly to the spot to avoid disturbing evidence. The body was about 300 yards west of the large chain motel and 100 yards south of Interstate 40.

Thinking the dead man had probably been dumped in the field, the investigators were cautious to avoid possible tire tracks or footprints. The victim appeared to be a man in his 20s with dark hair. Still viewing the nude form from a distance to protect the scene until crime scene technician could photograph it, Sergeant Morris observed that the victim's left eye was swollen and bloody. It appeared to be a gunshot wound. Blood had also run from the man's mouth and nose.

No clothing or jewelry was visible in the area, nor was there any sign of a weapon. Sergeant Joe Allen, an investigator/crime scene technicians, began taking pictures with both a still camera and a videocamera.

Noting the victim's youthful appearance, Sergeant Morris speculated that he might have been a recent high school graduate. With that in mind, a Polaroid was taken of the young man's face to be shown to any representatives of local schools who could be reached on Sunday.

While the investigators sought to identify the victim, uniformed officers jotted down license numbers of all vehicles parked on the motel lot. They began checking registrations to see if the car owners could be accounted for at the motel. Sergeant Soltis supervised the check of the parked vehicles.

One car in particular drew his attention. It was a white-over-blue-green Oldsmobile Cutlass bearing 1989 Texas tags 910RGH. The car drew Soltis' attention for several reasons. It was on the southwest corner of the parking lot, adjacent to the field where the body was found, directly opposite the body's location.

The car appeared to have been abandoned. It was unlocked, one door was ajar, the window on the driver's side was down, and clothing and other items were scattered inside. A check of the motel records revealed no guest had registered who listed the Cutlass on the registration card.

Sergeant Soltis got on the radio and called the tag number in to the police dispatcher. A fast check of auto registration records revealed the car was registered to a Kurt Mason, who listed an Amarillo address.

Following up this lead after the body had been taken to the Special Crimes Unit office to be examined under a laser light for trace evidence, Soltis checked a crisscross phone directory and obtained the number of Kurt Mason, the registered owner of the suspicious-appearing Cutlass on the motel parking lot.

The detective talked to the wife of the car owner. She said that her husband Kurt had given the car to their daughter and that several days before, she had loaned it to her ex-husband, Barnard Joseph Oberbrockling III. He hadn't returned the car yet, the woman said.

Sergeant Soltis asked Mrs. Mason to describe Oberbrockling. She said he was 26 to 27 years old, 5 feet 7 or 8 inches tall, weighed about 140, and had black wavy, medium-length hair, brown eyes, and a mustache. The description matched perfectly with the body in the field, Soltis thought.

Mrs. Mason promised she would have her daughter call the SCU when she returned home. Meanwhile, after Soltis advised his supervisor that the description of Oberbrockling sounded like he was the slaying victim, a quick computer check revealed that Bernard Oberbrockling had a minor record with the police department.

Sergeant Morris went to the police department and obtained a mugshot and a fingerprint card. Comparing the prints with those taken from the dead man, the investigators confirmed the corpse's identification as 26-year-old Bernard Joseph Oberbrockling III.

Finishing the body exam at the SCU office for trace evidence, the investigators had the body moved to a hospital morgue for the autopsy. The pathologist found that the murder victim had died sometime between midnight Saturday and the early-morning hours of Sunday.

Two gunshot wounds were found. One bullet had entered the man's upper right arm and angled upward into his chest cavity, from right to left. Blood at the wound was stippled, indicating the shot was fired at close range.

The other shot had entered the victim's left eye, and the stippling blood pattern also revealed it had been fired from a short distance. The slug's course was horizontal through the back of the head. The pathologist recovered the slug that was lodged in the chest. It proved to be a metal-jacketed, .25-caliber automatic projectile. But the head wound was listed as the cause of death.

In the meantime, Oberbrockling's wife was interviewed by investigators. She said that they had been separated for almost a year but had remained friendly. The young woman had loaned her estranged spouse the Olds Cutlass on Friday evening, October 7th. As a chef, he was cooking that night for a party at a friend's house, it was reported. On the evening that the body was found, the victim's wife was out looking for her unreturned vehicle.

When the detectives talked to several people who were at the party, they learned that Oberbrockling had left at about 3:30 a.m., accompanied by a friend. The friend said that the chef-turned-chauffeur drove him home, and he hadn't seen him since.

On Sunday, darkness had fallen before the crime scene could be thoroughly processed, so Sergeant Soltis and other investigators had to return to the field the next day to go over the area. The spot where the body had been found was marked by small orange surveyor flags, and the field was kept under police watch overnight to protect any possible evidence.

The following morning, Sergeants Soltis and Allen backtracked a trail that the victim and his killer apparently left through the field. Starting at the spot where the body was found, Soltis and Allen began following a trail of bare footprints, obviously those of the victim, and some tennis shoe impressions that showed that another person was chasing the fleeing man. The trail led toward the north. The officers observed that the tennis shoe prints closed in on the bare footprints as the deadly pursuit neared its end. There were also blood spots along the flight trail, indicating that the victim had received his first gunshot wound at the start of the trail.

A short distance from where the body was found, the detectives located a spent .25-caliber shell casing on the ground.

The path of flight through the field had apparently been preserved because the ground had been damp on Saturday night. The two sets of imprints in the earth remained after the ground dried the next day.

Continuing to comb the area, the investigators found other items belonging to the dead man on the north shore of the drainage lake. These included a temporary driver's license and a torn Social Security card bearing Oberbrockling's name. His wallet was also discovered.

The search turned up another spent .25-caliber shell casing, as well as a live round of the handgun ammunition. Later, a black-and-white slip-on loafer identified as the victim's was found on the lake shore. No clothing was found, however, and the officers speculated it might have been tossed into the lake.

From the evidence, it appeared to the detectives that Oberbrockling had been shot the first time, apparently in the arm, on the lake shore. The shooting probably happened after he had been forced to strip. The barefoot prints showed that the victim had tried to escape from the gunman, only to be overtaken by the killer and shot point-blank in the face.

The reconstruction of the crime pointed to a ruthless execution of the victim. The motive remained obscure, although the wallet on the ground pointed to robbery.

"When the first shot didn't kill him, the killer had to run him down to finish the job," one detective speculated aloud. But the big unanswered question was, where had Oberbrockling encountered his killer?

As far as could be determined, Oberbrockling had no reason to go to the large chain motel where his car was found abandoned on the parking lot. But, the sleuths wondered, had he driven there without telling anyone to meet with a guest? Or had he gone there with someone else, someone who robbed and killed him?

The victim's estranged wife told detectives that Oberbrockling was living with two other men at a home in northeast Amarillo. These men and other witnesses failed to shed any light on the victim's activities on the Saturday before his death.

Probers learned that the victim's last contact with friends had been on Friday, when he and two other men got together to plan a female impersonator contest. One of the witnesses said he and Oberbrockling had competed in such contests "in drag."

In the meantime, news of the murder had spread rapidly following the first TV newscasts featuring video of the crime scene on Sunday night. Since then, every local TV news program had something on the mystery of the nude dead man in the field and all the local papers carried related stories. Pleas for the public to come forward, for anyone who might have seen something that might be connected to the murder to contact the investigators, were made in a news conference.

Not to rob forensic science of its due, but one of the most effective anti-crime tools that a good detective has is still his CIs, his confidential informers. Every investigator cultivates them. Detective Mike Dunlap, assigned to the detective division of the Amarillo Police Department, was no exception.

Although not a member of the Special Crimes Unit, Dunlap, like every officer from uniform on up, had his ear out for any information on a breaking homicide. A CI who had given him good information in the past called Dunlap on the day after the body was found.

"I've got something for you on that dead man in the field," the caller said. "A guy named Paul Vaughn can tell you all about it. I heard him say that a relative of his did it."

The CI said the suspect was named Thomas and lived at an address on East Fourth Avenue.

Detective Dunlap wasn't familiar with the murder, nor had he read the report. He picked up the phone and called Sergeant Hudson at SCU to pass along what the informant had related. Hudson confirmed that the information fit the case well. The tipster had given certain details about the crime that had been kept from the news media.

Dunlap and Hudson launched a search for Thomas. The name of Thomas' relative, Vaughn, was found in some old incident reports. It was learned that Paul Vaughn worked at an auto dealer's.

The detectives drove in an unmarked car to the auto dealer. They explained their mission to the manager and requested that Vaughn be brought to the office quietly so they could talk to him.

Vaughn admitted that what the investigators had been told was true. He agreed to accompany them to the SCU office and give a statement. But once there, Vaughn said he was afraid to talk because he feared Thomas Schumacher, the "Thomas" involved. After being assured that he would be protected, Vaughn let go with his story.

Thomas Schumacher had admitted to him, said Vaughn, that he and a teenage boy, whose only known name was Mark, shot Oberbrockling during a robbery in the field. Schumacher was worried that the boy might talk and was thinking about shooting him, too, said the witness.

According to the witness, Schumacher and the teenager had met Oberbrockling at a downtown park, a popular rendezvous for homosexuals, and had accompanied Oberbrockling to the motel in his car, the Olds Cutlass. There, after walking to the field, Schumacher pulled a gun and ordered Oberbrockling to take off his clothes. Then Schumacher shot Oberbrockling in the arm or shoulder, and the wounded man started running. The gunman pursued, overtook him, and shot him in the face, said the witness.

Suddenly, the case proved to be one where informants were popping up everywhere. About the time Detectives Dunlap and Hudson were pursuing Dunlap's tip, Sergeant Morris received a call from a tipster. The man said he had been at a beer-drinking party at which Thomas Schumacher had bragged about shooting a man and dumping his body in a field near T-Anchor Lake.

Based on the details from the two informants, the SCU detectives presented their findings to the district attorney's office and obtained a warrant for Thomas Schumacher's arrest on a charge of murder. The suspect's description was broadcast to all police agencies in the Amarillo area. The house where Schumacher lived on East Fourth was kept under surveillance by two uniformed officers assigned and briefed by SCU investigators.

The patrol unit parked where it wouldn't be seen by anyone coming to the residence. Shortly before 10:00 p.m. on Monday, October 9th, a white Chevrolet stopped in front of the address. A man jumped out, hurried into the house, and returned a few minutes later to the waiting car driven by another man. The officers, watching through binoculars, saw that the passenger matched Thomas Schumacher's description.

The patrol unit fell in behind the car as it pulled away and stopped it. One officer approached the driver and asked for identification. Then he turned to the passenger with the same request. When the man handed him a driver's license bearing the name Thomas Foster Schumacher, the officer stepped back, drew his revolver, and ordered Schumacher and the driver from the car.

The officers ordered both men to lie on the ground and put their hands behind their heads. After the police dispatcher advised the Special Crimes Unit that the murder suspect had been nabbed, Detectives Dunlap and Hudson drove over to where the officers held the pair.

When questioned, Schumacher asked, "What's this all about?"

"There's some warrants outstanding for your arrest," the detective replied, referring to some prior traffic violations that the suspect had against him.

Saying that the arresting officers told him he was wanted for questioning about a murder, Schumacher told Dunlap, "I don't know anything about a murder. I worked all weekend. The only thing I know is that someone broke into my house over the weekend and stole my gun."

The detectives quizzed the car driver briefly, long enough to find out that he was not the other suspect, the juvenile Mark, who was reportedly involved in the slaying. The man signed a consent-to-search form for his car.

Schumacher was taken to the SCU office, where Sergeant Hudson read him his legal rights. After signing the form, the suspect talked briefly with the detectives, then volunteered to give a statement admitting to the killing.

The 25-year-old suspect, who said he worked as a roofer, related that the teenager boy named Mark Lewis came by his house on Saturday night, and they decided to go downtown. The suspect said the boy was 16 years old, a slim, 6-foot-1 inch youth with short brown hair who, since getting kicked out of his home, was living on the streets. Schumacher said he knew nothing about the boy's background.

He related that they went to Polk Street, the city's main street where young people congregate and get rowdy on Saturday night. They remained there and "just walked around" drinking beer and smoking marijuana until about 2:30 a.m. Sunday.

After that, they went to a large park in the downtown area, where Mark later asked a man in a two-tone car for a ride. Schumacher said they stopped at his own house so he could pick up a pack of cigarettes. While there, he also picked up a small-caliber handgun.

From there, they drove to the motel on Interstate 40 and parked on the west lot. After sitting in the car for about 10 minutes, Schumacher said, he got out to use the restroom. When he returned, the driver—who was in fact Bernard Joseph Oberbrockling, though Schumacher and his friend didn't know this at the time—walked with the two others to the nearby lake.

Schumacher said the trio talked for a few minutes, when all of a sudden, he struck the driver of the Cutlass and knocked him down.

"I really don't know why I did this," Schumacher said.

Mark pulled a knife and told the man to get undressed, Schumacher said. As the man took off his clothes, the boy searched through them and then tossed them in the lake. Schumacher stated that as he was holding his gun on the victim it accidentally went off, wounding the naked man in the right arm.

The victim fell down, Schumacher said, then jumped up and started running toward Interstate 40. Schumacher said he was scared, so he chased the man to see if the shot had struck him. As he pursued the fleeing victim, he saw the bloody wound on the man's arm.

Schumacher overtook the runner. The wounded man turned around and offered to do anything Schumacher wanted. The suspect related that his gun was pointed at the victim, and he pulled the trigger.

"I just meant to scare the guy, but it hit him," said Schumacher.

Schumacher said the victim fell to the ground. He ran back and told Mark they needed to "get out of there." They tried to find the victim's keys to start his car, but when they couldn't, they ran to a field across the interstate, where Schumacher threw the gun in a drainage ditch. They also threw away their jackets, fearing they were bloodstained, then returned to Schumacher's house.

The detectives didn't think Thomas Schumacher had told them the whole story, but they had him on paper as admitting to the shooting.

Quizzed about his accomplice, Schumacher told the detectives he didn't know much about Mark Lewis or where he lived. He did give the names of the boy's two older brothers. The suspect later led the investigators to a spot near the shooting scene where he had discarded the murder weapon and a jacket. The jacket wasn't found, but the weapon was where Schumacher said it would be. ID officers were called to photograph the gun before it was moved.

Detectives Hudson and Dunlap escorted Schumacher to his house. They recovered from a closet a pair of tennis shoes that the suspect said he wore on the murder night.

After Thomas Schumacher was arraigned on a

charge of murder and remanded to jail in lieu of $25,000 bond, the investigators started the hunt for the juvenile, Mark Lewis. First, they found that his older brothers, who were not involved in the murder case, had police records. Pulling the files, they obtained an address for the family. But relatives said they hadn't seen Mark for some time.

Since the boy had a juvenile record, the sleuths turned to the police juvenile department for assistance. Corporal Linda Smitherman of the juvenile division, who had dealt with the youth previously, obtained a detention order to take the teenager into custody. She and the detectives checked several addresses but were unable to find him.

Meanwhile, following up Schumacher's statement that the victim's clothing had been thrown in the lake by Mark Lewis, the police scuba diving team, a special unit, was assigned to search the small lake.

It didn't take long for the divers to come up with the waterlogged clothes, including a pair of blue jeans, a long-sleeved black shirt, a charcoal-gray sweater, and a black-and-white loafer. The right pocket of the jeans was turned inside out as though it had been searched. The man's shoe matched the other one found earlier at the scene.

The Raven .25-caliber semiautomatic pistol taken from the drainage ditch culvert and the victim's clothing were taken to the SCU office for processing.

On October 14th, while Corporal Smitherman and a uniformed officer were making a call not related to the Oberbrockling case, they were contacted by radio that Mark Lewis might be in the east Amarillo area, in the vicinity of a fast-food drive-in. With Smitherman driving, the two officers headed for the location.

"There he is," Smitherman said.

A tall, slim youth wearing a T-shirt and shorts and carrying a small stereo-cassette player was walking along the street. The uniformed patrol officer stepped out and ordered the youth to put down the cassette player and place his hands on the patrol car. He told the boy he was wanted for questioning about a murder.

Patting down the suspect for possible weapons, the officer found several items in both of his socks, among them a folded pocketknife.

Mark Lewis was taken before a justice of the peace, who read him his legal rights and appointed an attorney at the youth's request. The attorney came down to the SCU office and conferred with the teenager before the investigators questioned him. He instructed the boy not to discuss the case.

The detectives then took the youth to the juvenile detention center. On the way, Lewis asked them to stop at a north Amarillo park to pick up belongings he had stashed there, since he had no place to stay. The officers retrieved a gym bag that contained clothing and a pair of combat boots. (Schumacher had said Lewis was wearing combat boots on the night of the slaying.)

Based on Schumacher's confession, the youth was charged with aggravated robbery with a deadly weapon in the robbery at knifepoint of Bernard Oberbrockling. At a juvenile hearing handled by the county attorney's office, Lewis pleaded "true" to the complaint and was sentenced to the Texas Youth Council's correctional facility for not less than one year or beyond his 21st birthday.

Thomas Schumacher was indicted by a Potter County grand jury on a charge of murder. In December 1988, Mark Lewis was returned from the juvenile correctional center on a bench warrant for an interview by SCU investigators and an appearance before the grand jury.

On December 15th, he gave a signed confession to Sergeant Morris. Lewis' statement differed in details from that given by Schumacher.

After they drank beer and smoked marijuana that night, said the boy, they decided to rob someone. He said they walked to the park intending to "roll a queer." While there, they accepted a ride with a man later identified as Bernard Oberbrockling.

The boy told the driver to go to a motel on I-40 East, where he said he had a room. The trio stopped first at Schumacher's house, then went to the motel, where the driver was instructed to park on the west lot.

Mark Lewis said he suggested walking around the lake nearby. As they walked across the field, the boy said, Schumacher knocked Oberbrockling to the ground. Schumacher pulled his gun and Lewis pulled a knife. Then, Lewis said, Schumacher unzipped his pants and urinated on the man on the ground. The victim was crying and begging not to be hurt.

The youth related that he held his knife at the victim's throat and searched him for money. He found a wallet, but there was nothing in it.

It was then, Lewis continued, that Schumacher ordered the victim to undress. Schumacher told the crying victim that he was going to tie him with his clothing and toss him into the lake. The victim tried pleading with Schumacher, telling him he couldn't

329

swim.

Schumacher pointed the gun toward the victim and pulled the trigger. The shot hit him in the arm. The victim was screaming and Schumacher tried to shoot him again, but the gun jammed. As Schumacher injected another bullet into the chamber after ejecting the jamming projectile, the nude, screaming victim started running, the boy said.

Schumacher caught up with the fleeing man, spun him around, and shot him in the face. The victim fell to the ground. The youth said they tried to drive the victim's car but they couldn't find the keys. Then they fled on foot, tossing their jackets away because they had been spattered with blood when Oberbrockling was shot in the arm.

Mark Lewis had been expected to be called as a witness at Schumacher's murder trial, but on August 15, 1989, Thomas Schumacher entered a plea of guilty to the murder charge to escape what he believed would be a much more severe sentence if the case went to trial. Judge Samuel Kiser of 181st State District Court sentenced Schumacher to 50 years in the Texas penitentiary, a sentence he is serving at this time.

EDITOR'S NOTE:
Kurt Mason, Mrs. Mason, Paul Vaughn, and Mark Lewis are not the real names of the persons so named in the foregoing story. Fictitious names have been used because there is no reason for public interest in the identities of these persons.

"MONEY-HUNGRY MURDERESS"

by Joe Koenig

BURLINGAME, CA.
SEPTEMBER 3, 1988

Damn, but he had to go bad.

Scanning the chaparral and manzanita growing at the edge of the road, the young man leaned a bit more heavily on the gas. He was looking for a spot where he could park his car and scramble down the shoulder to answer one of nature's most urgent calls away from the curious eyes of passersby. Noticing a promising location off the southbound lane of Skyline Drive, a scenic highway balanced atop the ridgeline of the coastal range of mountains just south of San Francisco, the man killed his engine and scrambled down the steep slope.

As the motorist sought shelter in the dry, brittle undergrowth, his eyes widened at a thoroughly unexpected sight that greeted him in the weeds. Lying on its belly at the foot of the incline were the partially decomposed remains of what in life had been a gray-haired man of smallish stature. Sprawled with the head downhill, only the thick stump of a large tree had prevented the body from sliding all the way down the hill. Although small animals and insects had begun to do a job on the remains, the body still was clothed in the fine, vested brown suit in which the man apparently had died. The jacket was down around the arms, nearly even with the waist, as though it had slipped off the man's shoulders as he tumbled down the incline. Not far away from the body was a necktie which seemed to go nicely with the dark suit.

The motorist took another look at the body, then inched further in the woods to do what he had come to that out-of-the-way spot for in the first place. Then he scrambled up to the road shoulder, and made a beeline for the nearest telephone from which he could inform the police of his grisly discovery.

Not long after, on that cool afternoon of November 14, 1982, San Mateo County Sheriff's Detective Sergeant Robert Morse and Detective Bryan Cassandro, veteran homicide probers, arrived at the lonely road shoulder. Although a hasty search of the dead man's pockets turned up no identification, sets of automobile and house keys were retrieved from the victim's trouser pocket.

Joining the detectives at the scene were Criminalist Mona Ng of the San Mateo County Crime Laboratory, lab technician Stan Baker, and Robert Jesson, an investigator with the San Mateo County Coroner's Office. While the technical crew inspected the body and then recorded the site on film and videotape, the detectives pressed their hunt for evidence. By late evening, however, the lawmen had nothing to show for their efforts other than the two sets of keys.

"It's hard to say what to make of this," one prober said. "I mean, the body's been out here so long there's hardly any blood left, even though the victim appears to have suffered some kind of head wound. It's been raining recently, so there aren't any footprints around either, and the trail that the body must have left when it slid all the way down from the road has also been obliterated."

It was nearly midnight by the time the investigators called a halt to their initial search of the scene and the body was transported to the morgue where the autopsy would take place. The following day, Dr. Arthur Lack, a pathologist working with the San Mateo County Coroner's office, reported that the cause of death was a subarachnoid hemorrhage of the right cerebrum, under the right temple, which evidently was the result of two blows to the head inflicted with a flat, heavy object.

Later that day, as Detectives Morse and Cassandro plotted the moves they hoped would lead to a quick identification of the apparent murder victim, they spoke with a reporter from a San Francisco newspaper who was a long-time veteran of the Peninsula beat south of the city. It was the reporter's theory that the body might be that of 56-year-old Constantine "Gus" Georgakas, the general accounting manager at the Nabisco Brand Company's regional accounting center in Burlingame. Georgakas, the reporter reminded the officers, had been reported missing several weeks earlier, on October 28, 1982, after informing the supervisor of office services at the giant firm that he had discovered a number of checks that had been written without proper documentation and paid to a company he was unable to locate. Although he had not been able to determine exactly how much money was missing, Georgakas had said that it was at least several hundreds of thousands of dollars.

It was not until Georgakas disappeared that it was determined that some $2,800,000 had been paid out to the fictitious company.

Acting on the reporter's hunch, the officers hurried to Constantine Georgakas' home in a San Bruno condominium. It took only a short time to discover that one of the sets of keys found with the Skyline Drive murder victim opened the doors of the condo. The other set fit the front door of the home of a relative of the missing man who lived nearby. It was that same relative, who, not long afterward, identified the dead man as the missing controller for Nabisco, an identification that had to be confirmed through the use of dental charts because of the massive destruction of the body caused by the woodland animals.

At Nabisco, detectives learned that Constantine Georgakas was a dedicated, well-respected employee with a spotless reputation for integrity and honesty. After many years with the firm, he had been preparing to take early retirement, when, on October 26th, he had reported to the supervisor of office services that the firm appeared to have been victimized by a massive embezzlement. Just two days later, he had disappeared, and while his personal car—a 1965 Chevrolet—remained parked in its assigned spot in the company lot, his company car, a 1981 Chevrolet, was missing.

At the age of 56, the investigators were told, Gus Georgakas had spent a lifetime with Nabisco, where he had become a ranking executive. When the company decided to consolidate its operations in Wilkes-Barre, Pennsylvania, a continent away, Georgakas had been offered a transfer to the eastern headquarters. Reluctant to leave his northern California home, he had decided, instead, on early retirement.

From interviews with the office staff, San Bruno police learned that when the office manager had arrived for work on October 28th around 7 a.m., Georgakas' 1965 Chevrolet was in its accustomed spot behind the building. In fact, it still was there on November 18th, when Detective Cassandro went to Burlingame to delve into the dead man's background. Cassandro learned that on November 3rd, nearly a week after Georgakas' disappearance, Officer Tom Wood of the San Francisco Airport Police Department had recovered the 1981 station wagon Georgakas usually drove on company business. The vehicle had been parked in the third level of the airport garage.

At Nabisco, Cassandro learned that the station wagon normally would not have been parked at the airport had Georgakas gone there to pick up company employees or visitors. Because Nabisco was located barely five minutes from the airport, directly across the Bayshore Highway, it was Georgakas' habit to call the airline involved when an employee or visitor was flying into town, find out if the flight was on time and then drive to the airport with five minutes at the most to spare. If the passenger was not there when he arrived, Georgakas would kill the time driving around the circular parking area. On no occasion was he known to have parked at the airport garage.

On October 27th, Detective Cassandro learned, Georgakas left work several minutes early and then visited with a relative in nearby Millbrae. Around 5 p.m., he told the relative that he was returning to the office to catch up on some work. Later in the evening, he explained, he had to drive to the airport to pick up someone who was arriving on a plane from the east, someone he planned to dine with.

Cassandro then returned to Nabisco headquarters in Burlingame, where he spoke with a janitor. The janitor would remember seeing Georgakas entering the building shortly after 5 p.m., and then again at 8:30 p.m.

When he spoke with other employees of the giant baking company, Cassandro was unable to learn who Georgakas had planned to see for dinner that night. No one had been slated to arrive at the airport, that evening, so far as anyone knew.

To Cassandro, it was beginning to appear highly likely that whomever it was that Georgakas had met at the airport that evening, had killed him, then dumped his body off Skyline Drive and ditched his car at the parking garage where it was found.

Digging deeper, Cassandro learned that on October 22nd, a check had been issued through the company computer in the amount of $19,987, made out to a fence company. An authorized company "check signer" had reviewed the payment and, finding no supporting documents, had forwarded the check to Georgakas—his immediate supervisor. Georgakas' own investigation into the authenticy of the check had continued until his disappearance.

Other employees of Nabisco reported that Georgakas had been greatly troubled by the check. A day or two before he vanished, one co-worker recalled, Georgakas had told her he was deeply concerned about the check and that it could mean his job, as well as those of the woman who shared his duties as controller and the man in charge of the entire Burlingame operation if the mystery wasn't resolved. Reportedly,

Georgakas had said that he had found a number of cancelled checks of a suspicious nature and that he planned to contact the bank and find out who had opened the account to which they were paid.

One day later, the witness said, she had spoken again with Georgakas, who informed her that he had cut short his investigation. Georgakas explained that he had spoken about the incident with Sally Hasper, his fellow controller, whom he had trained and brought up through the corporate ranks, and that she had told him that there was a letter in her files documenting the checks.

"He told me to put a hold on everything," the witness informed Cassandro.

On Thursday, October 28th, the executive in charge of the operation had returned to Burlingame with Sally Hasper from a week-long meeting in Chicago, an organizational gathering whose purpose was to prepare the company for the shift to Pennsylvania. By that time, however, Georgakas had been reported missing. That afternoon, other employees of Nabisco reported seeing Sally Hasper enter Georgakas' office. Not long after, when a search of the office was made at the insistence of Georgakas' assistant, the file containing the records of the investigation into the $19,987 check and everything relating to it was missing.

At that point, the executive in charge of the Burlingame office called the company security police. They, in turn, sent in a couple of retired New York City homicide detectives to investigate. Soon, the Federal Bureau of Investigation was brought into the rapidly expanding probe, to provide additional assistance.

With the help of the security investigators, the feds were able to trace the bogus company to whom the checks were paid. The account was opened by Sally Hasper, who, in time confessed to the scam. After pleading guilty to a federal offense stemming from the embezzlement, she was sentenced to a three-year term at the federal penitentiary at Pleasanton, California.

With Sally Hasper behind bars, the feds were able to turn their full attention to the hunt for the missing money. For Detectives Cassandro and Morse, however, the investigation was only beginning. For, although Sally Hasper had conceded that Gus Georgakas had questioned her about the checks, she still claimed to know nothing about his murder. How could she, she asked, when she was in Chicago at the time the controller was slain?

As the feds and security officers pressed their search for the $2,800,000 believed to be stolen by the woman from her employer, Cassandro and Morse continued their hunt for Gus Georgakas' slayer. They began, logically enough, with a November 23, 1982, interview with Sally Hapser. Once again, the woman insisted that she had arrived in Chicago on October 25th. After checking into a hotel, she had phoned her secretary, who told her that people were looking for her check vouchers, and so she had called Gus Georgakas, who asked about the company on which the $19,987 check was drawn. Sally Hasper told the detectives that she had told Georgakas she had the vouchers out of the file and wasn't sure where they were. Georgakas, she said, had told her that he would have her secretary look for them.

The following day, her story continued, she had spoken again with Georgakas. He had told her that not only had the vouchers not turned up, but vouchers for other checks issued to the same company were also missing.

On October 27th, Sally Hasper had phoned another company employee and had been told that additional cancelled checks made out to the bogus firm had been found and that Georgakas had ordered people to look for the vouchers. The employee had told Sally Hasper that Georgakas was in a terrible mood.

Around 2 p.m., October 27th, the detectives learned, Sally Hasper, complaining that she felt ill, had suddenly left the meeting she was attending with other employees. The woman told Cassandro and Morse that she had returned to her hotel room, where she lay in bed for some time, until going out to a shopping mall around 5:15 p.m. Remembering that she was scheduled to go to dinner with company executives that evening, she had phoned the Chicago office and informed a young woman that she would not be able to show up at the restaurant. Then, she told the detectives, she went back to the hotel, and to bed.

When they contacted executives at Nabisco, the detectives learned that between 6:15 and 6:20 on the morning of October 28th, Sally Hasper had called to say that she was checking out of her hotel. An executive who had been staying at a different Chicago hotel was puzzled by Hasper's call. He had made arrangements to meet Sally at the airline gate and there had been no reason for her to call him two hours ahead of time.

Sally explained to the detectives that she had spoken by phone with Gus Georgakas on October 27th, asking him to report that the manager of the Oakland Office would be arriving in San Francisco the next day and to ask him to provide a lift from the airport, because she would be unable to do it herself.

339

Now Detective Cassandro began checking flight manifestos of all the major airlines, concentrating on flights that would have allowed Sally Hasper to fly from Chicago to San Francisco on October 27th. Soon he learned that a Ms. Turner had paid cash for a ticket on United flight 135 out of Chicago, which had departed around 6:40 p.m., Central Time, arriving in San Francisco at 8:46 Pacific Time. A further search of United's passenger lists revealed that the ticket for the flight in question had been purchased by one Susan Visa at 10:30 p.m., but that the credit card with which payment for the return flight to Chicago had been made was issued to one S. Hasper. To Detective Cassandro, the implication was clear—Sally Hasper had brought along with her only enough money to pay for a one-way flight to the coast.

Sally, however, had reported that her credit card was stolen. And, in truth, the signature on the credit card slip did not appear to have been hers.

After serving slightly more than a year and a half of her three-year term for embezzlement, Sally Hasper was released from prison. While the woman found employment with a new firm, Morse and Cassandro continued their attempt to link her to Gus Georgakas' slaying.

Using United Airline's ticket office and the airline's complex numbering system, Cassandro was able to track down a man who had been standing in line behind "Sally Visa" on the red-eye flight to Chicago shortly after midnight on October 28, 1982. The man described the woman he had seen at the time, and the description seemed to fit Sally Hasper to a T. Asked to view a photographic lineup, he selected Sally's picture and that of another woman as possibly those of the

340

woman he had seen.

Hoping to link Sally Hasper more closely to the Georgakas slaying, Morse and Cassandro now drove the route that Gus Georgakas' slayer would have had to take from the San Francisco Airport to the place off Skyline Drive where the controller's body was discovered. Morse was behind the wheel as the investigators took Highway 101 south to Highway 92, turned west and climbed to Skyline, which they followed south to the crime scene. One way, the journey took exactly 38 minutes, indicating that the round trip would have taken an hour and 16 minutes. This was plenty of time for Sally Hasper to purchase her ticket, transport the body to its resting place below Skyline and then return to the airport in time to catch her 12:05 flight back to Chicago.

It was no secret to the investigators that no one in Chicago had seen Hasper from the time she left the meeting at 2 p.m., on October 27th, until she met the company executive for the flight back to San Francisco at 8:15 the next morning.

It was not until September of 1986 that 41-year-old Sally Hasper formally was charged with the murder of Gus Georgakas. At her trial, which got underway in Redwood City, California, in the third week of January 1987, Deputy District Attorney Chuck Smith, in his opening remarks, told the jury that Sally Hasper had slain Georgakas to prevent him from exposing the embezzlement scheme she carefully had plotted to allow her to live a luxurious life-style.

"She killed Gus Georgakas because she knew that, had he continued his research, he surely would have found out that she was stealing millions of dollars from Nabisco. Her millionaire's life-style was more important to her than the life of Gus Georgakas."

During the years she was embezzling money from the firm, D.A. Smith said, Sally Hasper was considered a "trusted, loyal employee.

"She was so confident that she would not get caught that she almost flaunted what she was doing. Her motive was greed. She wanted to surround herself with fancy clothes, fancy cars and a fancy house. She was so comfortable in her role as a thief . . . that she came to work every morning smiling, congenial and efficient."

D.A. Smith went on to tell the jury that it was quite conceivable that Sally Hasper had delivered the blow to the head that claimed Gus Georgakas' life.

"Sally Hasper, in 1982, looked much different than the Sally Hasper you see today," Smith continued, pointing toward the defendant. "Sally Hasper, in 1982, was a heavy woman who weighed 215 pounds."

Gus Georgakas, on the other hand, was a 56-year-old man carrying barely 140 pounds on a five-foot, six-inch frame.

"What's more," the prosecutor said, "Georgakas' guard was down because he was too admiring and trusting of Sally Hasper to have suspected her of the embezzlement that he was in the process of investigating.

"The fatal mistake he made was that he trusted Sally Hasper and was loyal to her," Smith added. "He had no idea that she was willing to kill him that night to protect her millionaire's life-style."

On Tuesday, January 27th, a former Nabisco payroll supervisor in Chicago told the court that late in the afternoon of October 27, 1982, Sally Hasper had called her to bow out of a business dinner slated for that evening because she was ill. However, the witness said, when she made several attempts to call Sally Hasper at her hotel between 5 and 9 p.m., she received no answer and quit trying.

Also testifying that day was another former Nabisco employee who said that Sally Hasper had claimed suddenly to have become ill that afternoon after receiving a call during a business meeting with other Nabisco execs. The witness further testified that Sally Hasper had left the meeting to accept the phone call and that when she returned moments later she appeared "visibly shaken," said that she was ill, and left.

It was Deputy District Attorney Smith's contention that the phone call that had unnerved the defendant was from Gus Georgakas, who was beginning his investigation of the embezzlement.

On Wednesday, January 28th, a freelance document examiner told the court that after comparing the signature on the ticket receipt for a flight out of San Francisco signed Susan Visa with several examples of the defendant's signature, he had concluded that the same person had signed all the documents.

"The same person who wrote the comparative studies that I used was the same person who signed the airline ticket," the witness said.

On Thursday, February 5th, after some two and a half days of debate, the jury of six men and six women found Sally Hasper guilty of the first-degree murder of Gus Georgakas. The jurors also found the woman guilty of the special circumstance allegation that the murder was committed in order to prevent the victim from testifying against her. Because prosecutors did not seek the death penalty against her, it was noted, Hasper faced a maximum term of life imprisonment when she came up for sentencing.

On Wednesday, March 4th, Superior Court Judge Robert D. Miller sentenced Sally Hasper to a term of life in prison without the possibility of parole.

"2 BUCKS AND A TIFF . . . REASON TO KILL?"

by Robin Williams

WINTER HAVEN, FLORIDA
APRIL 20, 1983

He hadn't become a millionaire yet, but Wade Huffard Miles Jr. was doing all right for himself in fall, 1982. Not every 20-year-old could boast a reasonably secure job, his own apartment and enrollment in a college program training him for the high-demand hospital field. With the condition 1982's economy was in, the Winter Haven, Florida, resident had a lot to be grateful for.

Even better, he wasn't out battling the world on his own. His parents and other relatives lived within the same country, close enough to provide emotional and financial support without breathing down the neck of a young man striving hard to become a full-fledged adult.

The closeness meant a lot to his family too, especially since he was one of four children and the only son. He held a special place in his family's heart.

When classes ended October 18, 1982, at the elementary school where she was a teacher, a relative of Miles' decided to pay him a short visit. Smiling happily to herself, she got into her car and headed north to Winter Haven.

It appeared she'd been lucky enough to catch busy Miles at home that Monday afternoon. Rock music was blaring through the closed door of Apartment Seven, Brigham Apartments, an attractive complex where Winter Haven Hospital provided temporary living quarters for its new employees. The air conditioning unit for Miles' ground-floor apartment also was humming steadily.

But the woman felt strangely uneasy as she stood outside the apartment. She hadn't thought Miles liked that kind of music. It certainly seemed unlike him to be playing it so loudly in a hospital zone.

There was no response to her knock. Then her initial uneasiness changed to fear as she looked at the door handle. Although the elementary school teacher was no doctor, it didn't take a medical opinion for her to realize the brownish stains looked like blood.

Backing away, trying to smother a rising terror that threatened to engulf her, she headed for a telephone. Maybe a phone call could bring her reassurance. It was possible some friend of Wade's had left the stereo going while he was at his job as a hospital orderly.

But the telephone call to Winter Haven Hospital didn't set her mind at rest. The nurses working Wade's floor also were wondering what had happened to him. Knowing how prompt the young orderly tried to be, they couldn't understand why he hadn't shown up for the 3:00-11:00 p.m. shift.

A hospital security guard was paged about 3:30 p.m. and told to check out Miles' unexplained absence. But he was standing guard for the cashier and couldn't leave.

At 4:34 p.m., the hospital operator paged him again and told him to stop by Miles' apartment. His relative was worried because she couldn't get any answer, the operator explained.

So the guard left his hospital post and walked the short

distance to Brigham Apartments. When he arrived, the guard saw the same dried stains Miles' relative had discovered.

Deciding that whatever lay behind that locked door was more than a security guard was trained to handle, he called the Winter Haven Police Department. Officer Harold Parker was dispatched at 4:57 p.m. to investigate what was termed a "suspicious incident" at the hospital's employee quarters.

Arriving at the nearby hospital within minutes. Parker met with the guard and was taken without delay to apartment seven. Like the others, Parker had no trouble hearing the raucous music or spotting the suspicious stains.

Fortified by having a police backup, the guard used his hospital key to open the door to Miles' apartment. Officer Parker needed only a glimpse inside to know he'd be calling for assistance from his fellow officers almost immediately.

"It was apparent and obvious there had been great violence in the room," he noted in his report. Telling the security guard to stay by the front door, Parker went inside to search for whoever or whatever had shed the blood smeared across walls, carpet and furniture in the small apartment.

Finding no bodies in the living room or bedroom, he walked to the bathroom and stared down at its blood-soaked floor. A young white male, his once-handsome face distorted by blood and ugly blue-black swellings, lay motionless on his back. Detective Ernest Mincey would recall the victim as being in a "pool of blood."

Automatically, Parker checked the body for signs of life. Finding none, he left the apartment and stationed himself at its door. He reported the situation to a dispatcher, asking for detectives and evidence technicians.

Before the long night ended, all but one of the department's detectives would become involved in tracking down the killer or killers. Veteran Detective Darrell Kirkland, who served as chief investigator, later would describe the killing as "the most gruesome, gory, unnecessary and brutal homicide" he had worked in ten years as a police officer.

Since most of those years had been spent as a detective, Kirkland isn't a stranger to murder investigations. But this killing, for sheer violence, went far beyond what he and other Winter Haven officers were used to encountering.

Court records show that Detective Ray Ditty, another who helped break the case, also found it "hard to believe that human beings could do this to each other."

Among the investigators pouring into the apartment that night was Nancy Hutzell, who'd gone from communications through road patrol to become crime scene evidence officer. An enthusiast on explaining why proper evidence collection cam make or break a case, she would find this one—the first homicide she'd collected evidence on—contained enough possible clues to use almost every skill she'd learned.

Hutzell, Detective Mincey, and Detective Sgt. John Stanton would spend hours packaging everything from bloody beer cans to a 13-inch serrated knife that was bent and smeared with blood. The knife was found beneath a sofa.

They found the apartment a shambles. Furniture was overturned. There were sofa cushions, papers, clothing, pottery and broken glass scattered throughout the living room.

Scattered macaroni spilled from a cooking pot was on the living room floor amid bloodstains. There was no way the officers could turn without spotting some blood.

That was just in the living room. The kitchen floor tile was smeared with possible bloodstains, as were the door frame, stove front and lower cabinet doors.

Miles' bedroom hadn't escaped the whirlwind of violence either. Blood had splattered on bedding and a closet door. More blood smears were obvious on the air conditioning unit and the wall below it. And a bloody trail led them along the walkway to the bathroom, where the young man's ravaged body lay face up to the artificial light.

The body was that of a young man, probably in his early 20s, slender but not overly thin. He was fully clothed in a hospital-type shirt, white underpants and blue jeans with the pockets turned out. The jeans were unzipped and partially pulled down around the victim's hips.

The face, like the rest of the apartment, was covered with blood. Some had puddled in the eye sockets, while his short, dark hair was damp from still more.

Judging by the body's condition and how warm a jug of milk on the kitchen counter felt, the sleuths speculated it had been hours since the attack had taken place.

There could be no doubt the young victim had been attacked, beaten and savagely murdered. Marks from the beating and possibly cuts were visible on the body, but the extensive blood made it impractical for officers to try identifying wounds on their own.

Some couldn't help wondering what would have happened if one of Miles' neighbors had called in a complaint earlier about the blaring music. Since their victim didn't appear to have died instantaneously, he might have been able to get medical help. Hadn't anyone been curious why the same stuck record kept playing?

The dead man was identified quickly as Wade Miles. The security guard knew it was Miles because, he said, he'd seen him in the hospital emergency room three days earlier.

Hospital records revealed Miles was brought to the emergency room at 3:27 a.m. October 15th after a security guard found him in the main lobby. The youth complained of pain in his left leg. He also admitted to having drunk a large amount of vodka that night.

Drinking isn't unusual for a young man in the first flush of adulthood, so the detectives had no reason to treat news of his inebriated state as anything more than another piece of miscellaneous information. Its importance would grow in their minds, however, before the investigation's end.

When Dr. James L. Holimon, the associate medical examiner, arrived to make a preliminary examination, he saw what appeared to be a stab wound in Miles' right chest. A cut about the same size was visible in his shirt. Dr. Holimon told them death probably had occurred with 24 hours.

Interviews with Miles' relatives would confirm it couldn't have been much longer than that. He'd been with them until three the previous afternoon.

Before a funeral home vehicle carried the body to Lakeland Regional Medical Center for autopsy, Hutzell secured its hands in bags to preserve hairs, blood and other material around the fingertips. Mincey contacted the hospital's security chief to arrange for another lock on the door.

They continued collecting evidence and taking photographs as detectives began fanning out into a several-block area surrounding the apartment complex.

One of Miles' relatives arrived at the apartment soon

after it was opened for the police. Detectives broke the sad news and asked if he could help in any way with the investigation.

That relative supplied the names of three men whom he believed had been Miles' closest friends. He mentioned that he and another female relative of Miles' had been called to the hospital a few days ago when Miles was at the emergency room. The female relative would have more information, he added, because she'd been the one talking with Miles that day.

Before asking the grieving family any more questions, Kirkland went to the hospital and began interviewing Miles' stunned co-workers. He and Detective Robert Frazier came away from those interviews with the impression Miles could have been under some stress.

Several employees knew about the drinking incident. Others said Miles had told them some people were imposing on him. Another mentioned a relative Miles hadn't gotten along with. They told the detectives Miles had been dating a young woman who worked at the hospital.

Detectives Jerry High and Ditty, meanwhile, were interviewing his neighbors. One woman recalled having noticed loud music a couple of times during the past 24 hours. A man described the yellow, older-model station wagon he'd seen at the apartment a few days earlier. There had been a white couple and two small children inside, he recalled.

Another neighbor remembered seeing two white men knocking on Miles' door about 10:00 a.m. the day before his body was discovered. He described one man as about 5'10" weighing about 150. The man was wearing a bandanna, blue jeans, but not a shirt.

The bandanna could be significant, since some had

351

been found at Miles' apartment, but the detectives would need to learn whether those morning visitors ever located Miles.

Kirkland performed the sad task of seeing the victim's family after finishing his hospital interviews. They wanted to see Wade's body, but Kirkland gently refused. He knew it would be better for them to remember Wade as the handsome young man shown on his driver's license.

A female relative confirmed their impression that something had been bothering the young hospital orderly. When she'd gone to the emergency room, she said, Wade had been close to incoherent. He had warned her "they" were after him. When she asked who "they" were, he had named one of his friends and some other people whose names she didn't recognize.

Hoping to help, she asked why he spent his paychecks buying alcohol and partying with these people. He told her he called them when he got lonely, but then said he was going to stop. "I don't want to get mixed up in this crowd again," he assured her, adding that he loved his job and wanted to keep it.

Under the circumstances, the relative told police, she and her husband had decided Wade would be better off spending the weekend with other relatives. They'd picked him up about noon, Saturday, October 16th, and taken him there.

The victim's immediate family were able to tell detectives he'd stayed with them until Sunday afternoon. They had taken him to dinner and he'd sung with the choir at church. But he'd turned down their plea to stay until Monday morning, insisting he had things to do at his apartment.

So they dropped him off at the apartment complex

about 3:00 p.m., mercifully unaware it would be the last time they'd ever see him.

A relative said Wade had become involved with friends who had a bad influence on him. He singled out Simon Lord, a man in his late 20s, who also lived in Winter Haven.

The name was familiar to Winter Haven sleuths. Lord was one of the three men Miles' relative had mentioned as being the victim's closest friends. He also was the one his female relative said Miles had been talking about at the hospital.

Lord's supposed influence on Wade Miles Jr. had worried his family so much, detectives learned, that they had visited the man and told him to leave Wade alone.

One other thing emerging from Kirkland and Lt. James Tugerson's interviews with the family was some confused information about people from Ohio who had stayed at the apartment a few days. Although no one really knew much about them, the family had gathered Miles was growing tired of their company. But the Ohioans had been gone by the time Miles came home for his last weekend.

A minister who'd arrived to comfort the family told Kirkland he might be able to help him locate two of the three friends. The third was living in another county. They went to a Winter Haven church, where the minister checked his records and found some addresses.

In talking with the minister, Kirkland concluded Lord was a confused young man with problems of his own to work out. Specifically, he'd recently separated from his wife and taken a separate residence.

Armed with the addresses and background information, Kirkland returned to the hospital apartment. There he conferred with Hardy Pickard, an assistant state attorney for Florida's 10th Judicial Circuit. Pickard, who conscientiously made an appearance at major crime scenes within his area, heard Kirkland's summary of the investigation to date before examining the apartment himself.

Kirkland was pleased to learn large quantities of physical evidence had been collected while he and Lt. Tugerson, supervisor for the 4:00 p.m. to midnight patrol shift, were out. There would be numerous items checked for fingerprints and blood. Two in particular might be immediately useful in pinpointing a suspect.

One was the clearly defined shoe prints in blood surrounding Miles' body. The other, spotted by Detective Ditty, was a bloody trail leading from the apartment out into the complex's parking lot. From the trial's pattern, they speculated it had been made by someone who had left Miles' apartment with a cut foot.

Ditty checked with the hospital emergency room to see if anyone had been treated for that condition within the past 30 hours, but received little useful information.

Kirkland, Frazier and the others gathered outside the disheveled apartment to discuss their next step. This was what Kirkland loved about detective work — digging into the facts, pooling and shaping them until a concrete pattern started emerging.

They lacked any solid evidence connecting Lord to the slaying although the relatives' suspicions couldn't be overlooked. Before interviewing Lord, whose visit from Miles' relatives might have left him unfriendly, they decided to see the other friend.

Finding Allen Blair wasn't as easy as they'd hoped, however. When Detectives High and Ditty arrived at the south Winter Haven address they had for him, they learned he didn't live there anymore. Fortunately, a relative at the address was persuaded to tell the detectives where he could be found.

Blair was home at the second address and readily agreed to talk with them. He'd already heard about the killing from his dead friend's family and wanted to point them toward a possible suspect.

After learning about the murder, Blair said, he'd gone to Lord's house about 7:30 p.m. to tell him about it. Lord appeared nervous, he said, and had what appeared to be a swelling under his left eye.

Blair told the detectives he had asked Lord whether he knew anything about the killing and when he'd last seen their mutual friend.

Lord's response, or so Blair claimed, had been to deny killing Miles and insist he hadn't seen him in a while. He'd shown his hands, Blair said, telling Blair to look at them and asking rhetorically if he saw blood on them.

Although he hadn't, Blair said he left that encounter feeling uneasy. In his opinion, Lord wasn't telling the truth, or at least had something to hide.

One other thing he told them also sparked the detectives' interest. He described some people from Ohio—two men, two women and two children who'd been staying with Lord in his south Winter Haven rental home. The description sounded remarkably like the couple a neighbor had mentioned seeing at Miles' apartment.

The sleuths realized they were developing good reasons to suspect Lord. Kirkland, Frazier, High and Ditty met in a bank parking lot to pool their information one more time. That led them to a nearby pharmacy, where they called for a uniformed patrol officer to meet them. Officers Mike Schreiber, Buddy Waters and Roger Dennis showed up with two dogs.

They carefully circled the modest home where Lord was living. Detectives Kirland and Frazier, accompanied by Officer Schrieber, went to the residence's back door. The second detective duo, Ditty and High, were watching the front door from the north side. And the remaining officers were on either side of the block in case Lord tried to escape.

With their careful advance preparation, the actual meeting with Lord proved somewhat anticlimactic. They knocked on the back door and were invited in about three minutes later by a man identifying himself as Simon Lord.

But what Kirkland saw when light came on was anything but routine. There were blotches of blood across the carpet in what seemed to be an every-other-step pattern!

Kirkland followed this second bloody trail to the front porch. There he saw an area on which the blood already had solidified into a thickened mass.

Swallowing an instinctive feeling of excitement, Kirkland and Frazier informed Lord they needed to talk with him about a homicide. He agreed to accompany them to Winter Haven's detective annex.

Meanwhile, High and Ditty would remain with two women also found at the house. Two children were there, sound asleep, but there was no sign of the two Ohio men Blair had mentioned.

When Lord arrived at the annex, detectives there quickly realized he was scared, nervous and upset. Kirkland, a former road patrol officer, had seen that kind of fear before. He doesn't want to bring the heat down on himself or anyone else, Kirkland mused. Along with Frazier, the detective proceeded into a long and increasingly frustrating interview with their chief suspect.

They made only slow progress the first hour. Lord wasn't asking for a lawyer, but he wasn't doing much talking either. Kirkland drew some response when he talked about the criminal penalties for withholding information, but at that rate it would take hours for the suspect to reveal anything.

Kirkland stepped out for a short break about 75 minutes into the interview. Waiting for him was Ditty, eager to disclose that one of the women had claimed Lord wasn't the killer. She was accusing the two Ohio men of having attacked Miles Sunday night when they took him home from a drunken afternoon partying at Lord's house.

Kirkland could believe that version. As the session with Lord had worn on, he'd begun to suspect the frightened man was shielding someone. But he closely cross-examined the woman, who was related to one Ohio man.

The woman told a chilling story that reinforced Kirkland's conviction the killing was "the most uncalled for murder" he'd ever seen.

She said all of them—herself, the other woman, that woman's children, the Ohio men—had been staying with Lord at another house until his landlord objected. So they'd moved in with Miles temporarily until their first host could find another house.

Although they'd left Miles' apartment before the fatal Sunday, he ended up spending the afternoon with them at Lord's. Miles had brought half a bottle of vodka and they'd picked up some beer at a convenience store.

"Everybody was just generally having a pretty good time until . . . Bobby started talking about wanting to beat Wade up," she recalled. "They had been arguing and I could tell by the way they were acting that they were going to beat him up."

"Bobby" was Bobby Louis Spriggs, a 20-year-old who had hitchhiked to Florida in August of that year, accompanied by the woman now admitting to Sprigg's involvement in murder. The other man was a friend, 18-year-old Chester Alan Dummitt, who'd left his home in Ohio against his family's wishes only nine days before the murder. He'd been accompanied by the second woman and her two children.

The two men left about 9:30 p.m. Sunday, she said, ostensibly to give Miles a ride home. About 45 minutes later, she looked out the window and saw Dummitt on the patio. He'd told her to take the second woman to a different room so he could come in without her seeing him.

After doing what he asked, she met him at the door and saw he had a cut hand. Spriggs had a bandanna wrapped around a cut on his foot. Their hands and clothing, she said, were covered with blood.

Spriggs tried to say he'd cut his foot on a piece of a broken ornament, but she didn't believe him because the porch had been swept recently. And Dummitt, she told the detectives, had "said that they had beat Wade up pretty bad and he thought that he might be dead."

Lord had taken her to work and gone home to talk with his guests. About 6:00 a.m., the woman recalled, he called her at work to tell her Miles might be dead.

"Bobby and Alan had told him they killed (Miles), that they beat him to death. And Bobby had stated that he stabbed him."

Although that sounded pretty definite, she and Lord had trouble believing it. They didn't accept its reality, she said, until Blair arrived with the news that Miles was dead.

Confronted with her statements, Lord finally agreed to tell the detectives what he knew. His statement basically reinforced what the woman had said.

He said he'd met Spriggs through neighbors only a

month or two earlier. She'd found a job but Spriggs had no steady income.

Admitting Spriggs had told him that evening he planned to mess Wade up, he confirmed their reappearance at his house — covered with blood — after taking Miles home.

"I said, 'What the hell happened?' They said they messed him up pretty bad."

After taking the woman to work, Lord had returned home to hear more than he really wanted to know.

"They just kept beating on him until he was unconscious and then they started looking for some money around the apartment," he said in one statement.

Lord described how the pair had told him they hit Miles with fists, feet and an ashtray.

"Alan went to the kitchen, got a butcher knife, grabbed Wade's head, pulled it back and was going to slash his throat and put him out of his misery," Lord maintained.

"And Bobby got mad, grabbed the knife and stabbed him (Miles). Alan said he had to get out of there because he started getting sick from the smell."

That was the version, Lord said, he got from Dummitt.

As Lord was admitting his knowledge of the murder, High and Detective Sergeant Stanton were waiting at his residence for Spriggs and Dummitt to return from visiting a friend in another city. But their waiting wasn't in vain. Stanton collected blood samples from the porch. High found a pair of blood-soaked camouflage pants, identified as belonging to Spriggs, and a bloody handkerchief in one bedroom. The second woman revealed that there were several bloodstained towels in a bathroom hamper.

About 2:15 on the morning of October 19th, a goldish-tan 1976 station wagon with an Ohio license and two men inside arrived. They proved to be the missing men, who were transported to the annex by Officer Timothy Clouse.

Dummitt, the younger, was interviewed first. Kirkland went over the events following discovery of the body, pointing out how the evidence led to him and his friend. After some initial hesitation, Dummitt confessed.

The statements both Ohio men made, shown in police and court records, make it clear Miles had no suspicion anything was amiss until his supposed buddies turned on him with their fists and anything else they could find. He'd invited them into his apartment, played music and had given Dummitt milk.

Dummitt said it was nothing Miles said or did at the apartment that touched off their attack. He said he was just trying to scare Miles when he held the knife to his throat.

In a statement his lawyers later tried to get stricken, Dummitt recalled that moment and said he "just went crazy."

"I got the knife and I put it under his throat and I was just trying to scare him. I didn't . . . I didn't have no plans to kill him."

Spriggs and Dummitt had started hitting Miles on the side of his head and he'd followed suit. Spriggs confessed to having stabbed the youth about three times.

In an almost emotionless voice, he continued describing the attack, including how they'd taken the body to the bathroom.

"Was he still alive after you took him in the bathroom?" Frazier asked.

"Yes."

"How do you know that?" Kirkland followed.

"Well, every once in a while, I seen him breathe."

"What, gasping for air?" pressed Kirkland.

"Yeah."

Spriggs said he'd felt no desire then to help Miles. Instead, he took the only money he could find at the apartment, $2 and some change, and left with Dummitt.

Dummitt tried to offer some justification for hitting Miles by claiming it was retaliation for Miles having spanked one of the children. No one else remembered Miles doing that and the police firmly discounted it. Examining the younger child didn't disclose any bruises, either. The older child said Miles had been nice to them.

As far as the Winter Haven police were concerned, the motive had been robbery. They theorized that Miles, spending freely in his desire to be liked, had given the Ohioans the impression he was richer than he was.

As the detectives continued learning about young Miles, he came across as someone eager to do things for others. His friends and co-workers described him as neat, hard working and prompt. His family remembered him as a sensitive, outgoing Christian who had sung in the church choir and was continually trying to help someone.

The youth's tragic experience dramatized what families fear most when they warn their children not to get involved with the wrong crowd.

Dummitt and Spriggs were arrested about 4:00 a.m. on charges of robbery and first-degree murder. Officer Hutzell, also having a long night, came over to take photographs of the suspects and their injuries. The detectives didn't need to feel apologetic about waking her up; she'd already been taking photos and processing items in the station wagon.

That evidence included a plastic garbage bag containing two pairs of wet pants and one size-12 pair of red and white tennis shoes with possible bloodstains on them. The tread pattern on those shoes' soles appeared to match the bloody shoe print impressions found on the floor beside Miles.

By 9:30 a.m., Officer Hutzell was attending the autopsy on Miles. Dr. Holimon determined for the record that Miles had died of numerous injuries. There were many bruises, broken ribs and a chest wound consistent with the serrated knife edge. A charred pattern outside the victim's right eye might have been caused by being hit with a hot kitchen pot.

The autopsy also revealed his blood level as .185, almost twice as high as the level ruled for legal intoxication.

Kirkland spent the next three weeks learning all he could about Miles and firming up the testimony from their two main witnesses. The grand jury returned an indictment November 12, 1982, charging Dummitt and Spriggs with first-degree murder, robbery and burglary. It accused them of taking money, cigarettes and an identification card.

Four days later, Prosecutor Pickard filed a motion seeking blood and hair samples from the suspects to match with those found in the apartment, car and clothing.

Circuit Judge Thomas Clarke Jr. ordered December 6th that the two men go on trial separately. The next month, he ordered them to provide the prosecution with palm and fingerprints.

Before the first trial began, Pickard offered a deal under which he'd refrain from seeking the death penalty if they'd plead guilty to first-degree murder. Both refused.

Dummitt's trial began March 15, 1983, in Bartow, Polk County's county seat. His family had come from Ohio and were supplying him with a private lawyer. The defense had presented hundreds of letters from people in Dummitt's home town intended to show the killing was out of character.

The defense attorney didn't try to claim Dummitt hadn't been involved. Instead, he painted the picture of a young man sent out of control by consuming 11 glasses of vodka and a six-pack of beer. He hinted that an alcohol-induced blackout might have prevented him from realizing his actions.

But the prosecution contended Dummitt had led the attack, which had been planned before leaving the house. Pickard said the time needed to inflict Miles' many injuries gave Dummitt time to know what he was doing.

The jury took a middle ground. It decided March 17th that Dummitt was guilty of second-degree murder, a lesser offense, and acquitted him of robbery. A burglary charge already had been dismissed.

Spriggs went on trial the first week in April. He also would contend drinking impaired his judgment. The older defendant also admitted to having hostile feelings toward Miles.

The second jury was harsher on Spriggs, finding him guilty of first-degree murder and robbery with a deadly weapon. But it recommended life imprisonment rather than the possible death penalty for Spriggs.

Judge Clarke took that advice and sentenced Spriggs to two concurrent life sentences. Under the sentence for murder, he must serve at least 25 years.

Dummitt's sentencing came on April 20th. He received 75 years in prison for the second-degree murder conviction with the court retaining jurisdiction over his sentence for 25 years.

The judge listed several reasons for retaining jurisdiction. Dummitt's blows would have killed Miles even if Spriggs hadn't stabbed him, he said, and neither man made an effort to seek help for Miles.

"The court can discern no reason to believe that the defendant, Mr. Dummitt, would not again engage in similar conduct if he were to gain his freedom," concluded the judge.

EDITOR'S NOTE:
Simon Lord and Allen Blair are not the real names of the persons so named in the foregoing story. Fictitious names have been used because there is no reason for public interest in the identities of these persons.

"MUTILATED MOLLY FOR FRUIT PUNCH!"

by Benison Murray

JOHNSON CITY, TENNESSEE
JANUARY 24, 1984

The last days of May, 1983, were about to usher in what Captain Rick Gordon of the Johnson City Police Department would term, "our bloodiest crime that has occurred in ten years."

The May landscape in the extreme northeastern part of Tennessee is a tapestry. Apple trees in blossom stud the valleys. Mountain laurel runs like a pastel crown. The tobacco beds hemstitch each harrowed acre like living gems. For the farmer dreaming of the fall harvest, it always looks like it will be the best cash crop ever.

May means many things to different people. For Molly Hawk, a 92-year-old resident of Washington County, the penultimate day of May was a source of great satisfaction. She had seen another spring.

Padding about in worn house slippers, still in her nightgown, Molly peered from her window in order to see who had knocked at her kitchen door. Visitors were always welcome to gossip and to share a cup of coffee. Arranging her face in a welcoming smile, Molly Hawk opened the door.

The shove took her by surprise. The blow aimed at her

face was both swift and deadly. The frail old woman was tossed up, then fell to the floor as limp and weightless as her own kitchen curtains. It was only the prelude to a murderous assault.

Jerked upright by her assailant, the helpless woman was levied into position and battered repeatedly. The unequal struggle carried both the victim and her aggressor through the first floor of the two-story dwelling, his blood and hers spattering the walls, the floor and the furniture.

Nothing in Molly Hawk's life had prepared her for this. There was no defense possible because of her extreme age and state of health. Mute from terror and shock, the elderly woman reeled under the onslaught, and was left unconscious on the floor of a store room, her face pulped beyond recognition.

She never heard the house being ransacked, drawers pulled out and papers strewn about. She never knew when the door opened and shut leaving her alone once again.

Early the next afternoon, a relative came to check on the old woman. She pushed open the door, took one step into the kitchen, then backed hastily out. She had seen enough. There on the kitchen floor were Molly's house shoes—some five feet apart. A bloody pillowcase was on the floor too. Spooked at the utter silence, and sure a murder had been committed, the woman fled the house in terror intent on a phone and help from the Johnson City Police Department.

Shortly, she was rewarded by the pulling in of a patrolcar. One look through the house brought the officer on the run to his vehicle where a call alerted Capt. Rick Gordon, the commander of the Criminal Investigation Bureau. He assigned Detective Sergeants Bill Dickover and Trent Harris who raced to their own vehicle in order to beat the summoned rescue squad to the Unaka address.

Brushing past the terror-stricken relative who was told to stay put for questioning, both men leaped the stairs literally neck-to-neck with the paramedics.

They found the badly beaten Molly Hawk lying partially nude, her face covered with a newspaper and battered beyond recognition.

The real surprise was that she was alive at all. Molly was carefully carried out to the rescue vehicle and rushed to the emergency room of the local medical center.

Orders were snapped out by the attending doctor while his practiced eye assessed the damage done to his patient.

Brain damage was possible as she was convulsing. Her left jaw was obviously fractured, both her eyes were swollen shut and there was a deep depression on her left cheek. In addition, the doctor noted Molly Hawk had sustained cuts on both arms while her skin was peeled back from the tops of both hands, exposing bone on one of them.

The ME performed what was necessary for maintenance. Surgery was out of the question. All the doctor could do was hope for the best and make a copy of his notes for the detective assigned to this case who was sure to come by.

With the victim gone, grim-faced homicide detectives began the basic evidence gathering they'd need to process the case. They first recorded the scene exactly as it was found for a permanent record.

Photos were taken of the house slippers, the bloody pillowcase, the calendar unturned to a new day. The camera was used to show blood patterns on the floor, the walls, and the furniture. Best of all, a series of photos were taken of a bloody footprint standing out on the kitchen tiles. Later, Dickover would pry up the tiles and preserve the footprint in the hope of finding a suspect with shoes that would match the damning print.

More than sufficient photographs were taken because homicide investigators know a crime scene can change as if by magic. The major axiom in any crime setting is "show it like it is." Many times a blown-up photo will show things not seen by the eye, and in time, their significance will be shown to be pertinent to the solving of a case.

A crime scene sketch was made which showed the relative distance from the body of Molly Hawk to the blood splashes, the house shoes, the footprint and the pillowcase. The fact that the phone line had been cut was noted on the schematic drawing as well as all doors and windows which could have afforded entrance or exit to the assailant.

A fingerprint search was carried out. All potential locations for prints were carefully dusted and a fiberglass brush applied to them. As the print became visible the brushing was continued in the direction of the friction ridge impressions, cleaning out the space between the ridges. The prints were finally lifted with transparent tape and transferred to a clean white card for storage.

This finished, the house was sealed and Sergeants Dickover and Harris began interviewing anyone who might have heard or seen anything relative to the beating of Molly Hawk.

Back at the hospital, Mrs. Hawk's condition was listed as critical. X-rays and a brain scan showed, as her physician had feared, a fractured jaw and multiple fractures of her left cheek. The good news was that there was no evidence of inner cranial bleeding in spite of the savage

368

beating she had sustained.

Molly Hawk was administered antibiotics, her fractured jaw was wired together and she was connected to a breathing machine. When Dickover checked back with her doctor, he was told the woman was in intensive care and they could only sit back and wait.

Meanwhile, city investigators were disheartened that after checking, no prints could be found that didn't belong to the victim, her family or friends. But this was not unexpected. Detectives know that good legible prints are found in less than three percent of crime scenes worked. In these days of TV murder and mayhem, it is a backward burglar indeed who would leave such a signature.

And the attack on Molly Hawk was considered to be a burglary. The theory was that an unknown intruder had entered, brutalized the old lady, then ransacked her dwelling for money.

Dickover and Harris hour after hour had interviewed every close neighbor and no one had heard anything. No screams, no sounds of the terrible beating being administered to their elderly neighbor—nothing. No one had seen a person or persons leaving the Hawk residence that would have led them to believe a crime was taking place in the Unaka street home.

For the sleuths it was very disheartening, but par for the course. If they had learned anything in the course of being detectives, it was that old cliche—"Rome wasn't built in a day"—and neither was a case against a vicious perpetrator.

But if the two detectives had no eyewitnesses, and no fingerprints, they still had the bloody footprint found at the scene, plus the various blood scrapings taken from the Hawk house. With luck, something would be determined from lab tests that would allow them to zero in on

369

the assailant, or damn a suspect, when found.

Dickover and Harris true to investigative tactics wore out shoe leather slogging to every place and questioning every person their experience told them might know something. They needed leads badly. Lab tests had now shown there were two kinds of blood at the scene—one of them Molly Hawk's. A great deal of hope was put on the kitchen tiles holding the bloody footprint—if they could just find a suspect whose shoes matched the print.

Although non-productive to this point, the two sleuths had brought 25 people to Capt. Rick Gordon for additional questioning. It was hoped that shortly one interview or another would net them the jackpot.

They finished canvassing the neighborhood of Molly Hawk. Now they started on what would become the bulk of the investigation. Post office employees were questioned, delivery trucks run down to the businesses they represented and the drivers given a hard look. Family members were re-questioned in the hopes something would be remembered, some lead found that wasn't ferreted out on the first go-around. Friends of the old lady were interviewed together with employees of any store where the woman was known to trade. Power company employees, meter readers, and the young girl clerks at the local mini-marts were asked what, if anything, they had seen on the day Molly Hawk had been assaulted.

Over 100 hours of intensive investigation were put in by Dickover and Harris and they felt they deserved a break, and one was about to take place.

On June 5th, two men intent on money, once again returned like predators to the same Unaka area where they had been before. They were intent on burglarizing another home occupied by an elderly woman. Fortunately, the 91-year-old lady had been transferred to a local home for oldsters, and was not in the position of Molly Hawk.

The house belonging to the old woman was being watched by their neighbor, Robert Wigham. Wigham was playing cards with his friend, John Shoemaker. Both were points away from a winning hand when the phone rang. It was yet another neighbor who told Wigham the residence he was housesitting had lights on.

Alarmed, the game between the two friends came to an abrupt halt. Lights shouldn't be on in the house. Wigham knew for a fact his elderly neighbor was still in the residence for the aged, and if this was so, then who had turned the lights on in the house and what were they doing?

Wigham, his friend Shoemaker, and the latter's wife, made the decision to investigate — but cautiously. As added protection, Wigham's wife was left behind to notify the Johnson City Police Department.

The three would-be detectives made their way to the driveway of the dwelling just in time to see two men coming out of the house. From the way they were walking it looked like they were drunk. What was more, neither seemed aware they were under observation.

At that moment, sirens of a responding patrol car could be heard coming rapidly through the night. Wigham and his party watched as the two intruders, hearing the siren, jumped into some concealing bushes.

Uniformed officers made a hasty capture of both men and their arrest on suspicion of burglary. The officers noted on their incident report the battered and swollen hands of one of the suspects.

All officers in the city and county were aware of the Molly Hawk assault and had been on the lookout for any suspicious character showing evidence of a brawl of any kind.

After detectives read them their rights, both suspects were taken to the Johnson City Jail for incarceration and further questioning. No one at that point thought they were more than a pair of dirty-neck drunks out to pilfer some cash hockable items to buy booze—but they had possibilities.

At the local lockup, the men were identified as James William Barnes, 44, and his companion, Kenneth Skeene, a 34-year-old ex-Vietnam helicopter pilot. Both were well known to area law enforcement officials.

Three months before, Barnes had been released from jail after serving seven months of a two-year sentence for aggravated assault. Lawmen learned he had a past record of destroying property, battery and disorderly charges, 32 of which had been dismissed in Sessions court between 1974 and 1980.

Barnes was known as a public drunk—and a mean one. The man had been in and out of alcoholic rehab programs like a human yo-yo. He was violent too. He had been convicted and served 11 months for dragging a 17-year-old relative by the hair from her wheelchair and threatening to kill her grandparents.

Skeene was as charming. He had a record, probers found out, which included threatening city police on at least two occasions, and in 1981 he had threatened to kill a news reporter at the Johnson City Press Chronicle newsroom. As if this wasn't enough, he had been arrested by the FBI for making verbal threats against the life of the president.

With this record of violence, plus the fact that both suspects were found in the Unaka Avenue area where Molly Hawk had been assaulted, and with the marks of battering evident on Barnes' hands, Captain Rick Gordon, Sgt. Sam Reed, Dickover and Harris huddled. They decided to question them to determine if both were involved in the Hawk assault.

Confronted with Barnes, each lawman noted the deep marks of violence that were on both of his arms. They looked at his swollen and battered hands, particularly his right hand.

The lawmen approached the interview with caution. The whole thrust of the questioning was intended not to spook the suspect or anger him so that he would refuse to cooperate or deny everything.

But the best interrogation was not going to get Barnes to admit anything. By the time the detectives gave up, they felt they had been lucky to get him to admit his name.

With Skeene, however, the interview went smoothly. Alternating between tough and tender, officials got Skeene to pour forth a veritable fountain of information. This covered not only the burglary on Unaka Avenue on June 5th, but the earlier attack on Molly Hawk.

Joined by Assistant District Attorney General Bill Mooney, Skeene admitted the motive behind the Hawk assault was to secure Kool-Aide to use as a mixer with Lysol.

Smiling winningly at the men clustered around him, Skeene said he and Barnes saw Mrs. Hawk sitting in her house that afternoon, but he did not go inside.

"I never touched Molly Hawk and I never went into the house," he told investigators.

He elaborated on his story by telling the officials Barnes went to the kitchen door and when the old woman opened it, Barnes shoved her, then began hitting her with his fists. According to Skeene, he wanted no part of the affair and told Barnes so. He then left and returned to a building where Barnes and he did most of their drinking. Later, he said, Barnes joined him and he had blood on his hands.

"I asked him what happened and he said, 'If she'd done what I asked her and sat . . . she'd been all right,' " Skeene said.

Skeene told the silent men that he had watched long enough to see Barnes hit the old woman "four or five times." He also told them that when Barnes came to the downtown location, he had told Skeene, 'I didn't get anything!"

Jubilant at this good news, investigators were still cautious. Hard evidence was needed, not self-serving statements by an accomplice. If Barnes had shoes that would match the incriminating tiles, the probers knew they would be home free. They would be able to charge Barnes with the June 5th burglary, plus the assault on Molly Hawk and the burglary in her house.

And this is exactly what happened. The shoes belonging to Barnes matched the bloody footprint on the tiles. Skeene remained held on $5000 bond on the first-degree burglary charge on the second house they had pilfered. Barnes was charged with both that burglary and assault with intent to commit murder and second-degree burglary at the Unaka address of Molly Hawk. Barnes was ordered held by Judge Stewart Cannon with $10,000 bond on the assault charge and $5,000 bond on the burglary charge.

Barnes did not go gentle into his cell. Once there, awaiting his preliminary hearing, he pulled the insides from his mattress in a rage, and for whatever reason, tore the metal stays from a wristwatch he was wearing. He was promptly burdened with an additional charge of destruction of city property.

In the preliminary hearing, evidence showing probable

374

cause were presented by police. The court was told that Barnes' shoes matched the bloody print found on the kitchen tiles preserved by Dickover, plus the sworn statement of his drinking buddy, Skeene.

In court, Skeene recanted the shocking story of the two lifelong acquaintances who, having finished their first bottle of Lysol, decided to get a chaser for the second.

According to Skeene, he and Barnes went to the Hawk home where Skeene saw Barnes hit Molly Hawk with a chair. Skeene told the court, "I said, 'Bill, don't hit that old woman.' I started to help her, but he told me to get back outside. I tried my best to talk him out of it."

Later, Skeene said, when Barnes joined him at their favorite drinking spot, Skeene noticed his hands were bleeding.

"He told me to keep my mouth shut and if anybody asked me, he cut his hands fighting a bunch of black people," Skeene testified.

Barnes was bound over to the grand jury on five charges of assault to commit murder, two counts of burglary, and two counts of destruction of city property. His bond was set at a total of $25,000 on all charges, while Skeene had his bond reduced to $2,500 as he was not considered an escape risk.

On July 6th everything changed. At the local medical center, Molly Hawk, the gallant old lady who had been making such a gutsy fight for life, lost her battle. The charge against Barnes was immediately amended to first-degree murder. He was now held on $1 million bond.

James William Barnes was indicted by the grand jury on the amended charges, and his trial, set for January 3, 1984, was re-scheduled to January 24th to allow Assistant DA Bill Mooney to locate Skeene who was to be the state's key witness.

Bill Mooney, the hard-hitting young prosecutor, said the state intended to ask for the death penalty for what he termed was a "torturous" crime committed by the defendant against the 92-year-old Molly Hawk.

In the defense's opening statements in the murder trial, a plea was made urging that jurors judge Barnes "as if they were being tried." The jurors were told "our defense is that Bill Barnes did not commit this crime. Our offense is that Kenneth Skeene murdered Molly Hawk — that *he* beat her to the extent she later died."

Arresting officer Sgt. Bill Dickover told the jury about the bloody footprints which were preserved by him at the crime scene.

"We also think the blood all over the house came from her walking around and falling. Whether that happened during or after the beating, we don't know," he testified.

The emergency room doctor gave a graphic account of the elderly victim's injuries, telling the jury Molly had been so badly beaten she was unrecognizable.

A relative of the victim testified she had seen a bloody pillowcase and Molly Hawk's house slippers lying five feet apart. It was she who called police.

Kenneth Skeene testified against his good buddy and told the court when they went to the Unaka address they were looking for Kool-Aide to mix with a bottle of Lysol to drink. He denied ever touching Molly Hawk.

Skeene recalled that when the beating began he said to Barnes he wanted no part of it and left. Barnes later joined him and his hands were bleeding.

An FBI lab agent told the court that tests proved Barnes' shoes matched the bloody footprint in comparisons of shoe defects, design and size.

The defense countered, saying Skeene had beaten

Molly Hawk and only stopped when Barnes stopped him. He was accused of having bragged about the beating he did in Johnson City.

Skeene argued this by saying, "I'm not that mean and I'm not that sick."

The defense tried to bring out the fact that the victim had not died of the beating but of pneumonia that developed.

Pathologist Bob McGee said dryly, "What I found didn't kill her but it didn't do her any good."

Police officials testified that blood scrapings taken from the Hawk home matched both the victim's blood and that of the defendant.

The defense elicited an admission that in fact a third type of blood could have been present without detecting it. "It's not like fingerprints," the FBI lab agent said. "If the blood flow was constant, it would have shown."

Barnes took the stand in his own defense and told a story diametrically opposed to that of Skeene.

Barnes testified Skeene had told him they were going to his grandmother's house. He said the only thing he did when they got to the house was stand outside the door and smoke.

"I didn't go in until I heard someone holler twice, 'Don't kill me,' " Barnes said.

Barnes said he then went into the kitchen and saw Skeene hitting the woman. He said he yelled and hit Skeene across the room, partially knocking out Skeene's false teeth. He said Skeene crawled through his legs and left the house.

Barnes said the only time he touched Molly Hawk was to lay her down on the floor and tell her, "No one's going to kill you."

Barnes denied any knowledge of the cut phone wire,

nor could he explain how his blood got throughout the house. His explanation of his swollen hands was that it was because of a fight he had prior to the Hawk beating.

Concluding defense testimony came from a prisoner who connected Skeene to the Hawk beating. He told jurors Skeene had admitted he had beaten the victim when the two were together in a cell.

With closing arguments terminated, instructions were given to the jury and the six-day trial with its total of 18 witnesses came to the moment of decision.

Now it would be up to the panel to determine if James William Barnes was guilty or innocent of the death of Molly Hawk.

If found guilty, Barnes could receive a life sentence, or if aggravated circumstances were found, he could be given death under Tennessee law.

When the jurors filed back into the Washington County Courtroom, James William Barnes had no better luck than Molly Hawk. Barnes was found guilty of the first-degree murder of Molly Hawk and sentenced to death by electrocution based on three aggravating circumstances proved by the state.

EDITOR'S NOTE:
Robert Wigham, John Shoemaker, and Kenneth Skeene are not the real names of the persons so named in the foregoing story. Fictitious names have been used because there is no reason for public interest in their true identities.

"GREEDY BANDIT
EXECUTED TWO!"

by Jack Heise

PORT ARTHUR, TX.
AUGUST 19, 1985

It was more than just official duty that drew Patrol
Officer Ken Carona to the Park Place Plaza Shopping
Center in Port Arthur, Texas, shortly after ten o'clock on
Tuesday morning, July 16, 1985. He stopped at the
branch of the Jefferson Savings and Loan where one of
the three young women employees was a very special
friend.

Carona entered the lobby and then stopped with a
puzzled frown. The bank was open, but none of the employees were at their desks, in the tellers' cages or at the
drive-in window.

Waiting for a few moments for someone to appear,
Carona crossed the lobby and went back to where the
door to the vault was open. He stopped again, this time
with a gasp as if having been hit in the solar plexus.

The bodies of two young women were sprawled on the
floor in a welter of blood.

Carona recognized them immediately. One was his
very special friend, 23-year-old Diana Joy Jackson. The
other was 28-year-old Helen Jean Barnard, supervisor of
the branch bank.

Racing to a telephone, Carona called headquarters requesting assistance and an ambulance. "I think Diana is still alive," he said.

Officers and medics were at the bank within minutes. Diana Jackson, who had been shot in the back, appeared to be still breathing. Helen Barnard, shot in the forehead, was dead. Diana was rushed to a hospital a short distance away.

Captain Jim Heubel, with Lieutenants Bill Edmonds and K. J. Landry and Homicide Division Sergeant Cedric Clayton, took command at the scene. The bank and the area around it was roped off while officers were sent to the other businesses in the large shopping center to locate any possible witnesses.

Calls were placed to the Texas Rangers and the FBI office in Houston, 90 miles away, requesting assistance.

It was learned that, normally, there were three women working at the bank branch. Only two, however, were shot, presenting the possibility that the third employee might have been taken as a hostage. An alert went out covering all of the police agencies in Texas and neighboring Louisiana.

Waiting for the technicians to arrive to process the scene, the detectives observed that the tellers' cages had been looted and cash boxes taken.

It appeared the bandit must have entered shortly after the bank opened, forced the employees into the vault and executed them in cold blood, then picked up the cash boxes and left.

"What a monster," one of the detectives said. "He could have tied them up, locked them in the vault, but he must have planned to kill them before he ever stepped a foot inside."

The deliberate shooting of the victims suggested the possibility that he may have been known to them and had eliminated them to prevent them from identifying him.

A call was placed to the hospital to learn if the victim who had been shot in the back might have regained consciousness and possibly provide information about the holdup and shootings.

The detectives learned that Diana Jackson had died in the emergency operation room shortly after she reached the hospital.

The third employee, who it was thought might have been abducted, came to the bank. She explained that she had been called for jury duty and that Diana Jackson, who normally would have come in later, had taken her place.

When the technicians arrived to check out the bank for fingerprints and other physical evidence, one of the first things they noted was a surveillance camera on a wall. Someone apparently had tried to dismantle it, but had been unable to jerk it free from the brackets holding it to the wall.

"Let's hope it was on and the film hasn't been exposed," one of the detectives said.

The camera was carefully removed from the wall and rushed to a local television station. After the film had been processed, it was played on a screen. The quality of the film wasn't good, but a technician said he could enhance it and have it ready within a short time.

Technicians located two spent .45-caliber shells in the vault that had been fired from an automatic handgun. The shells were carefully preserved so that the slugs that killed the victims could positively identify the murder weapon, if it could be found.

Officers checking out the shopping plaza failed to locate any witnesses who had seen a person entering or leaving the bank. Most of the shops were just opening for the day at the time the slayings had taken place, and there were only a few early customers in the mall.

The enhanced videotape was played for the investigators. The camera had been turned on and showed Helen Barnard at her desk and Diana Jackson at the drive-in window when the first customer entered the bank. It showed the time as 10:10 a.m.

The person who entered the bank was a tall man, weighing at least 200 pounds with a pronounced potbelly. He was wearing sunglasses with dark lenses, a light-colored shirt and dark slacks. The camera recorded him smiling as he came into the lobby and then walked over to the desk where Helen was seated.

The tape rolled on showing the man talking to Helen for a few minutes. Then he drew a handgun and apparently announced the holdup. He pointed the weapon at Diana and signalled her to leave the drive-in window and come out into the lobby.

The camera caught the two young women complying with the orders. Expressions on their faces showed fear, but not panic, as the man talked to them, most likely assuring them if they followed orders they would not be harmed.

Both young women were aware of the bank policy that they should not resist a holdup or do anything to jeopardize their lives, or the lives of customers if it took place while others were in the bank.

With the two women in front of him, the bandit herded them into the vault. The camera did not cover the vault area. There were several minutes of tape that showed only the empty interior of the bank.

The robber again appeared on tape as he came out of the vault. He methodically scooped up the money in the

382

cash drawers and placed it in the reserve boxes of cash in each of the tellers' cages. He walked out of the bank with the loot, but returned within moments.

The camera recorded him crossing the lobby again and coming directly up to where the camera was located. The film stopped at that point as the bandit apparently shut off the camera and then had tried to rip it off the wall.

"What a heartless, cold-blooded killer," Captain Huebel said as he viewed the film.

"It looks like a real professional job," one of the FBI agents said. "He knew exactly what he was going to do before he ever entered. He was going to eliminate any witnesses, but he blew it when he didn't get the camera off the wall."

The investigators played the film again, taking note of every movement of the killer. The camera had caught him as he left the bank and showed a light-colored pickup truck parked in front. It was assumed that it was his vehicle, but the image wasn't clear enough to positively identify the make or model.

"We know what the guy looks like," Landry said. "Now all we've got to do is find out who he is and where he is."

A description of the killer was immediately broadcast over the police network.

The bank employee who had escaped the holdup and slaying by being called for jury duty was shown the film. She studied the features of the killer but could not place him as anyone she knew or who might have been in the bank previously.

Single prints of some of the best frames showing the killer were made. They were given to officers to show to employees in the shopping mall on the chance that the killer might have cased the bank before actually pulling the robbery.

Bank officials arrived at the branch. They were able to tentatively put the loot that had been taken as being around $7,000. One of the officials explained that because it was a savings and loan bank, it did not keep the large amounts of cash that are required for commercial banks. Most of the customers were either making payments on loans, deposits, or withdrawing smaller sums from their savings account.

Each of the boxes in the tellers' cages contained "bait money," which are packets of currency with the serial numbers recorded and the bills marked.

An FBI agent, with training for bank robbery cases, however, said that "bait money" most often is only of value when the bandit is caught shortly after the holdup and has it in his possession. If it is spent some distance from where the robbery took place, it could be days or even weeks before it passes through the hands of merchants and then to banks where it might be recognized and identified.

"If the guy is as cool and professional as he looks on the film, he'd know about 'bait money,' explosive dyes and that sort of thing," the agent said. "He'll probably be a long way from here before he checks out those packets of cash or attempts to spend any of the loot."

In the meantime, residents of Port Arthur were first shocked and then angered by the callous slaying of the two young women. There was some criticism that the bank should have employed more security for the employees.

Bank officials, however, explained that the branch was located in a large shopping area and the employees had been instructed not to resist any holdup. It was doubtful that even if a security guard had been on duty the tragedy could have been prevented. Most likely, the killer would have taken the guard by surprise and he would have been executed along with the young women.

And as horrendous as the slaughter had been, it was fortunate that no customers had come in or the death toll would have been larger.

As the tedious task of dusting the interior of the bank for fingerprints continued, the investigating officers were faced with a number of unanswered questions.

Why had the bandit selected the small branch in Port Arthur? He must have realized that, as a savings and loan institution, it would not have as large amount of cash on hand as would a commercial bank.

Had the robbery been planned in advance, or had the branch been selected at random by some transient who just happened to be passing through the area?

The primary question, however, was why the robber had deliberately killed the two employees. There was no evidence that they had struggled or resisted him. The slug that felled Helen Barnard had been fired within inches of her forehead. Diana Jackson had apparently turned away from the bandit and had been shot in the back. Only two shots had been fired, and with deadly accuracy.

The videotape showed that the killer had remained completely calm after the slayings as he picked up the cash boxes.

"It just doesn't make any sense for him to have killed the women," an officer said.

One of the FBI agents agreed and said, "There's no way a sane person can get into the head of a psychopathic killer like him. He has absolutely no regard for human life."

It was also possible the murders might just have been the start of a bloody rampage if the killer followed the routine of many serial killers.

Prints from the videotape were sent to the National Crime Information Center for a computer check to determine if there had been previous holdups or slayings fitting the pattern in other parts of the country.

Despite the fact that the surveillance camera had caught the bandit-killer on tape, it appeared that it would be a difficult task to identify and locate him as he apparently had managed to get out of the area. Road blockades that had been set up earlier around the Port Arthur area were recalled.

Then, late in the afternoon as the videotape was being shown, one of the Port Arthur officers suddenly exclaimed, I think I know that guy or somebody that looks a hell of a lot like him!"

The officer named a person and said he had known the man several years earlier while the person had been working as a truck driver in Beaumont, a larger city 25 miles north of Port Arthur.

But as the officer studied the features of the killer captured on the videotape, he said, "I can't figure him for a cold-blooded killer. He was a pretty decent guy, as I recall, I think he had a couple of stepdaughters who should be about the same age or maybe a few years younger than the women at the bank."

An immediate check was made of the criminal files to determine if the possible suspect might have a criminal record.

The man's name did appear in the criminal file. He had been charged and entered a plea of guilty to passing a not-sufficient-fund (NSF) check. There was no record that he had ever engaged in any violent crimes.

"We'll have to check him out," an agent said. "Although it could be just a case of being a look-alike."

The police in Beaumont were contacted with a request for any information they might have on the man and where he could be located.

The Beaumont police knew the possible suspect. They said he had been employed for a time as a security guard at the main office of the savings and loan company in Beaumont. They did not know his present address but would make inquiries to locate him.

The investigators in Port Arthur went into a huddle. Was it possible that the man the officer recognized as resembling the killer was actually the cold-blooded murderer, or was it just one of those rare coincidences in which he looked like the man and had also been employed as security guard for the bank in Beaumont?

"If we can get to him before he gets rid of the cash and the gun, we'll known for sure," an agent said. "We might not be able to make a positive identification from the videotape, but the gun and marked money is solid evidence."

While the search went on to locate the possible suspect, the investigating officers conferred with Jefferson County District Attorney James McGrath. If and when the man was located, they would need an arrest and search warrants.

"That is if he is the guy we're looking for and he's still in this part of the country," an officer said. "My guess is if he did pull something like this, he'd put a lot of distance between himself and around here."

McGrath said he would prepare the warrants, and, as soon as additional information was obtained, he would take them to a court to have them issued.

A new lead in the case developed later in the evening with a call to the Beaumont police by the manager of a foreign car agency. He said he had just read about the bank robbery in Port Arthur and the slaying of the two women employees.

"I'm not sure this has anything to do with it," the caller said, "but it's sort of strange and I thought it best if I let you know about it."

He related that, about a week earlier, a young woman had purchased a new sports car from the agency and paid for it in cash with a check.

The check had bounced, and a relative of the woman had deposited a check for $5,000 to her account to cover the insufficient funds.

The relative's check had also bounced.

"I called them and told them if the checks were not made good we would press criminal charges," the man said. He related that the relative of the young woman had come in to see him. The relative promised that he would make good on the checks by bringing in cash.

"He told me he had some kind of a deal going down and he would have the cash by today," the automobile agency manager said. "And sure enough, he came in this afternoon with $5,000 in cash."

The caller said he did not want to cause any trouble for the man, but the man had been evasive about where he had obtained the cash.

"I guess you guys could check it out, and if it is on the level, he wouldn't have to know that I called you," the informant said.

Assured that the call would be confidential, the caller named the man who had made good on the NSF check by covering it with cash.

The man that the automobile agency manager named was 50-year-old David Lee Holland, the same man the officer in Port Arthur had named as looking like the killer who had been captured on the surveillance camera videotape and who also had been employed as a security guard by the main office of the bank in Beaumont.

When the information was forwarded to the investigators in Port Arthur, they immediately contacted McGrath and asked him to have the arrest and search warrants issued. They had ben able to obtain from the automobile agency manager the home address of David Holland, who was living in Nederland, a suburb of Beaumont.

They had also learned that the money given to the automobile agency had been deposited in a bank in Beaumont shortly before closing time. Bank officials were contacted and asked to open the bank so that the deposit could be examined to be checked against the serial numbers and secret markings on the "bait money" that had been taken in the robbery.

It was shortly before three o'clock in the morning when agents with the FBI, Port Arthur police and Jefferson County sheriff's officers met in Beaumont.

The check with the bank on the cash that had been deposited by the automobile agency revealed that the deposit contained marked and recorded currency that had been taken in the "bait money."

D.A. McGrath obtained an arrest warrant naming David Holland as a suspect for the bank robbery and the murders of Diana Jackson and Helen Barnard. The search warrant covered his home and car.

The officers had already ascertained that Holland was at his home, and police had been stationed in the area to keep the house under surveillance. "This guy is a cold-blooded killer," an agent told the group. "We're going to have to handle this carefully so that we don't get anyone else killed."

The plan was laid out that 15 officers armed with automatic weapons would go to the area in unmarked cars and take up positions around the house. Two officers would go up to the house to serve the warrants on Holland. Backup officers would be close by to rush in in the event Holland resisted the arrest.

"We want the guy alive," one agent said. "It's the only way we can wrap up the case. Hold your fire unless you are actually in danger yourself."

It was shortly after three o'clock in the morning when all of the officers were in position and the two investigators went up to the house. Lights were on inside. They rang the doorbell, and Holland, fully clothed, opened the door for them.

He did not appear to be surprised when the officers identified themselves. He was quoted as saying, "I guess I know why you are here."

He turned and held out his hands for the cuffs to be placed on his wrists.

With Holland in custody, officers and agents searched his house and pickup truck. They claimed in an affidavit filed later that they found money in the house that had been identified as part of the "bait money."

The affidavit also alleged that they discovered a .45-caliber automatic handgun in the house which ballistic experts identified as the weapon used in the murders of Diana Jackson and Helen Barnard.

Confronted with the evidence from the surveillance camera videotape, the marked money and identification of the murder weapon, it was alleged in an affidavit that Holland confessed to the robbery and the murders of the two bank employees and had voluntarily taken officers to a spot on the Lower Neches Valley Authority Canal outside of Beaumont, where he had discharged the empty cashiers' boxes.

Captain Heubel and D.A. McGrath announced to the news media that Holland had been taken into custody and had been charged with the robbery and murders.

"It has been a terrible tragedy," Heubel told the reporters, "but we are fortunate to have solved the case so quickly, due to the cooperation of a number of citizens and police agencies."

Asked if Holland had made any statement as to why he had gunned down the bank employees in cold-blood, McGrath said that he could not comment on that. He confirmed that Holland had confessed to the crimes, but the statement he had given would not be made public prior to the time he went to trial on the charges.

Separate funeral services were held for the two victims. The services for Diana Joy Jackson were held in her home town of Port Neches and for Helen Jean Barnard in her hometown of Groves. Both chapels were crowded with hundreds of mourners paying their last respects.

McGrath presented his evidence that had been obtained by the investigators to a special Jefferson County grand jury. The panel returned indictments charging Holland with two counts of capital murder and one count of bank robbery. He was convicted and sentenced to death.

"WAS THE KINDLY WIDOW WASTED FOR HER WHEELS?"

by John Railey

HARBINGER, NORTH CAROLINA
APRIL 29, 1986

Ethel Sumrell Owens was missing. Throughout that hot Tuesday, April 29, 1986, in North Carolina, the family and friends of the 79-year-old Currituck County woman had been trying to telephone her in vain. Her faded burgundy Impala, a 1968 model with a dull white top, had been missing from her driveway since early that morning, as near as the neighbors could tell. The last time anyone had talked to Ethel had been when a relative telephoned about eleven o'clock the night before. Ethel had sounded fine then.

It wasn't like the warmhearted woman, whose mind was as sharp as ever, to go off for so long without telling any of the friends she kept in touch with. They were all worried. Ethel Owens lived alone in a neat white frame house smack-dab in the middle of Harbinger, a close-knit community of a few hundred residents in northeastern North Carolina.

Her house sat by U.S. 158, a busy road that crosses the Currituck Sound a few miles south of her residence and shoots through the Outer Banks, a nationally known resort area on the Atlantic. In 1986, development was creeping into Ethel Owens' corner of the county, but not at an alarming rate.

Everyone still knew everyone else in Harbinger, and they were worried about their elderly friend, who had spent all her hardworking life in the community. She and her late husband once ran a general store in the front of their home, catering to locals and beach-bound tourists.

About 7:15 p.m. on Tuesday, Ethel's worried friends and relatives filed a missing-person report with the Currituck County Sheriff's Department. At that time, the department had only about eight to ten deputies. With such a small staff to patrol his large, sprawling county, Sheriff Norman Newbern often works cases himself.

Upon listening to the details of Ethel Owens' case, the dispatcher realized that there were serious implications. He immediately called Sheriff Newbern.

Newbern was then 47, a quiet country gentleman who'd logged 22 years as the elected sheriff. A Currituck native, he had known and liked Ethel since he was a boy. The sheriff hurried to join some of his deputies who were already at the widow's home.

Entering the missing woman's house with a relative's key, Newbern quickly determined that there had been trouble in the house. The sheriff and his deputies found that someone had broken in a south-side window in what had once been the store area of the house. Ethel had been using it as a storage room. A door, usually locked, led to the rear, which was the living area of the house.

That door had been broken down.

As Newbern and his men moved through the usually tidy house, they found furniture in disarray, suggesting the aftermath of a violent confrontation. In Ethel's bedroom, they found the bed covered by bloody sheets. What they did not find was any sign of the widow herself. They did determine that her purse was missing, and they found the back door standing open.

Theorizing that Ethel Owens had been abducted in her own car, Sheriff Newbern had his deputies broadcast a computer lookout, listing a detailed description of the Impala right down to its new tires and new license tag, as well as a description of the missing widow herself.

Then the sheriff focused on what physical evidence was present in the house. He hoped that the evidence would include telltale fingerprints left behind by the intruder, particularly in the whitewashed, clean front area of the house.

Convinced that he had a serious case on his hands, Newbern called in agents from the State Bureau of Investigation, North Carolina's top enforcement agency. Doc Hoggard, the SBI agent who was assigned to the area and whom Newbern had often worked with, arrived late that night. So did Agent Dennis Honeycutt, who then supervised the deputies dusting for prints through the night.

Honeycutt lifted a number of prints that tracked the intruder's path through the house. The deputies photographed the interior of the house.

Meanwhile, other deputies went door to door, interviewing neighbors about anything they might have seen or heard. From those interviews, the deputies determined that Ethel Owens' car was last seen in her driveway by a newspaper carrier about 6:00 that morning, and a neighbor noticed the car missing from the driveway about 6:45 a.m.

So Ethel must have been abducted sometime during that 45-minute span. With little else to go on, narrowing down that time span would save a lot of work as Sheriff Newbern made an appeal through the press for the help of anyone who had noticed anything unusual or suspicious near the house during that time. Newbern told reporters he believed that Ethel Owens had been abducted, and he didn't think robbery was the motive.

The next morning, a tired Sheriff Newbern telephoned his counterparts in neighboring jurisdictions, alerting them to the situation. One of those calls was to his old friend, Davis Sawyer, the sheriff of nearby Pasquotank County.

Sawyer, then 58, had logged 24 years at his own post. Before joining the sheriff's department, he had left his job as an auto-body man and spent 10 years with the police department in Elizabeth City, the Pasquotank County seat.

Sawyer was a Currituck native himself, and he and Newbern had blossomed together in their law enforcement careers. After finishing his chat with Newbern that Wednesday morning, Sawyer called his nine deputies into his Elizabeth City office and told them to be on the lookout for the Impala and Ethel Owens.

Like Newbern, Saywer often investigates cases himself. He joined his deputies out on the miles of Pasquotank roads, lines of blacktop and yellow sand winding through the neatly plowed fields and dark swamps of the sprawling coastal plain.

Meanwhile, Sheriff Newbern also called Elizabeth City Police Chief Clarence Owens, who put his own officers on the hunt. (Chief Owens was not related to the victim.)

Time was of the essence in the search, and because the missing-person report wasn't filed until over 12 hours after Ethel Owens' disappearance, the sleuths were seriously handicapped.

Ethel had health problems that required daily medication. A check of her prescription bottle revealed that she hadn't taken her drugs since Monday.

News of the apparent abduction, spreading like wildfire through Harbinger, left residents shocked and outraged. The last crime in their community had been a break-in a couple of years earlier. Violent crime was relatively low throughout the whole county, which might mark two or three murders in a "high" year and then go a few years without a single homicide.

The community's shock notwithstanding, the close-knit character of the neighborhood would support the investigators' efforts. The deputies continued interviewing residents, focusing on little things they might have seen or heard in the days before the crime, hoping to turn up the small pieces of the puzzle that would crack the case.

Some residents remembered seeing Ethel Owens in church recently, hugging friends and chatting away. Relatives and friends told reporters that all they could do now was pray.

By Friday morning, Sheriff Sawyer was doing what he had been doing since Wednesday — cruising his county, looking for Ethel Owens and the elusive Impala. About 11:30 a.m., he wheeled his cruiser through a staff parking lot behind Albemarle Hospital in Elizabeth City.

There, he spotted a parked car matching the description of the Impala. The sheriff parked his own car and got out for a closer look. He saw that the right front door had been left half-open, as if the driver had made a quick exit.

As he walked around the auto, Sawyer saw blood on the passenger-side door. Peeking inside, he spotted more blood on the front passenger seat. And on the floorboard lay a bloody paring knife. Sawyer didn't touch the weapon. From what he could see, Ethel Owens' missing pocketbook was not in the car.

Next, Sawyer turned his attention to the locked car trunk. There were no keys in the car, so he sent for a locksmith.

As far as Sawyer was concerned, it would snow in July if this wasn't Ethel Owens' car. Just to be sure, though, he radioed Chief Deputy Jackie Manning and had her check the license-plate number, confirming that it was in fact Owens' Impala.

Then Sawyer contacted Sheriff Newbern, who met Sawyer and the locksmith at the scene a few minutes later. Sawyer braced himself to see Ethel Owens' body in that trunk.

But, as the locksmith finished his task and the trunk lid popped open, all the two sheriffs saw was empty space.

After impounding the car, Sheriff Newbern had SBI agents retrieve the knife for further analysis, take samples of the blood in the car, and dust for fingerprints.

Meanwhile, the watchful residents of Harbinger had led the investigators to a suspect. Eazed Rudolph "Zeb" Meekins had known Ethel Owens all his life and lived near her. In fact, a relative of Meekins' had worked as a maid for Ethel for 26 years—right up until the time of Ethel's disappearance.

Sheriff Newbern learned that Ethel had tried to help 28-year-old Meekins, who was a troubled, unemployed man. A check revealed that Zeb Meekins had a record of convictions for assault and rape dating back to 1974.

In the days before her disappearance, Ethel had told friends and relatives that Zeb had been threatening her, and she was scared of him. But Ethel had not reported the incidents to her friend, Sheriff Newbern, because she was scared that doing so would only make matters worse.

Sheriff Newbern had dealt with Zeb Meekins in the past. He believed the man to be as bad as Ethel Owens was good. In fact, Currituck deputies had been seeking Meekins for weeks in connection with the April 2nd rape of a local 20-year-old woman. The victim had told deputies that she'd been driving Meekins, an acquaintance, home when the incident occurred.

Through the press, deputies had appealed to the public in that case for help in finding Zeb Meekins. The suspect was described as a stocky black man, standing 5 feet 6 inches tall and weighing about 155 pounds.

With Ethel Owens' disappearance, the stakes in the hunt for Zeb Meekins went up. The investigators speculated that Meekins might have killed Owens in order to get a car and some cash so that he could flee from the rape charge.

The deputies had come agonizingly close to catching their man several times. They had tracked his movements, believing that he was staying with friends in Elizabeth City during the day and returning home under cover of night.

The lawmen also believed that Ethel Owens had journeyed to Norfolk, Virginia, and New York in April.

By the Thursday after the kindly widow disappeared, the trail was getting hot. One witness told sleuths he had seen Zeb Meekins driving Ethel Owens' car after Ethel had disappeared. Another witness said Meekins had come by his house to change some bloodstained pants the day the elderly woman disappeared. Unfortunately, the sleuths were never able to locate those pants.

Finally, on Thursday afternoon — the day before Sawyer found the car — a clerk at a store just outside Elizabeth City had called the police after a man tried to cash an apparently forged check belonging to Ethel Owens.

The clerk, having read all about Ethel's disappearance in the newspapers, refused to cash the check, and called the Pasquotank Sheriff's Department as soon as the man left.

The deputies, realizing the man fit Zeb Meekins' description, notified their counterparts in Currituck and Elizabeth City. On Thursday night, police officers and Pasquotank deputies found Meekins at a relative's home in Elizabeth City. He surrendered without a fight.

The officers arrested the suspect on the Currituck rape warrant and brought him to the Elizabeth City jail.

After checking out the car on Friday, Sheriff Newbern dropped in at the jail to have a chat with Zeb Meekins about Ethel Owens' disappearance.

Meekins, an obnoxious, arrogant man, was still wearing the clothes he'd been arrested in — a pair of blue jeans. Otherwise, he was barefoot and barechested.

The suspect didn't talk at first. Then he began to let out bits and pieces in the conflicting stories he told.

Ethel Owens was dead, he said. He was present when she was killed — he didn't say where that was — but he denied doing the killing himself. He was paid to dispose of the car, he said.

Where, Sheriff Newbern asked, was her body?

It was "overboard" — that was all the suspect would say. He did admit he knew where the body was, but he said it would never be found.

Sheriff Newbern brought a tearful relative of Zeb Meekins' to appeal to him. The suspect also refused to tell her where the body was.

Newbern finally walked out of the room feeling utterly disgusted.

Ethel Owens "was a sweet woman — honest, kind," the suspect's relative later told a reporter outside the jail.

"She treated everyone nice."

Now the sheriff changed the focus of the search. Instead of looking for the car and Ethel Owens, deputies and police now began to look for the widow's body. On Friday afternoon, spotters in planes were straining their eyes, peering into the swamps and fields below. Officers were rattling their street cruisers over bumpy farm paths and driving slowly down rural roads, looking into ditches. Other deputies were searching otherwise inaccessible areas on foot.

They concentrated on areas around the victim's home, and also checked around the hospital where her car had been found.

By Saturday afternoon, the deputies still didn't have a body. But SBI agents had tentatively matched the fingerprints lifted from Ethel Owens' house and car with Zeb Meekins' prints. And the store clerk, working from a photo laydown, had identified Meekins as the man who tried to forge one of Owens' checks.

Sheriff Newbern charged Zeb Meekins, who was now being held in the Currituck Jail, with the first-degree murder and kidnapping of Ethel Owens, as well as with the first-degree burglary of her home and felonious larceny of her checks. Meanwhile, the suspect still refused to give the location of the body.

About 7:10 p.m. on Saturday, a cool dusk was falling, dissipating the heat of the day. A Currituck deputy slowly cruising a curve on U.S. 158, several miles north of Owens' home, spotted what looked like a human figure lying in a roadside ditch. After getting out of his car and climbing over a guardrail, the deputy found that it was the body of an elderly woman with several apparent stab wounds. Her dress was hiked up around her waist.

As cicadas whined from the black, snake-infested

swamp falling off from the highway, the deputy radioed Sheriff Newbern. The sheriff, arriving scant minutes later, immediately realized that the dead woman was his old friend, Ethel Owens. Newbern and his men shot photos of the grim scene. Then they searched for other evidence, but in vain.

The sheriff had the body sent to the office of the state medical examiner in Greenville, North Carolina.

In the days ahead, Zeb Meekins, being held without bond, still refused to talk. While the blood in Ethel Owens' house indicated that Meekins had probably assaulted her before dragging her to the car, Sheriff Newbern felt that the killing had taken place in the Impala. Forensic scientists said that a study of the bloodstains in the Impala backed up Sheriff Newbern's conclusions.

Pathologists determined that Ethel Owens had been stabbed 19 times. They found no evidence of sexual assault.

SBI forensic scientists were unable to lift prints from the knife, but they did find that the blood on the weapon matched samples of Owens' blood taken during her autopsy.

Newbern and his deputies continued to strengthen their case by re-interviewing various witnesses. Meanwhile, an Elizabeth City man told the detectives that Meekins had confessed killing Owens to him.

Other witnesses said that Zeb Meekins had been drinking heavily at a party in a home near Ethel Owens' dwelling the night before the elderly woman disappeared.

All the while, the residents of Harbinger and Currituck County remained outraged over the case. Recognizing the tension, the authorities held Zeb Meekins in lockups outside the area, pending his trial.

The court appointed Elizabeth City lawyers Lennie Hughes and O.C. Abbott to represent the Meekins. Longtime District Attorney H.P. Williams Jr., serving several counties from his Elizabeth City office, said he would be seeking the death penalty against Meekins.

On a request from the defense team the following summer, doctors at Dorothea Dix, a state mental hospital in North Carolina's capital of Raleigh, evaluated Zeb Meekins to determine if he was competent to stand trial. The doctors ruled the defendant competent.

In November 1986, a judge granted a defense motion to have the trial moved to Currituck. The defense lawyers argued that community outrage would make it impossible to seat an impartial jury within the county.

The trial began in mid-February 1987 in Chowan County Superior Court in Denton, North Carolina, a historic sound-side town about an hour's drive from Ethel Owens' home. Despite the change of venue, Chowan Sheriff Fred Spruill took extra precautions with courtroom security. Many Currituck residents remained outraged about the case, and some of them were attending the trial. To prevent any incidents, the deputies used a metal detector to scan each person entering the courtroom.

It took until early March for a six-man, six-woman jury to be selected from a pool of 144 candidates.

The case began well for the prosecution. Key witnesses included Sheriff Newbern; the Elizabeth City man who said that Meekins had confessed to him; and SBI Agent J.L. Leonard, a finger-printing expert. Leonard told the jury that Meekins' prints were found in Ethel Owens' car and in her house. Relatives of the victim said that Meekins had visited her several times in the days before her disappearance, and that she was scared of him.

402

Zeb Meekins chose to testify in his own behalf. He repeated what he'd told Sheriff Newbern the previous May—that he didn't kill Owens. He'd been paid $50 to dispose of her car, Meekins testified.

While Meekins had told Newbern earlier that he'd been at the scene the night Owens was killed, he now claimed he hadn't been there at all.

In his closing argument on Thursday, March 5th, Prosecutor Williams asserted that Meekins had killed Owens and robbed her because he needed cash and wheels to flee the Currituck County rape charge.

That night, the jury came back with their verdict. They found Meekins guilty of first-degree murder, kidnapping, burglary, and larceny. As the clerk polled each juror, Meekins began rising from his chair, looking at the prosecutor and saying that he would "get him."

Suddenly, the defendant ripped off his coat and dived across the aisle at the startled prosecutor. As bailiffs lunged for Meekins, one of the defendant's relatives also hopped into the melee.

It took six law enforcement officers to break up the scuffle. Neither D.A. Williams nor anyone else was injured.

Judge J. Fred Williams (no relation to the D.A.) ordered the bailiffs to handcuff and shackle Zeb Meekins. The defendant repeatedly tried to stand back up until the bailiffs shackled his leg irons to his chair. Then Meekins wept softly.

The relative who'd joined the fracas told Judge Williams that he'd only been trying to break up the fight, but the judge found him in contempt and gave him 30 days in jail. Then the judge recessed court. The attorneys would come back the next day and argue for and against the death penalty.

Sheriff Spruill told a reporter that night, "We've been running pretty tight security all the time of the trial. I think the incident . . . proves that the security measures we used were necessary."

Ethel Owens' family members, who sometimes sobbed through the graphic testimony, knew that tension only too well. "It's all been a very grueling, gut-wrenching, emotional experience for all involved," one relative told a reporter.

The attorneys came back Monday for penalty-phase arguments. Called by the defense, an Elizabeth City psychologist testified that Meekins had been diagnosed as schizophrenic. The defendant had the mental abilities of an 11-year-old, the doctor said.

In his closing argument, Prosecutor Williams sought to secure a one-way ticket to the gas chamber for Meekins. The prosecutor noted the brutal circumstances of the kindly victim's death. He pleaded with the jury to return the ultimate punishment.

The jury began deliberations on the next day, Tuesday, March 10, 1987. They deliberated for nearly two hours before coming back with a life sentence. Judge Williams tacked 94 years on that sentence for the convictions of kidnapping, burglary, and larceny. Since the judge ordered all the sentences to be served consecutively, Zeb Meekins will not be eligible for parole for 45 years. D.A. Williams dismissed the charges of rape in connection with the April 2nd incident, considering the amount of time Meekins faced for Ethel Owens' murder.

Defense Attorney Hughes told reporters that his client was relieved the jury didn't give him death.

Things have been relatively quiet in Currituck since the Meekins case. Ethel Owens' house still stands by bustling U.S. 158. Her relatives keep it maintained, painted in the crisp white that its elderly occupant liked so well when she was alive.

Local folks still talk about the case now and again, a trace of anger slipping into their usually friendly tones when the subject comes up.

In showing just how much an alert citizenry can aid law enforcement, they may have given other would-be felons the sense that someone is always watching. Communities filled with helpful, caring neighbors may be a thing of the past in many parts of the country, but not in this coastal area.

And Sheriffs Newbern and Sawyer and Chief Owens proved once again that small-time law enforcement agencies can rise to the occasion just as well as their counterparts in the big cities. Newbern and Sawyer carry on with their work, enjoying the continued respect of the communities in their bailiwicks. Owens has since retired.

Zeb Meekins is currently serving his sentence.

"$2 — WAS IT WORTH A CABBIE'S LIFE?"

by Charles Lynch

MOON TOWNSHIP, PA.
FEBRUARY 8, 1984

It was a cold, dark night, brightened only by a light dusting of snow when Officer Michael Price pulled his cruiser off a desolate area of Montour Run Road to catch up on some paperwork. He no sooner parked when a car drove up, and the driver told Price that a cab was parked off the road a short distance away. The officer put his paper work away — it was shortly before 1:00 a.m. — and headed for the direction of the cab.

It was sitting alone in a clearing with its headlights on. As Price pulled up, his lights picked up the figure of what appeared to be a man lying on the ground on the driver's side of the cab. Price thought that perhaps the man was drunk, but when he got closer he noted wet blood around the man's head and upper body.

After checking the man's pulse and determining he was dead, Price quickly examined the area and cab interior for signs of anyone else. He then went back to his cruiser and notified his base dispatcher, who called Moon Police Chief Tom Krance and the medics. When the medics arrived, they checked the body once again, and the scene was roped-off to await the arrival of investigators.

Allegheny County Homicide detectives Henry Watson and Dave Schwab were dispatched to the scene from their headquarters in downtown Pittsburgh, about 10 miles away, at 1:45 a.m. on December 19, 1982.

As soon as Watson and Schwab arrived they put in a call to headquarters for their boss, Inspector Charles Mosser, and the county's mobile crime unit. Mosser ordered four more detectives to the scene, and the investigation was underway. Chief Krance also had four of his detectives summoned to the scene.

Watson and Schwab walked carefully to the cab, No. 337, and observed the body of a man lying on the ground. There was a pooling of blood under the victim's head, staining the newly fallen snow, and indicating that the victim had suffered, if nothing else, a fatal head wound. Two opened cans of beer were lying on the ground on the passenger side of the cab.

The officers also noticed in checking the cab that there was a pooling of blood on the front seat, several fractures in the windshield, and some evidence of shotgun wadding. It looked as though the victim had taken a shotgun blast to the head as he sat in the driver's seat. Then, fatally wounded, he stumbled or fell outside and died.

Watson noticed that the victim's clothing had not been disturbed. The detective was particularly concerned whether the victim's pockets had been "turned out" by a robber looking for money and other valuables. Later, in a close examination of the body at the morgue, it was discovered that the victim had been carrying almost $160 on his person. If robbery had been the motive, then the robber fled empty-handed. At this point, although it might have seemed logical, the investigators weren't going with the robbery motive.

Criminalists Dr. Robert Levine and Jean Austin, and

Photographer Kay DiNardo, from the Allegheny County Crime Lab, arrived at the scene at about 2:00 a.m. They did what they could at the outdoor scene, working under portable lights set up by the Moon Township Volunteer Fire Department. The cab was towed later to a county maintenance garage, where the examination was completed under more suitable conditions.

About an hour after the police arrived at the scene, and after the immediate area had been searched, two county policemen heard a "moaning" coming from over the hillside. Sgt. William Wolverton and Patrolman Robert Clark climbed over the railing to investigate and saw a man struggling to climb up the hillside where they were standing.

When they reached the man, the officers could see that he had suffered a severe face wound: the lower half of his face was gone, and he was bleeding heavily. The man was unable to talk and, naturally, was incoherent. The victim appeared to have suffered a wound similar to the one that killed the cabbie. One investigator noted in his report that "the victim lacked facial features."

When the medics arrived and examined the man, they called for a helicopter to transport the patient to a Pittsburgh hospital. The chopper, however, was unable to respond because of the bad weather.

The man was rushed in an ambulance to Allegheny General Hospital, with a police escort.

Detectives John Flaherty and Thomas Fitzgerald followed the ambulance to the hospital, where they collected as evidence the victim's clothing which, for some unexplained reason, was soaking wet. The clothing was bagged and its wet condition noted in the officers' report.

During the ride to the hospital, the victim could not speak but he indicated to Medic Jeff Busch, while in the

Valley Ambulance, that he wanted to write something. Given a pencil and paper he wrote, "Put me under." Twenty minutes later, when they arrived at the hospital, the patient's vitals signs were good and he was admitted to surgery.

Meanwhile, back at the scene, Detectives Watson and Schwab were examining the cabbie's log book. They were concerned with the entry indicating where the last fare had been picked up. They were hoping it would help explain what the cab was doing in the area and lead to the identity of the passenger. The detectives figured that there was a passenger because of the $12.40 registered on the fare meter.

Mosser, not knowing what else was lying over the darkened hillside and in the woods—weapons or maybe even another body—ordered the area searched. Police and volunteer firemen, 25 by number, combed the area, right up to the first crack of dawn. Nothing of value to the case was found, however.

Shortly after 5:00 a.m., Watson and Schwab left the murder scene and headed for Fusion Street in the Sheraden area of Pittsburgh. Fusion Street was the last entry, a one-passenger pickup, in the dead cabbie's log. They wanted to know if anyone at that address had ordered a taxi. The cab company had confirmed that someone at that address had ordered a cab by phone at 12:08 a.m.

The detectives apologized for the early-morning intrusion and asked the man who answered the door if anyone from his house had ordered a cab earlier and was now missing from the home. After a quick check, the resident confirmed that Walter Cooke, 20, was gone.

The man said he and Walter, an unemployed machinist, had been watching a Saturday night football game on television and, when it was over, at 11:30 p.m., the relative went to bed. He said he assumed Walter had done the same, but apparently that wasn't correct.

The detectives asked the man if Walter owned a gun and, if so, where was it? The man told the officers that he bought Walter a new, 12-gauge shotgun with interchanging barrels two months earlier and gave it to him as a present. The gun was not in the house.

The officers also wanted to know if Walter had any ammunition for the gun in the house. The relative handed over about 50 shells.

When Watson and Schwab left the residence, they wondered if the mysterious man in the hospital, the man who stumbled out of the darkened woods with his face half shot off, was Walter Cooke.

At 9:00 a.m., after everyone was recharged with cups of hot coffee, Mosser ordered a second search of the area. Four hours later, with nothing positive to show for the effort, the search was called off. The snow, which continued through the early morning hours, didn't help the detectives.

It was pretty much confirmed at the scene, through records and other information provided by the cab company, that the dead driver was William Koontz, 36, who lived in the Sheraden area of Pittsburgh. The fact was later made official at the county morgue, where the body was identified by a relative.

By coincidence, both the cabbie and Walter Cooke lived in Sheraden. Police had no reason to believe the men knew each other.

In a background report on the dead cabbie, detectives learned he had quit a job as a computer programmer three years before when he had decided to drive a cab for a living. During that time, he had performed his job well. There were no complaints against him either from passengers or the taxi company. His record indicated he had been robbed once before.

Detectives also learned that, for the past few weeks, Koontz had been working overtime in order to surprise his wife with some extra money for Christmas presents. In fact, on the day of his murder, before leaving home at 3:00 p.m., he had given his wife money to buy Christmas presents for his two small children.

On Monday, December 20, the day after the murder occurred, Detectives Flaherty and John Markell interviewed a Yellow Cab driver who stated he thought he had Walter Cooke as a fare two days earlier.

The cabbie said he picked up Walter at about 5:00 a.m. at his home on Fusion Street and took him to the same area where Koontz was slain. The witness said Cooke was carrying a shotgun, bow and arrows, a box of shotgun shells and several cans of beer. Walter reportedly told the cabbie he was going to hunt for doe.

According to the driver's log book, the fare was $10.40. The fare registered on Koontz' meter was $12.40. Apparently the cab took different routes and there was a $2 difference in the fares. In retrospective theory, the two bucks might have cost a man his life.

Also on December 20th, at about 4:00 p.m., County Policeman Robert Clark searched the wooded area and found an interchangeable shotgun barrel lying on the ground about 300 yards from where the cab was found. Walter Cooke's missing gun had interchangeable barrels.

Mosser, who had a gut feeling that the gun was still lying somewhere in the woods, ordered another search on December 21st. The searchers included volunteer firemen and two scuba divers who "cleared" the creek, which ran below the hillside from where the cab was found. The area was searched for six hours. Nothing was found.

411

On December 22nd about 40 Yellow Cabs, containing 100 drivers, turned out for Koontz's funeral. Following services at St. Nicholas Church, the cabs formed a long funeral procession on their way to the cemetery where their fellow driver and friend was buried.

Koontz's murder was a telling blow to the many cabbies who came to pay their respects. One said, "He (Koontz) was like a brother to us, and it could have happened to any of us . . . he was a very, very nice guy."

Most of the drivers considered it inevitable that they would become crime victims, but what happened to Koontz was hard to take. Koontz died of a single shotgun blast to the neck.

The investigation, meanwhile, was hampered by the inability of the key figure to communicate with the police. Detectives were hoping an interview with Walter Cooke would help unravel some of the questions about Koontz's death. But Cooke, three days after he was found seriously wounded, was still unable to talk and a hospital spokesman said Cooke possibly suffered brain damage and loss of speech. Nevertheless, the investigation continued.

Finally, on January 6th, investigators got a big break. A large, black and white Allegheny County Police horse van pulled into the murder scene area at 10:00 a.m. and unloaded six horses.

Six mounted police officers, under the direction of Lt. William Coe, started a systematic search of the large area. The mounted patrol was called into service because the officers could cover more territory than men on foot, and see more from their higher, saddle positions.

The idea of using the horses, which was approved and encouraged by Superintendent of County Police Robert Kroner, paid off. The horses are normally used to patrol the county's parks. Seventy-five minutes into the search the elusive shotgun was found by Officer Dave Fuchs, lying on a grassy knoll overlooking the creek—about a quarter mile from where the cab was parked. It was Walter Cooke's gun. The gun's serial number on the sales slip found at the Cooke residence matched the numbers found on the weapon in the woods.

And there was more: the gun held a spent shell and a live shell in the chamber, and the wadding was consistent with the wadding found at the murder scene. The mounted patrol also found a piece of flesh clinging to a shattered tooth and four cans of beer attached to a six-pack plastic holder. Two cans had been found lying on the ground next to the cab. Mosser was delighted.

Sgt. Mike Stowell, one of the homicide detectives said, "Finding the gun was a big plus . . . we had other physical evidence, but without the gun we would have had to believe his (Cooke's) story about the third man; the gun discovery clinched it." It was only a matter of time until someone else walking in the woods would have found the gun and taken it.

On February 10, 1983, at 10:30 a.m., Investigators Watson and Schwab, along with Sgt. Joseph Balough, arrested Walter Cooke in his hospital room, where he was still confined. Deputy Coroner Floyd Coles arraigned him on a charge of criminal homicide. Cooke's jaw, tongue and part of his nose were severely damaged, and he communicated during his arraignment by writing on a pad. Coroner Coles, at that time, told a reporter that Cooke appeared alert and responsive at the arraignment.

Superintendent Kroner, at a press conference, said that the shooting resulted from an attempted holdup by Walter Cooke or a fight over the fare. Asked what led investigators to suspect Cooke, Kroener said, "You try to eliminate all persons at the scene, and we had great difficulty eliminating him as a suspect."

At the preliminary hearing on February 28th, because Cooke was unable to speak for himself, Watson presented Walter's version of what happened the night Koontz was murdered. Cooke had explained earlier to Watson, by writing, that a cab came to his home to take him to Montour Run Road. Cooke admitted he ordered the cab. When they reached the road where the cab eventually stopped, Cooke asked the cabbie to pull over so he could relieve himself.

"He (Cooke) said when he got out, a white male appeared from nowhere, shot him and the cab driver," Watson said. This story was doubted by detectives from the very beginning. Detectives theorized that Cooke headed into the woods after the killing, planning to walk home, and shot himself accidentally — possibly while climbing a hillside and using the shotgun as a support.

Dr. Robert Levine, criminalist for Allegheny County, determined that Koontz was shot while still in his cab. The gunman was in the rear seat, and Koontz's head was to the right and turned partially around toward the backseat when the weapon was fired.

Levine determined that the muzzle of the gun was about one foot away from Koontz's collar area when it was fired. Along the same lines, Schwab theorized that "Koontz had turned around to get his money, and to tell Cooke 'it was the end of the line,' and unfortunately it was."

Although a motive for the killing was never definitely pinned down, Watson had his own theory, one supported by most of the other investigators who worked the case: There was a discrepancy in the two cab fares on the same trip from Cooke's home to the site at Montour Run

Road.

In Watson's second interview with Walter at the hospital, the detective asked the suspect, "Walter, do you want to know what I think?" This was after Cooke had written that he didn't want to answer any more questions.

Watson: I think it was all over $2 difference in the fare.

Cooke: You're crazy. You don't shoot someone over $2!

Watson: I've seen it done for less.

The trial judge would later rule that the conversation between Watson and Cooke should not be considered by the jury.

Dave Schwab, Watson's partner, said Cooke's alibi, when he eventually was able to communicate, of what happened on that lonely road was "filled with gaping holes." The detectives said they couldn't see Cooke getting out of the cab, after he asked the driver to pull over at a desolate area so Cooke could relieve himself, and climbing over a railing, down a steep hillside where he supposedly was out of view.

Schwab reasoned Walter could have accomplished the same thing, as most any man would have done under the same circumstances, by standing alongside the cab, where it came to a stop.

According to Cooke, while he was over the hillside, he heard a shot, and while scampering back up to the cab, a man standing at the top shot him. Nowhere throughout the intensive investigation was there any evidence of a third person being present.

Watson and Schwab also theorized that after Koontz was shot, Cooke attempted to flee the area through the woods. He had to wade in knee-high water to reach a knoll, where he accidentally shot himself in the face. Cooke waded in the creek again to get back to the cab to seek medical help, and into the arms of the police, where they were still working. The question of how Cooke's clothing got wet, was easily answered.

At a pre-trial hearing, on February 2, 1984, Cooke's attorney argued that the statements his client made to detectives not be allowed as evidence. The judge denied the request despite the defense argument that Cooke was under the influence of a pain killer at the time of the interviews.

Walter Cooke, wearing a mask of gauze to cover his face from the nose to the chin, went to trial in Allegheny County Common Pleas Court on February 6th, before a jury and Judge Henry R. Smith.

Sitting prominently in the front row of the courtroom for every day of the trial was the victim's widow and her two small children. The widow, in discussing the courtroom vigil during a recess in the trial, told a reporter, "I think it is important that they (the children) are here to see some of this . . ." Their appearance, no doubt, reminded the jury that the cabbie's death created a void, in at least three lives.

The jury also had to cope with the image presented by Cooke, with half of his face blown away with a shotgun blast, and his ability to communicate dependent upon a mechanical voice box he was just learning to use.

Police testimony based on investigation, and incriminating physical evidence, as presented by Deputy District Attorney Christopher Conrad, put Walter Cooke's hand on the trigger and gun that killed Koontz.

Detective Watson testified that a check of Koontz's log book, which was located in the cab, determined Walter had been picked up at his home by Koontz and taken to Montour Run Road, where the murder occurred.

Watson told the jury how he and his partner visited

416

Cooke's home and talked to Cooke's relative, who permitted them to retrieve shotgun shells belonging to Walter's gun that was missing from the home.

Crime lab specialists testified that the shells matched those found at the murder scene and in the shotgun.

In his closing arguments, Conrad argued that Walter had gotten into the cab with the intention of committing suicide, and that for some unknown reason, had decided to kill Koontz before he walked off into the woods familiar to him from previous hunting trips and take his own life.

Defense Attorney Nicholas Radoycis told the jury that the long line of county detectives, firearms and pathology specialists whose testimony linked his client to the shotgun and shotgun shells that killed the cabbie, did not put his hand on the trigger.

The defense suggested that much of the evidence presented in court did not rule out Cooke's original statement to police—that Cooke had asked the driver to pull off the road so he could relieve himself over a hillside, and that when he returned, he was shot by the same gunman who killed Koontz.

The jurors, however, believed Conrad's presentation of evidence and the belief that it would have been illogical and unreasonable for a gunman to commit a robbery in the manner in which Walter claimed it had occurred.

The trial came to an end on Wednesday, February 8th, when the jury convicted Cooke of third-degree murder. The verdict showed the jury believed Cooke shot Koontz to death with malice, but without premeditation. The conviction in Pennsylvania carries a maximum sentence of 10-to-20 years in prison, and a crime committed with a gun requires a mandatory sentence of a least five years.

Then, in a rare courthouse move for a man just convicted of murder, at least in Allegheny County, Judge Smith continued Cooke's $14,000 bond and permitted him to go home for the weekend. The district attorney's office objected strongly and argued that Cooke's injuries were not severe enough to warrant freedom from jail.

Cooke's attorney countered that Cooke had been under bond for more than a year of court proceedings and had never failed to appear when scheduled. The attorney also claimed that the injuries his client must live with will be more of a burden than the jail sentence he just received.

Radoycis pleaded with the judge that Cooke must breathe and speak through a tracheal tube inserted in his throat and feed himself specially prepared food through a tube inserted in his stomach. Cooke's doctors estimated that four or five operations may be required just to rebuild his face.

Conrad, in one last move to prevent Cooke's release, told the judge to consider Cooke's new status—not as a surviving victim of a bloody robbery, as suggested during the trial—but as a convicted murderer. Judge Smith, nevertheless, released Cooke, but ordered him to be back in court on Monday for a hearing on whether he should be jailed.

In asking for leniency at that February 13th hearing in continuing Cooke's bond, Radoycis said that because of the extensive injuries Cooke sustained, a prison atmosphere could be harmful to Cooke.

The attorney explained that his client's food must be liquified and injected by a syringe into a tube in his stomach, and that he needed to have his extensive facial bandages changed 10 times a day to prevent infection.

But DA Conrad explained that Cooke could change the bandages himself and could feed himself. Conrad also argued that Cooke presented a danger to society and to himself and asked the judge to send Cooke to jail.

A representative from the county behavior clinic that questions all homicide suspects, said that he thought Cooke might become depressed if he was sent to jail. Conrad did not regard the observation too seriously and asked that representative if it wasn't true that everyone going to jail for the first time would suffer depression. The spokesman admitted that Conrad was probably right.

At the end of the hearing, Judge Smith revoked Cooke's bond and then remanded him to jail. One of Cooke's relatives in the courtroom began to cry, as did Koontz's widow, who had attended every court session.

"HE RACKED UP BODIES FOR COLD CASH!"

by Bruce Gibney

In the fall of 1987, Redding, California detectives had a frightening murder case on their hands. One of the victims was a pretty, middle-aged landlord. The other one was a young housewife and mother of an infant child. The women did not appear to know each other; as far as police could tell, the two had never met.

The thread that connected their lives — and violent deaths — was a raspy, distinctive voice that sounded familiar to the Redding Secret Witness Program. The voice would lead to the discovery of a third victim in a case that was as baffling as police had ever encountered.

"We got something real unusual here" is how Redding Police Chief Robert Whitmer described it.

The first victim was 48-year-old Averill Weeden. She was reported missing on May 25, 1985.

Police investigated the incident and found evidence that suggested Averill's family had reason to worry about her disappearance.

Averill's two-bedroom home was clean and tidy. But a search showed that the woman's closet was full of clothes. The house looked as though Averill would be back any moment.

Perhaps the most obvious clue that 48-year-old woman had not left town voluntarily was her friendly, if hyperactive, little dog, who yipped and jumped in circles when a detective arrived to check on Averill Weeden's whereabouts.

Averill, detectives learned, was very attached to her dog. She would not have left without first making sure the dog was properly cared for.

A description of the comely landlord was entered into the police telex. Investigators also checked the police wire for unidentified bodies of young women that had surfaced in northern California.

In August, Redding's Secret Witness Program offered $1,000 for information on Averill Weeden's disappearance.

A man inquired about the reward. The Secret Witness operator assigned him a secret code and told him if the information proved to be valuable, he could go to a local bank, present the secret code and collect the reward in cash.

"The cops won't know who I am?" the man asked guardedly.

"We guarantee anonymity," the operator responded.

"Are you a cop?" he asked.

The operator explained that she operated the Secret Witness Program but wasn't employed by a law enforcement agency. Actually, she owned and operated Redding's only answering service.

"Give us the tip," the operator pleaded. "If it pans out, you get the cash."

The caller gave directions to a rural section of forest north of Redding with the now-inappropriate name of Happy Valley. The caller described a distinctive rock formation under which the body lay.

Lawmen went to the spot, located off Bechelli

Lane near South Bonnyview Road, and conduced a grid search of the thick forest that grew along the road. After several hours, they found the formation described to the Secret Witness operator and carefully removed branches and leaves. A body lay underneath. Dressed in slacks, with a rope around the neck, the body's remains were badly decomposed and ravaged by animals. Officials wearing masks and protective clothing removed the rotting corpse to the coroner's office.

An autopsy was conducted that evening and the preliminary report was made available the next morning.

According to Coroner Margie Boddy, the victim was a female who had died of multiple traumatic injuries. Exposure to the elements and ravishing by animals made visual identification all but impossible.

But a set of dental charts sent to the Department of Justice identified the victim as the missing landlord, Averill Weeden.

Redding Detective Dave Mundy was put in charge of the investigation. He focused his probe on one person—Averill's onetime tenant, 27-year-old Robert Maury.

Maury had put himself in the hot seat when he told investigators that he gave Averill a lift into town the day she disappeared but gave conflicting stories about where he took her. He told sleuths he took Averill to the supermarket. But he told a relative of Averill's that he dropped her off in front of the post office, at the other end of town.

When asked why he told police one story and the relative another, Maury replied unconvincingly, "I goofed. It happens."

It wasn't the only goof. Maury told detectives that after dropping off Averill he had gone to a party. But the two friends he purportedly partied with said they hadn't seen Maury the entire day he was supposedly with them.

Maury again claimed bad memory for the apparent discrepancy.

"Do you mind taking a polygraph exam?" the detective asked.

"Not one bit," Maury replied.

Robert Maury was hooked up to a polygraph machine and questioned for an hour. Surprisingly, he passed.

"I found no deceptions at all," the polygraph examiner said, after examining the graph tape that recorded Maury's responses to the questions.

The polygraph appeared to clear Maury—but not in Detective Mundy's mind.

He went to the Shasta County District Attorney's Office and talked to D.A. Steve Carlton. "I don't care what the polygraph says," the detective said. "I think the guy is not telling the truth."

Carlton agreed. But except for their own suspicions, they had nothing connecting Robert Maury to Averill Weeden's gruesome murder—no statements, no physical evidence.

For two solid months, the two lawmen stayed as close to Maury as fleas to a dog. They thought their long hours had paid off on November 11th, when Maury confessed that he knew more about the Weeden murder than he had at first acknowledged to them.

Maury now said he had returned home on the evening of May 25th and had discovered Averill struggling with two men. Before he could open his mouth, one of the men showed him a gun and told him to sit down.

Maury said he watched as one of the men put a rope around Averill's neck and choked her to death. "I couldn't do nothing," Maury said. "They would have killed me if I had moved an inch."

After Averill was dead, Maury said the two assailants turned their attention on him. One of the killers suggested they kill him. Instead, Maury said, they loaded Averill's body into a car, then told him to get in.

He said they drove to Happy Valley where, with his hands tied, he watched the men crush Averill's face with a rock, then cover her body with brush.

"They made me come along so that I wouldn't talk," Maury said. "I guess they figured if I was along that made me as guilty as them."

Maury insisted that he was forced to go along and that he had not willingly participated. He said if necessary, he would agree to take another polygraph examination.

After Maury was gone, Detective Mundy asked, "You believe that?"

"About as much as you do," D.A. Carlton responded. "Unfortunately, I still don't have a case I can prosecute."

Two years went by and on June 22, 1987, Dawn Marie Berryhill, a 20-year-old single parent, was reported missing by her family.

The case was investigated by the Shasta County Sheriff's Office. Detectives questioned several witnesses, including a belligerent ex-boyfriend, without any success in finding the young woman.

In July, the Secret Witness Program offered a $2,500 reward for information on the missing girl.

On August 6th, a man called the Secret Witness Program and said he had information that might help law enforcement agencies. First, however, he wanted to know, "Can I get some money for turning in a body?"

By coincidence, the operator on duty remembered an almost identical question being asked in the Averill Weeden disappearance.

That was two years earlier—but the operator was certain it was the same man.

While explaining how the Secret Witness Program operated, she pulled out a pocket tape recorder and recorded the last bit of the conversation.

The tape was turned over to Shasta County detectives.

Sheriff's Detective Dick Newsome contacted Redding PD Detective Mundy, telling him about the search for Dawn Berryhill and the tape recording of the man seeking cash.

"The operator says she is certain it is the same guy who called you in the Weeden case," he said.

"Let's hear it," Mundy said.

The Redding detective listened to the tape and heard an old familiar voice.

"That's Maury," Mundy exclaimed. He filled Newsome in on the Weeden investigation and Maury's bizarre and lengthy statement.

"The D.A. said he was that close to filing charges," Mundy said, holding his thumb and forefinger about an inch apart. "But he was afraid they wouldn't stick."

Nodding, Newsome outlined developments in the

Dawn Berryhill investigation. The pretty brunette was last seen when she handed her baby to a neighbor, then roared off on the back of a big motorcycle driven by a slim man with brown hair and a beard.

Robert Maury, police noted, had a motorcycle and fit the description of the bearded biker to a T.

On August 17th, investigators went to a spot off Happy Valley Road. Following the Secret Witness instructions, they discovered a badly decomposed body under some brush and tree branches.

Lawmen believed the victim was the missing young mother and were surprised when she was identified through fingerprints as Belinda Jo Stark, 30, of Fall River Mills.

Stark was last seen alive on June 25th, hitchhiking to Nevada City to pay an overdue traffic ticket.

That was great, investigators agreed. But where was Dawn Berryhill?

That question was answered September 22nd, when police discovered another grave. It was located 250 yards from Belinda Stark's corpse and contained the decomposed remains of a young woman, identified as Dawn Marie Berryhill.

Redding police and Shasta County investigators formed a joint task force, the first of its kind, to solve the murders. Dave Mundy and Dick Newsome were the chief investigators. They didn't doubt for a minute that Robert Maury was the one who was supplying the tips to the Secret Witness Program.

After supplying the tip that led to the discovery of Dawn Berryhill's remains, the anonymous caller had collected his $2,500 reward at a local bank.

Police did not see Maury collect the money. But they did retrieve the discarded envelope that contained the cash—and found Maury's prints on it.

The print linked Maury to the payoff—but not to the murder. "We still don't have enough to make a case," D.A. Carlton told the sleuths.

Maury was placed under 25-hour surveillance while detectives search for evidence that would put him behind bars.

On September 29th, they searched a shed behind Maury's Palisades Avenue home. They confiscated clothes, bootlaces, restraints and pornographic photos depicting women being bound and assaulted.

Maury objected to the search. He also objected to being followed everywhere he went.

Investigators told him that they thought he was mentally ill and that the surveillance was necessary because he might be schizophrenic or have a dual personality.

Maury insisted he was not mentally ill. He agreed to undergo a psychiatric exam if he would get the cops off his back.

An exam was arranged with a psychiatric examiner with the State Department of Corrections.

The psychologist concluded after the two-day exam that Maury was not insane. However, the shrink admitted, Maury was more than a little strange.

During the exam, Maury had said he thought police encouraged crime by offering to pay people for information about criminal acts.

"You know they pay people for finding bodies and things like that," he commented to the psychologist. "Over a thousand dollars. They'll give you money. Heck, a person could actually make a good living that way, killing people and turning in their bodies."

He revealed to the psychologist that one of his informants had told him where to find the purse of the second victim, Belinda Jo Start. He said he would personally take the psychologist to the spot—for $200.

The two set out to Happy Valley where Maury pointed out a purse, laying in brush about 50 feet off the road, apparently tossed from a passing car.

The purse was taken to the crime lab, where Maury's prints were found on a wallet inside the purse.

As far as District Attorney Carlton was concerned, that was the last piece of the murder puzzle and the item of physical evidence that he needed to tie Robert Maury to the killings.

On November 6, 1987, Maury was arrested and booked into the county jail on suspicion of three counts of murder. He was also charged with the rape in June of a Redding housewife.

The rape victim came forward after she saw Maury's picture in the newspaper following his arrest. She said Maury was the man she had met at a lake on June 20th. He offered her a ride on the back of his motorcycle. After he told her that a mutual friend would be there, she said she decided to accept a ride to a party with Maury that evening.

The woman charged that instead of going to the party, Maury took her to Hidden Valley, put a noose around her neck and raped her.

Maury angrily denied committing the rape or the murders at his November 21st arraignment. "The cops said I helped them out and for helping them out I was put in jail," he said.

He said he was confident he would beat the rap—

and soon. "I'll walk out of these doors in eighty days, not guilty. You better have cause to get the real guy because I'm walking out a free man."

Maury did not walk free, and it was almost two years before he stood trial before Judge William Lund. It took 10 weeks to select a jury of 12 panel members and four alternatives. It took another five weeks for the state to present its 130 witnesses and more than 100 pieces of physical evidence.

In his opening statement, co-Prosecutor Jim Ruggiero told jurors that the prosecution had no eyewitnesses, no confession and no exact time as to when the murders were committed. He said they did, however, have an abundance of circumstantial evidence linking the murders and a solid motive — money.

"He killed them for the Secret Witness funds," Ruggiero said.

Jurors listed to graphic testimony and heard a tape recording made by the Secret Witness operator. They also heard from the psychologist, who told of her two examinations of Maury and his statement that "a person could actually almost make a living killing people."

On July 26th, the jurors left the courtroom and toured the dusty dirt roads off Happy Valley to see where the bodies of the three women were found. The trip was requested by prosecutors, who wanted the jurors to see the remote locations where the crimes were allegedly committed. The judge, lawyers, court personnel and bailiffs accompanied the jurors on the tour. They were shown where the police had recovered the bodies and the purse belonging to Belinda Jo Stark.

Maury had sought to accompany the jurors, but

decided not to because it meant he would have to wear shackles and handcuffs.

A high point was reached August 11th, when the defense offered as a witness Dr. Thomas T. Noguchi, a forensic pathologist for the Los Angeles Medical Examiner's Office and so-called "coroner to the stars." He had investigated the deaths of many famous personalities, including those of Robert Kennedy, Marilyn Monroe, William Holden, Natalie Wood and John Belushi.

Noguchi testified that Ms. Stark appeared to have died of "unnatural causes." He said although it appeared that Ms. Berryhill had not been strangled, "other causes are not completely ruled out."

Defense Attorneys Rolland Papendick and Stephen Kennedy said they asked Noguchi to review the autopsies because "he's an excellent pathologist."

Noguchi said he agreed to help the defense because it was a challenge. "I don't take a case unless it's a 'Mission Impossible' worthy of time and effort."

The dapper, diminutive celebrity ex-coroner created a sensation in the courtroom when a star-struck friend of one of the jurors asked him for an autograph on the juror's behalf. Noguchi complied, but the autograph was confiscated by a bailiff.

In final arguments, co-Prosecutor Ruggiero told jurors that Maury was a man "in the habit of killing women," who believed he could get away with the crimes and get paid at the same time.

But greed, the co-prosecutor contended, was the "beginning of the downfall for the defendant. He had the audacity, even when he was under suspicion, to call again."

Ruggiero noted that Maury provided an unusual amount of information about the murder victims to the Secret Witness Program. He knew, for instance, how they were killed — strangulation — and was familiar with the Happy Valley area where they were found.

"He thought the rest of the world was stupid," Ruggiero said. "Fortunately, he was wrong."

He asked the jury to consider the odds of one person coming upon three bodies and later proffering tips. "Not too many people come upon one body in their lifetime. Three times is a habit, and I think Robert Maury was in the habit of killing women."

The case went to the jury on August 24, 1989. Jurors had sat through five weeks of testimony, but spent less than 10 hours to reach a verdict: Robert Maury was guilty of three counts of murder and one count of rape.

The penalty phase followed. Jurors had to decide whether the defendant would spend the rest of his natural life in prison or would die in the gas chamber at San Quentin.

Robert Maury quickly made known his personal preference. On September 5th, taking the witness stand, against his attorney's objections, Maury stunned the packed courtroom when he asked for the gas chamber.

"I feel the only penalty you can conscientiously consider is the death penalty," he maintained. "If you think I'm guilty, then give me death."

Maury dismissed with a wave of his hand defense testimony that he suffered from mild clinical depression and had a rough childhood.

"I've never been depressed in my life," Maury said.

"I've taken medication before, but to sleep, not because I feel depressed." He said he thought his defense lawyers had done a good job, but added they had the responsibility of asking the jury not to give him the death penalty.

"I am asking you to ignore my attorneys," he told the jurors. "I want you to do the only right thing — vote for the death sentence."

Co-Prosecutor Andy Anderson agreed that Maury deserved the maximum sentence — not because Maury wanted it, but because he deserved it.

"He stands convicted of killing three women with special circumstances of multiple murder and murder during the course of a robbery," he said. "These killings were nothing more than a game. He killed, then he toyed with police."

It was time to pay the piper, prosecutors urged. And the price had been written in the Bible — "An eye for an eye, a tooth for a tooth."

Jurors began deliberations. When they emerged on September 8, 1989, they had reached a verdict that left prosecutors and the defendant satisfied — death in the gas chamber!

Robert Maury's reaction to getting what he said he wanted was a tight little smile. His eyes were clear and his jaw set. Like a character out of an old western novel, he remained tough to the end.

By state law, the case was automatically appealed to the State Supreme Court. Until it is ruled upon, Robert Maury will reside on San Quentin's Death Row.

APPENDIX

"They Butchered Benji in the Bathtub!" *True Detective*, March 1993

"The Exxon Exec's 5 Days of Hell!" *Official Detective*, February, 1993

"Evil Scheme of the Greedy Grandson!" *Inside Detective*, July, 1984

"Need a Car . . . Kill a Driver!" *Inside Detective*, September, 1983

"A Woman's Greed Laid the Dealer Low!" *Official Detective*, January, 1990

"Rodney was Hammered to Death for $14" *Inside Detective*, March, 1983

"The Killer Defiled, Bludgeoned, Then Called 911" *Inside Detective*, April, 1993

"How Many Victims for the Greedy Golden Girl?" *Inside Detective*, September, 1985

"Six Slugs for the Dixie Bookie" *Master Detective*, July, 1992

"Knifed Paul for his Ghetto Blaster!" *Front Page Detective*, March, 1985

"Sick Cokehead's Rob/Rape Rampage" *Master Detective*, April, 1993

"They Sawed the Homo's Head Off for 73 Cents!" *Inside Detective*, October, 1984

"Greedy Grandson and his Devil-Worshipping Gang!" *Front Page Detective*, July, 1986

"Manhunt for the Greedy Killers in the Red Corvette!" *Inside Detective,* May, 1985

"Shotgunned Her Four Times . . . for a Radio" *Front Page Detective*, May, 1982

"Flashy Widow's Lust for Cash Made Her Kill" *Official Detective*, February, 1993

"Greedy Killer Lurked in a Pine Tree and Pounced!" *True Detective,* April, 1993

"Naked Runner was Tracked Down and Shot!" *Master Detective*, April, 1992

"Money-Hungry Murderess" *Inside Detective*, May, 1989

"2 Bucks and a Tiff . . . Reason to Kill?" *Front Page Detective*, January, 1984

"Mutilated Molly for Fruit Punch!" *Inside Detective*, July, 1984

"Greedy Bandit Executed Two!" *Inside Detective*, January, 1986

"Was the Kindly Widow Wasted for Her Wheels?" *Front Page Detective*, November, 1992

"$2 — Was it Worth a Cabbie's Life?" *Front Page Detective* — October, 1984

"He Racked Up Bodies for Cold Cash!" *Official Detective*, November, 1990

**GOOD VERSUS EVIL. HEROES TRAPPING MONSTERS.
THIS ISN'T FANTASY. IT'S LIFE.
CAPTURE A PINNACLE TRUE CRIME TODAY.**

JEFFREY DAHMER (661, $4.99)
By Dr. Joel Norris

Everyone knows Dahmer's name, but how many of us know the man behind the headlines? Renowned psychologist Dr. Joel Norris sheds light on the dark forces that compelled Dahmer to butcher and consume the men he loved. Based on unpublished facts about the killer's lifestyle and background, it features extensive interviews with his friends and ex-lovers. Readers may never fully understand Dahmer's behavior or find him sympathetic, but Norris's book outlines how a seemingly normal man can degenerate and lash out while silently passing among us.

ARTHUR SHAWCROSS: THE GENESEE RIVER KILLER (578, $4.99)
By Dr. Joel Norris

Despite his parole officer's warnings, child killer Arthur Shawcross was released from prison early. He headed to Rochester, New York, to begin his next chapter. Shawcross's second chance at life spelled death for eleven women. He conducted a horrible slaying spree, reminiscent of Jack The Ripper, that targeted prostitutes and denizens of Rochester's red light district. Strangling them in remote wooded areas, his insane bloodlust drove him to butcher their naked bodies and to devour parts of their flesh before disposing of them. Ironically, police arrested him by luck when he was observed casually eating his lunch while the nude corpse of his latest victim floated past him in the Genesee River.

CHOP SHOP (693, $4.99)
By Kathy Braidhill

Generations of mourners brought their "loved ones" to Lamb Funeral Home. They trusted the sincere staff, appreciated the sympathetic directors, and knew without question that their relations were in capable hands. They were wrong. Grotesque mutilations and sadistic practices flourished at Lamb's. Like a ghoulish twist on a vampire novel, here the living merrily preyed upon the dead. Fingers were severed to claim expensive rings; teeth were forcefully pulled out for the ounces of gold filling; and organs were fiercely removed to be sold to research labs. The crematorium fires blazed fiendishly around the clock as multiple bodies were stuffed into the chambers for mass burnings. It was a scenario worthy of the Holocaust. *Chop Shop* recounts how unspeakable acts of horror were perpetrated against the ultimate victims: dead men who can tell no tales. Thankfully, Kathy Braidhill broke this case and gave a voice to these victims.

SEX, MONEY AND MURDER IN DAYTONA BEACH (555, $4.99)
By Lee Butcher

Florida's society set always makes a splash in the papers: debutante balls, charity auctions, MURDER. Beautiful heiress Lisa Paspalakis surprised her wealthy family by marrying for love. She wed Kosta Fotopoulos, a waiter, after a whirlwind courtship. This fairytale union was ripe with villains and greed. Fotopoulos and his mistress had already laid plans for Lisa's cold-blooded demise. This is an explosive indictment of greed, decadence, and amorality.

Available wherever paperbacks are sold, or order direct from the Publisher. Send cover price plus 50¢ per copy for mailing and handling to Penguin USA, P.O. Box 999, c/o Dept. 17109, Bergenfield, NJ 07621.Residents of New York and Tennessee must include sales tax. DO NOT SEND CASH.